# GLOBALIZATION AND DEVELOPMENT

# A GLOSSARY

Mike Mason

Fernwood Publishing • Halifax

Editing: Brenda Conroy
Printed and bound in Canada by: Hignell Printing Limited

A publication of:
Fernwood Publishing
Site 2A, Box 5, 32 Oceanvista Lane
Black Point, Nova Scotia, B0J 1B0
and 324 Clare Avenue
Winnipeg, Manitoba, R3L 1S3
www.fernwoodbooks.ca

Fernwood Publishing Company Limited gratefully acknowledges
the financial support of the Department of Canadian Heritage,
the Nova Scotia Department of Tourism and Culture and
the Canada Council for the Arts for our publishing program.

Library and Archives Canada Cataloguing in Publication

Mason, Mike, 1938-
Globalization and development : a glossary / Mike Mason.

Includes bibliographical references.
ISBN 1-55266-150-4

1. Globalization--Dictionaries. I. Title.

JZ1318.M374 2005     303.48'2'03     C2005-901426-1

*I believe we are on an irreversible trend toward more freedom and democracy—but that could change.*
— Governor George W. Bush Jr.


*Almost overnight, globalization has become the most pressing issue of our time, something debated from boardrooms to op-ed pages and in schools all over the world... Not only in trade liberalization but in every other aspect of globalization even seemingly well-intentioned efforts have often backfired.*
— Joseph Stiglitz

# Abbreviations

| | |
|---|---|
| *AJ* | *Alternatives Journal*, Toronto |
| *CAQ* | *CovertAction Quarterly*, Washington |
| *CCPAM* | *Canadian Centre for Policy Alternatives Monitor*, Ottawa |
| *Econ* | *The Economist*, London |
| *Econ 04* | *The Economist*, "The World in 2004" |
| *FP* | *Foreign Policy*, New York |
| *FT* | *Financial Times*, London |
| *Front* | *Frontline*, Chennai (India) |
| *G&M* | *Globe and Mail*, Toronto |
| *GW* | *Guardian Weekly*, London |
| *GM* | *Greenpeace Magazine*, Toronto |
| *HD* | *United Nations Human Development Report* |
| *HM* | *Harper's Monthly*. New York |
| *LBO* | *Left Business Observer*, New York |
| *LMD* | *Le Monde Diplomatique*, Paris |
| *LRB* | *London Review of Books*, London |
| *MR* | *Monthly Review*, New York |
| *Nat* | *The Nation*, New York |
| *NI* | *New Internationalist*, Oxford |
| *NLR* | *New Left Review*, London |
| *NS* | *New Scientist*, London |
| *NYRB* | *New York Review of Books*, New York |
| *Obs* | *The Observer*, London |
| *PS* | *Ploughshares Monitor*, Waterloo, ON |
| *TS* | *Toronto Star*, Toronto |
| *Wal* | *Walrus*, Toronto |
| *WB* | *World Bank Annual World Development Report* |

Note: all $ are US; Canadian $ are C$.

**acid rain.** A form of air pollution wherein rain contains sulphur dioxide, nitrogen oxide and ammonia. Industry is the main source of acid rain. In Europe acid rain reached its highest levels between 1950 and 1980; thereafter it was mitigated by protocols between states. After 1975, sulphur emissions in North America were reduced by as much as 25%. See pollution, environmental and links.

**Action Aid** (www.actionaid.org). One of largest UK aid agencies. Campaigns include lobbying World Trade Organization "to ensure international agriculture benefits poor people and protects farmers' rights to seed and plant resources." Concerned about impact of genetically modified crops and patents on genetic resources. An excellent site for discussion about food in general and genetically modified food in particular. See aid, biotechnology, blood diamonds, genetically modified food, organizations and publications, agriculture, lobbyists, Third World and links.

**Adam Smith Institute** (www.adamsmith.org.uk). Right-wing British think-tank. Its experts have been used by the World Bank to advise on privatization. Few of its enthusiasts seem to realize that Adam Smith was writing about a world where industrial capitalism was as yet unknown. See lobbyists, business, Canadian/US and links.

**Adbusters** (www.adbusters.org). Vancouver-based anti-corporatism and anti-globalism magazine with sales of 100,000 worldwide. Extraordinary artwork. Piercing perceptions. Organizes "Buy Nothing Day" but now markets its own products. Tends to self-exaggeration. According to one subscriber: "I am unclear as to how your group plans to 'topple existing power structures and forge a major shift in the way we will exist in the 21st century.' I do not think that providing a bad press about corporations will solve the problem" ("Letters," Adbusters, 34, Mar/Apr 2001, 6). See media, alternative and links.

**affluent alliance.** A euphemism for the association of rich countries, headed by the US; the club of the First World. See wealth, distribution of, world and links.

**Africa Action** (www.africaaction.org). US-based organization which works for political, economic and social justice in Africa. It is a coalition of the American Committee on Africa, the Africa Fund and the Africa Polity Information Centre. See organizations and publications, peace/arms control and links.

**agitprop.** Agitation and propaganda. A term associated with the Communist International but useful to describe lobbyists. See lobbyists and links.

**agreements, international, on arms control.** See arms, Canada, organizations, peace/arms control and links.

**agreements, international, on environment.** See Amsterdam Declaration, Bonn World Climate Conference, Kyoto Protocol, organizations and publications, environmental, pollution, environmental and links.

**agriculture, capitalist.** The production of foodstuffs, including organic foodstuffs, for profit as opposed to use. See fair trade, firms, agribusiness, genetic engineering, organizations and publications, agriculture and links.

**aid.** Gifts or loans given to Third World countries by Western countries, often in connection with development and thus called "development aid." Aid might be tied, in that it is given on the condition that the recipient spends it in ways determined by the donor, usually to the benefit of firms in the donor country. Untied aid has no such strings, at least in principle. In practice, all aid has strings attached. Aid can be measured as a percentage of the GDP of the donor country. The UN recommends that rich countries give a minimum of 0.7% of GDP. Only a few countries have managed this, notably Denmark, Norway, Netherlands and Sweden. In 1991, Japan surpassed the US as the single biggest aid donor, giving over $10 billion in 1998. The total aid given by the rich world in 1998 was $51.89 billion (*NI*, 332, March 2001, 19). For aid figures see United Nations' Development Program (UNDP), *Human Development Report*, which is published annually. See aid agencies, Canadian International Development Agency, development, alternative forms of, United Nations Development Program (UNDP) and following entries.

**aid agencies.** See Action Aid, aid, Canadian International Development Agency (CIDA), International Development and Research Council (IDRC), non-governmental organizations (NGOs), United States Agency for International Development (USAID) and links.

**aid, Canadian.** In 1950, at the genesis of the era of development, Canada gave C$11 million in aid. By 1967, this figure had reached $279 million; since then it has increased to several times that amount. OECD countries were to attempt to reach the UN established aid target of 0.7% of GNP and some did. The highest point attained by the Canadian government was 0.5% in 1986–1987. Since then, especially due to the ongoing cuts in the 1990s, this figure has fallen. The latest cuts, of $150 m., will have reduced by one-third the aid spending since the early 1990s. In the 1990s, a larger share has been going to Eastern European countries and for emergency humanitarian relief.

The 1990s has seen a practical abandonment of the goals of the UN. According to the United Nations *Human Development Index* (2003, 160), in 2001 Canada gave 0.22% of GDP as aid, lower than any developed world country except Greece. Denmark gave 1.03% (Government of Canada. Parliamentary Research...79-16E). See aid, lobbyists, Third World and links.

**AIDS.** See HIV/AIDS.

**AlertNet** (www.alertnet.org). "AlertNet provides global news, communications and logistics services to the international disaster relief community and the public." AlertNet is funded by Reuters Foundation, an educational and humanitarian trust created by the Reuters news agency. See media, alternative and links.

**Alternatives Journal** (alternat@fes.uwaterloo.ca). Quarterly publication about the environment produced by the Faculty of Environmental Studies, University of Waterloo. Excellent articles on local issues and good at debunking bogus environmental arguments written in the interests of Big Pollution. Useful information about courses in environment studies. See media, alternative, organizations and publications, environmental, press, non-business and links.

**Amazonia.** In Brazil, one of two of world's greatest tropical forests. For its destruction with the assistance of the World Bank (Hecht, 1989; McNeill, 2001, 232–33). See forests, destruction of, organizations and publications, environmental, World Bank and links.

**America.** "If we have to use force, it is because we are America. We are the indispensable nation. We stand tall. We see farther into the future" (Madeleine Albright, US Secretary of State, defending use of Cruise missiles against Iraq, quoted in Johnson, 2000, 217). "America, at its best, is not just a country. It's a spiritual value and role model" (Thomas Friedman, cited in McQuaig, 2001, 116). See America First, Americanization, Americans, rich, US and links.

**America First.** An ideology in full flower under George W. Bush's administration. America Firsters rallying around the vice president, Dick Cheney, include the vulpine Paul Wolfowitz and a wide range of think-tank pundits. They believe that all measures should be taken to ensure that the US remains the first and only world power. The invasion of Iraq in March 2002 is but the most egregious policy manifestation of this ideology. See America, imperialism, US, isolationism, US and links.

**American Enterprise Institute for Public Policy Research** (www.aei.org). Neoliberal US think-tank which produces essays ranging from the provocative ("Serbia is able and willing to try Milosevic. We are denying

Serbia the same rights we have claimed for ourselves...") to the predictable ("Bush is Right on Global Warming"). This institute employs Dinesh D'Souza, one of the most clamourous of pro-business gushers: "We know how to create wealth... but there is only one way to do it, and that is the American way of technological capitalism" (cited in McQuaig, 2001, 28). Two of the institute's hacks produced, a little prematurely, *Dow 36,000: The New Strategy for Profiting from the Coming Rise in the Stock Market* in 1999. The next year the stock market peaked (with the Dow Jones Industrial at 11,722.98 on January 14, 2002), and then slumped (reaching below 7000 in early October) (*TS*, August 26, 2002, D30). See America, bear market, ideology, lobbyists, business, think-tanks, and links.

**Americanization.** The process of becoming culturally Americanized. This usually entails adopting American individualism, anti-statism, susceptibility to violence, indifference to poverty and other side-effects of unrestricted capitalism (such as environmental degradation). At a more trivial level, Americanization involves eating junk food but also accepting the great, radical, popular innovations of 20th-century America from jeans to rock and roll. The French are probably more worried about this phenomenon than anyone else. David Held (2004, 4) makes the point that globalization does not mean Americanization. See globalization, McDonald's and links.

**Americans, rich.** "Ownership of the most valuable financial assets... like stocks and bonds, is densely packed in the upper crust. In 1995, the richest 1% of households—about two million adults—owned 42% of the stock owned by individuals, and 56% of bonds... the top 10% together owned nearly 90% of both.... In 1992 (the most recent year available), the top 0.5% of stockowners held 58.6% of all publicly traded stock; the next 0.5%, 11.7%, the next 4%, 24.2%; add those together and you discover that *the top 5% owns 94.5% of all stock held by individuals* (italics in original)" (Henwood, 1998, 66). See wealth and links.

**Americas Watch.** A division of Human Rights Watch, not to be confused with School of the Americas Watch. See Human Rights Watch and links.

**Amnesty International** (www.amnesty.org and www.amnesty.ca). An international NGO that concerns itself, in the first instance, with political prisoners but also with human rights abuses. See organizations and publications, human rights and links.

**Amsterdam Declaration** (www.sciconf.igbp.kva.se). Declaration by over 1000 scientists made in Amsterdam in July 2001, calling for greater protection of environment and resources. See agreements, international, on environment, organizations and publications, environmental, pollution, of the environment and links.

**analysts, financial.** From John Liscio, a former financial columnist: "Financial writers are nothing more than glorified recording secretaries. Unlike their colleagues in other fields like theatre, cinema, food, sports, politics, and fashion, financial writers and even columnists refuse to think for themselves. Because they cherish access to highly placed sources, they serve as nothing more than conduits for the received wisdom, which is almost always wrong.... Whatever the moron economists and analysts tell the financial press gets smeared across the page. There's no filter.

"Imagine how ridiculous it would be if a sports writer, assigned to a perennial also-ran, persisted in printing the absurdly optimistic views of the managers, owner, and aging pitching staff, and little or nothing else. Or if a food critic's review of a restaurant was built around the opinion of the master chef and maitre d'. Asking a Wall Street hack his opinion on the economy is like asking a producer how he feels about a play he just mounted, or a runway model what she thinks about the new line..." (cited in Henwood, 1998, 101–02). See capital and links.

**anarchism.** Political tendency with origins in the nineteenth century. Leading theorist was Mikhail Bakunin (1814–1876). Favours the destruction of capitalism and its organs and return to pre-capitalism. Abjured by both communist and bourgeois parties. Anarchists have been active in all protests against the World Bank, neoliberalism, globalism, free trade. Often they espouse "direct action." Noam Chomsky is the most famous contemporary anarchist. Unlike Marxism, anarchism lacks a sustained economic and social theory or any program for sustained collective action beyond the politics of protest and gesture. Post-capitalist anarchist society is unimaginable. "For contemporary young radical activists, anarchism means a decentralized organizational structure, based on affinity groups that work together on an ad hoc basis, and decision making by consensus. It also means egalitarianism; opposition to all hierarchies; suspicion of authority, especially that of the state; and commitment to living according to one's values. Young radical activists who regard themselves as anarchists are likely to be hostile not only to corporations but to capitalism. Many envision a stateless society based on small, egalitarian communities. For some, however, the society of the future remains an open question. For them, anarchism is important mainly as an organizational structure and as a commitment to egalitarianism. It is a form of politics that revolves around the exposure of the truth rather than strategy. It is a politics decidedly in the moment" (Epstein, 2001, 1). For an exposition of classic anarchism, see Daniel Guérin, *Anarchism*, 1970, and especially the Introduction by Noam Chomsky. See organizations, anarchist.

**anarchy.** Two meanings: (1) the object of anarchists, (2) general crisis, loss of economic order but not necessarily breakdown of capitalism. See anarchism.

**anti-Americanism.** Always a minority taste among Canadian intellectuals and in the 1990s growing in France and certain other European countries. "Since the collapse of the Soviet Union, it is the US that has taken over the mantle of oppressor and world's bullyboy..." (*Obs*, April 8, 2001, 25). Much opposition to US economic domination takes the form of nationalist reaction against US commercial institutions which are themselves innocuous, e.g., McDonald's and Starbucks, although some are not, e.g., genetically modified foods. According to Jean-Michel Normand in *Le Monde*: "McDonald's... commercial hegemony threatens our agriculture and its cultural hegemony insidiously ruins alimentary behaviour—both sacred reflections of the French identity" (Bhagwati, 2004, 106). See America, Americanization, genetically modified food, imperialism, US, nationalism, Canadian and links.

**anti-globalization movement.** Begun in Seattle, a loosely organized response on the part of civil society in both the developed and developing world against neoliberalism and globalization. While the anti-globalization movement is represented, unofficially, at all of the meetings where leaders of business and government congregate in order to advance the neoliberal agenda, the annual meeting of the World Social Forum is the most regular aspect of the movement. For further discussion, see Klein, 2000 and Veltmeyer, 2004. See Bové, José, Cancun, Doha, Free Trade Area of the Americas, globalization, organizations and publications, critical of capitalism and globalization, Seattle, Klein, Naomi, World Social Forum and links.

**Anti-Slavery International** (www.antislavery.org). Pioneer anti-slavery society based in UK. Sister organization in US is Free the Slaves. See slavery and links.

**arms.** See following entries, plus International Institute for Strategic Studies, lobbyists, business, military expenditure, US, organizations, peace/arms control, overcapacity and overproduction, Transparency International and links.

**arms, production and sale of, Canadian.** The top ten Canadian military contractors in 1999 (on the basis of total value of annual sales, in millions of Canadian dollars):
1. General Motors, London ($763).
2. CAE Inc., Montreal ($385).
3. Computing Devices Canada, Neapan ($315).

4. Bombardier Inc., Montreal ($250).
5. SNC-Lavalin Group, Montreal ($182).
6. Magellan Aerospace Corp., Mississauga ($180).
7. Bell Helicopter Textron Canada Ltd., Mirabel, QC ($136).
8. BAE Systems Canada Inc., Montreal ($126).
9. Spar Aerospace Ltd., Mississauga ($85).
10. Pratt & Whitney Canada Ltd ($60+)

Canadian arms production includes not only light armoured vehicles (LAVS) in which GM is especially active but also flight simulators produced by CAE and Computing Devices Canada (CDC, a subsidiary of the US defence giant General Dynamics), the world's largest producer of tank computers. In July 2001, CDC won a £1.7 billion deal to supply British armed forces with a new generation of digital communications equipment. Magellan Aerospace (which owns Bristol aerospace in Winnipeg as well as other subsidiaries), provides components and overhaul of military and civilian aircraft. BAE Systems (formerly Canadian Marconi) builds military and commercial communications and civilian navigation systems. Diemaco in Kitchener boasts that it is "Canada's centre for excellence for small arms." A major market for Canadian arms was Indonesia, Canada's largest trade partner in Southeast Asia during the period of the Timorese genocide. See arms, production and sale of, global statistics, arms, production and sale of, US, arms, sales to developing countries, Asia-Pacific Economic Cooperation and links.

**arms, production and sale of, global, statistics.** See Stockholm International Peace Research Institute, US Arms Control and Disarmament Agency and links.

**arms, production and sale of, US.** In 2003, the US spent $399 billion on "defence," compared to $219 billion for its NATO allies and clients. Russia spent $65 billion, China $47 billion, and the rogue states together, $11 billion" (*Econ, 04,* 93). "Arms sales are important to examine, because they create the very violence that the United States uses as an excuse to step into a conflict. Of the twenty-four countries that experienced at least one armed conflict in 1997 (the most recent year for which data is available at this writing), the United States sold weapons and/or provided military training for twenty-one of them at some point during the 1990s" (Tabb, 2000, 98). The leading US arms firms (with 1999 sales in $billions at constant 1998 prices and as the % of arms of total sales) are Lockheed Martin (17.6, 70%), Boeing (15.3, 27%), Raytheon (11.3, 58%), Northrop Grumman (7.0, 79%) and General Dynamics (5.5, 62%) (Burrows, 2002, 16). See arms, Keynesianism, military, organizations, peace/arms control and links.

**arms, sales of to developing countries.** The top five of the world's arms selling nations to developing states in constant 2001 US dollars (in $ billions):

|        | 1994  | 1996   | 1998   | 2000 | 2001 |
|--------|-------|--------|--------|------|------|
| US     | 8,431 | 11,008 | 11,412 | 8692 | 6006 |
| Russia | 1,789 | 3426   | 2075   | 3119 | 3400 |
| France | 833   | 3655   | 6988   | 1560 | 200  |
| UK     | 5595  | 6624   | 3603   | 4887 | 3300 |
| China  | 714   | 799    | 546    | 624  | 400  |

(*G&M*, August 10, 2002, A9).

The relative place of the 20 top arms-purchasing countries (in $billions, 1996–2000, at constant 1990 prices).

1. Taiwan $12,281 8. Malaysia $1,445 15. China $5,231
2. Pakistan $2,626 9. Brazil $1,346 16. India $4,228
3. Kuwait $2,063 10. Israel $2,890 17. Greece $3,619
4. Singapore $1,874 11. Saudi Arabia $8,362 18. Egypt $3,619
5. Thailand $1,771 12. Finland $2,787 19. Japan $3,558
6. UK $1,694 13. Turkey $5,664 20. UAE $2,983
7. Switzerland $1,612 14. South Korea $5,334

(Burrows, 2002, 17). See arms, organizations, peace/arms control and links.

**Asia.** See arms, Asia-Pacific Economic Cooperation, Association of South East Asian Nations, crisis, financial, East Asian, export-led growth, model, development, East Asian, Newly-Industrialized Economies, world economy, trends, since 1945 and links.

**Asia-Pacific Economic Cooperation (APEC).** Founded in 1987 on the initiative of Japan and Australia and dominated by the US. Comprises 22 Pacific nations including Canada, US, Mexico, Australia and New Zealand as well as Asian countries. "APEC has always been market driven and is heavily influenced by big business and the private sector free marketers. It mainly relies for its research on the tripartite think-tank of business representatives, academics and [state] officials" (Dobbin, 1998, 115). "Under American leadership, APEC became the leading organization promoting globalization in East Asia. At annual meetings in different Pacific Rim countries, it insistently propagandized that the Asian 'tiger economies' open up to global market forces, in accordance with the most advanced (American) theorizing about capitalist economies…" (Johnson, 2000, 208). By November 1998 at its Kuala Lumpur summit, in the midst of the Asian financial crisis, the organization became unglued with Japan taking the lead against any further market-opening schemes. By this time the US and Malaysia were at one another's throats over the suggestion by Vice President Al Gore that the Malaysian people should overthrow their president, Mahathir Mohamad, who had reimposed capital controls. Neither attended the 1999 APEC meeting of trade ministers in Auckland, New Zealand. "At the… APEC meeting in Brunei… in November [2000], it was obvious that the organization was in disarray, had lost its sense of purpose and that its defenders were desperately attempting to paper over cracks in a seriously flawed and foundering organization. If the Asian trading bloc envisaged by ASEAN materializes, it is difficult to see a meaningful role for APEC" (*G&M*, February 12, 2001, A13). The APEC summit in Vancouver in 1997 cost $57.4 million of which sixty-seven corporations contributed C$9.1. Among those which contributed C$1 million were Nortel, TD Bank and the Export Development Corporation. The Royal Bank contributed C$250,000 (Dobbin, 1998, 117). During the summit, the "pepper spray" incident took place, when demonstrators against presence of Indonesian dictator Suharto were attacked by RCMP, presumably on orders from Ottawa. Unsurprisingly, Prime Minister Chrétien was exonerated. The most recent meeting was on 18–22 October 2003 at Bangkok. See Asia, pepper spray and links.

**Asian crisis.** See crisis, financial, East Asian.

**Asian developmental model** (a.k.a. "the alternative model"). See model, development, East Asian and links.

**Association of South East Asian Nations (ASEAN).** A free-trade bloc founded in 1967 in the shadow of the Vietnam War, which has become the most important regional organization in East Asia. Original members were Indonesia, Malaysia, Singapore, Thailand and Philippines. Later joined by Vietnam, Laos, Cambodia, Myanmar and Brunei, with Japan, China and South Korea as associate members. Last meeting was November 7, 2001, in Brunei. At this meeting the ASEAN states agreed to create a free-trade area within ten years. "What we are aiming for is the biggest free-trade area in the world with 1.7 billion people, and it will be closer to two billion when it comes into effect," said Sultan Hasanal Bolkiah of Brunei. Japan and South Korea are expected to join ASEAN next year (*G&M*, November 7, 2001, B9). See Asia and links.

**Attac (Association pour la taxation des transactions financiers pour l'aide des citoyens)** (www.attac.org). French anti-globalization lobby group, founded in June 1998 by Ignacio Ramonet, editor of *Le Monde Diplomatique*, uniting citizens, associations, trade unions and newspapers. Helped found World Social Forum. Attac has become an international movement to support the Tobin tax. Web page is in English, German and Spanish as well as French. Quebec branch founded in 1999, had its first conference in Montreal on 8 April 2000. See *Campagne française pour la réforme des institutions financières international*, lobbyists, Third World, neoliberalism, tax, Tobin, World Social Forum and links.

**authoritarianism, soft.** Term used by political scientists, think-tankists and others to describe governments such as those of Japan, South Korea, Taiwan and Singapore. As opposed to "soft totalitarianism" of China, Suharto's Indonesia, Chiang Kai-shek's Taiwan. "Hard totalitarianism": Soviet Union, Hitler's Germany, Mao's China.

**Aventis.** Producer of genetically modified seeds. Owned by Bayer, the German firm which is one of the big four in the area of genetically modified seeds. See biotechnology, genetically modified food and links.

**Basle Convention.** Established in 1989 to regulate international trade in hazardous waste. According to the convention, every country should be responsible for its own wastes. "In 1995, in keeping with the Basle Convention, Canada banned PCB exports to the US but a US toxic waste company took Canada to NAFTA court and won" (*GM*, 9, 4, Summer 2002, 13). See Greenpeace, organizations and publications, environmental, waste, hazardous and links.

**Battle of Seattle.** See Seattle.

**bear market.** Condition of stock market when selling dominates buying. The contemporary bear market began in March 2000. Between that date and July 2002, stocks had lost 30% of their value; in the case of NASDAQ, the market for shares in TMT (technology, media, telecommunications stocks) it had lost 70%. This represents a total loss of $7 trillion. "This is shaping up to be the worst one since 1929, both in terms of duration and intensity," said Eric Kirzner of the University of Toronto's Rotman School of Business (TS, July 12, 2002, E1). The opposite of a bear market is a bull market. The longest bull market in history began on August 12, 1982, with the Dow Jones Industrial Average at 777. It peaked at 11,722.98 on January 14, 2000, and subsequently fell to 7702.34 on July 23, 2002 (TS, August 26, 2002, D1, D3). See bubble, bull market, crash , stockmarket and links.

**Big Mac Index.** Measure of labour time it takes to buy a Big Mac, in other words, real purchasing power. In Kenya it takes 10 minutes, in Thailand, one hour and in Kenya, three hours.

**biotechnology.** Field of science concerned with, among other things, genetically engineered plants and animals. There were 4284 biotechnology firms around the world in 2003, of which 622 were publicly traded. The US dominates the field with EU countries coming up fast. 96% of genetically engineered (GE) crops were grown in only three countries, the US (68%), Argentina (22%) and Canada (6%). According to a report by the accountancy firm Ernst & Young (*Beyond Borders: The Global Biotechnology Report 2002*) the US accounts for 72% of global bioscience revenues,

Europe 22%, Canada and Asia Pacific countries each 3%. Julie Daniluk of GENEaction (Toronto) (*TS*, June 12, A27) writes: "The notion that the developing world is eagerly awaiting the arrival of genetically engineered crops is misleading at best and has more to do with biotech public relations than agricultural sustainability." See genetic engineering, organizations and publications, agriculture and links.

**Black Monday.** October 9, 1987. Limited meltdown of New York stock exchange due in part to sudden retreat of large institutional investors. See crash, stockmarket and links.

**blood diamonds.** Also known as "conflict diamonds," these are diamonds that are mined in areas under the control of mercenary groups who have been financed by local diamond buyers and sold on the international market. The main source of blood diamonds is Sierra Leone and Angola. The European Commission, the executive body of the European Union, has announced that only diamonds certified by the Kimberley Process can be imported into the EU. Fat chance. There are a surprising number of sites which deal with blood diamonds: www.globalwitness.org, www.un.org/diamonds.com, www.amnesty.org/diamonds, www.actionaid.org, www.kimberleyprocess.com and www.conflictdiamonds.com. See organizations and publications, environmental, organizations and publications, human rights, organizations, mining and links.

**blowback.** CIA-speak normally referring to unintended consequences to initiator of action. Used regularly with reference to Iraq. See Johnson, 2000 for classic study and see foreign policy, US for links.

**bond market.** In early 1990s both the US Federal Reserve Bank ("the Fed") and the Bundesbank allowed generous money and credit growth. US short-term interest rates were at about 3%. Since the economies of both the US and Germany were in or near recession, the excess liquidity flowed into financial markets. Banks used short-term interest rates to borrow short and buy long—to borrow at 3% to acquire huge volumes of long-term bonds which yielded 6 or 7%. There was a bond spree. This rescued the banks from the consequence of the debt binge of the late 1980s but led to inflation. The resultant bubble collapsed in 1994; Soros got badly burned; bond marketeers want zero inflation, i.e., stable money. This makes job creation impossible (Greider, 1997, 296–97). See bonds, World Bank and links.

**bonds, World Bank, boycott.** Several institutional investors including cities, trade unions and religious groups have joined the World Bank Bond Boycott campaign on the grounds that the policies of the bank are environmentally harmful (CCPA *Monitor*, November 2001, 23). See bond market, capitalism, finance, World Bank and links.

**Bonn World Climate Conference.** Meeting of representatives of most of the states of the world on July 21–22 in an attempt to save the Kyoto Protocol on the reduction of greenhouse gases after it had been repudiated by US President George W. Bush. See agreements, international, on environment, organizations and publications, environmental, pollution, of the environment and links.

**boom, baby.** A significant increase in births, the classic period being in the years after the Second World War. The baby boom was followed by the "baby bust" in the 1970s, the epoch when contraceptive pills lowered the birth rate. The children of the "boomer" generation are known as the "echo generation," which peaked in 1990 and are now passing through the education system. As the "boomers" pass through society their priorities change and, because of their numbers, their effect on society, the economy and politics consequently shifts. The classic statement of this phenomena is in Foote, 1996. See population, world.

**boom, economic.** Economic expansion and prosperity. The longest postwar boom in the advanced capitalist countries lasted for twenty-five to thirty years from 1945 (although this boom in the US began in 1940) and was characterized by high profits and high employment. The French refer to *les trentes années glorieuses*. See wealth, welfare state, world economy, trends, since 1945 and links.

**Bové, José.** A French farmer who, at Millau in France, demolished McDonald's with a tractor, making himself a Jeanne d'Arc figure in the struggle against globalism, especially in agriculture. Regarded by globalizers like Jagdish Bhagwati as misguided (see Bhagwati, 2004, 106). See anti-globalization movement, Confederation Paysanne, McDonald's and links.

**Bretton Woods conference.** Conference held at New Hampshire resort in 1944 at which "Bretton Woods institutions" (World Bank, International Monetary Fund) were conceived. See Bretton Woods institutions and links.

**Bretton Woods institutions.** Institutions such as the IMF and the World Bank founded in the aftermath of World War Two whose purpose it was to guide postwar economic development and particularly international commerce. Over the next fifty years, their popularity plummeted. "To their enemies, the International Monetary Fund and the World Bank are indistinguishable; twin faces of the hydra-headed monster of the 'Washington Consensus,' dedicated to the defence of global capitalism and the oppression of the poor" (FT, July 6/7, 2002, 7). See International Monetary Fund, international financial institutions, Washington Consensus, World Bank and links.

**British American Security Information Council (BASIC)** (www.basicint.org). International research institute that analyzes government defence policies. See organizations, peace/arms control and links.

**Brookings Institute.** Centrist Washington think-tank. Writes commissioned histories for the World Bank. See think-tanks, World Bank and links.

**bubble.** Extreme inflation in the price of goods or shares. The great bubbles in modern history have involved tulip-bulb buying in Amsterdam in the 17th century and the South Seas Bubble, 1720. Keynes: "Speculators may do no harm as bubbles on a steady steam of enterprise but the position is serious when enterprise becomes the bubble on a whirlpool of speculation." The great stock market bubble in the US in the 1990s, which was stimulated by changes in financial deregulation and changes in wealth-holding patterns, popped in 2000. See bear market, bull market, markets, foreign exchange, stock market, world economy, trends, since 1945 and links.

**bull market.** See bubble, bear market, stock market and links.

**Business Council on National Issues (BCNI).** See Canadian Council of Chief Executives.

**Business Roundtable.** Right-wing US lobby group, founded in 1972. Spent over $10 m. to secure NAFTA and $30+ m. to secure unrestricted trade and investment in China. See Canadian Council of Chief Executives, lobbyists, business, US and links.

**Byrd amendment.** US law that allows companies filing antidumping cases to pocket the duties. Objected to by Canada and other countries. One of several US trade laws that protect uncompetitive US industries such as steel and lumber. Of the Byrd amendment, the fervent globalizer Martin Wolf writes (2004, 214): "Perhaps the most disgraceful episode in a long and shameless history [of anti-dumping legislation] has been the Byrd amendment in the US...." See protectionism, trade and links.

**Campagne française pour la réforme des institutions financières international** (www.globenet.org/ifi). See Attac and links.

17

**Campaign Against Arms Trade (CAAT)** (www.caat.org.uk). See organizations, peace/arms control and links.

**Campaign Against Depleted Uranium** (www.cadu.org). Seeks to ban use of depleted uranium in weapons. See arms, production and trade, Canada/ global/US, organizations, peace/arms control and links.

**Canada-Asia Working Group** (krcawg@web.net). Inter-church coalition involved in East Timor. See organizations and publications, human rights and links.

**Canadian Action for Indonesia and East Timor (CAIET).** (cafiet@interlog.com). Human rights pressure group. See organizations and publications, human rights and links.

**Canadian Biotechnology Advisory Committee.** Federally appointed and apparently sedated watchdog that has recently rejected calls for mandatory labelling of GM foods in spite of strong evidence that majority of Canadians are wary of such foods. This has been regarded as a victory for the GM industry. See genetic engineering, Canadian government policy regarding/ popular opposition to, organizations and publications, agriculture and links.

**Canadian Centre for Policy Alternatives (CCPA)** (www.policyalternatives.ca.). Nationalist, democratic, left-of-centre research centre; publishes *CCPA Monitor* and publications including "A Citizen's Guide to the WTO" and "Unsafe Practices: Restructuring and Privatization in Ontario Health Care." See Canada, blocking of international protocols by, lobbyists, Third World, organizations and publications critical of capitalism and globalism, water, Canadian and links.

**Canadian Council of Chief Executives (CCCE).** Formerly Business Council on National Issues. Powerful, extremely right-wing pressure group representing 150 leading Canadian corporations founded in 1976 by W.O. Twaits, chairman of Imperial Oil, and Alfred Powis, president of Noranda. Modelled on US Business Roundtable, the BCNI council included representatives of Canadian Chamber of Commerce, Canadian Manufacturers Association and the Conseil du Patronat du Québec. "(I)t would explicitly reflect the interests of multinational and transnational corporations under the leadership of finance capital, led by the chartered banks... the BCNI was organized to reinvent the Canadian state in order to facilitate globalization" (Dobbin, 1998, 166). In July 1984, at a meeting between leading business and government figures a secret pact was concluded which agreed on the lowering of corporate royalties (in the mining and oil sectors, in particular) and taxes and the deregulation of oil and gas prices (which destroyed Trudeau's National Energy Program). One major consequence was the lowering of the business contribution to the national coffers and the raising of the federal debt. During period of Conservative rule of Canada (1984–1993), with the help of the research facilities of the C.D. Howe Institute, it was said to write policy for the Canadian government. The BCNI later campaigned against Unemployment Insurance and public health care. The leading element of the BCNI is the Policy Committee which includes heads of major Canadian banks and resource companies as well as US firms such as Cargill and GM. In 1996, the Royal Bank contributed C$52,000 to the BCNI's C$2 million budget (op. cit., 207). Present chief is Thomas Paul D'Aquino. More recently the CCCE has warned the Liberal government, unsuccessfully, against signing the Kyoto Agreement. See Business Roundtable, C.D. Howe Institute, Fraser Institute, Friday Group, General Electric, lobbyists and links.

**Canadian Council on Social Development (CCSD)** (www.ccsd.ca). A think-tank concerned with social issues. See organizations, health and welfare and links.

**Canadian Institute of Strategic Studies** (www.ciss.ca). Branch-plant of UK International Institute of Strategic Studies that deals with Canadian issues. See International Institute for Strategic Studies and links.

**Canadian International Development Agency (CIDA)** (www.acdi-cida.gc.ca/index-e.htm). Canadian government aid agency which distributes around 10% of its aid through NGOs. See aid and links.

**Canadian Parks and Wilderness Society (CPAWS)** (www.cpaws.org). Advocacy group with 13,000+ members and 400 volunteers founded in 1963. Concerned with expanding and maintaining parks and wildernesses. See organizations and publications, environmental and links.

**Canadian Peace Alliance** (www.acp-cpa.ca). Founded in 1985, Canada's largest umbrella peace organization. Coordinated campaigns against Gulf War, war in Yugoslavia, bombing of Afghanistan, unnecessary military spending and Canadian participation in US missile projects. See agreements, international, on arms control, arms, organizations, peace/arms control and links.

**Canadian Peace Building Coordinating Committee** (www.cpcc.ottawa.or.ca). Ad hoc working group of NGOs involved in peace keeping. See agreements, international, on arms control, arms, organizations and publications, peace/arms control and links.

**Canadian Security and Intelligence Service (CSIS).** Secret police organization mainly concerned with spying on Canadians, not excluding trade unionists and students. For a survey, see Kinsman, Steedman and Buse (eds.), 2001. See organizations, human rights and links.

**Cancun.** Resort in Mexico that was the site for September 10–14, 2003, World Trade Organization meetings between trade ministers of over a hundred countries. Before they began, Justin Forsyth of Oxfam predicted: "The chances of success are slim. Rich countries have repeatedly stalled over key issues.... Cancun is already soured with frustration and anger over broken promises: rich countries must change course and take this vital opportunity to make trade fair" (Oxfam News Release, 2 September 2003). The talks collapsed after the poorer nations, organized into the Group of 22 (G22), demanded cuts to farm subsidies that the richer countries were unwilling to make. "The failure of talks is the second major defeat for the eight-year-old WTO, which tries to regulate and open up world trade. In December 1999, similar negotiations collapsed amid rioting in Seattle" (*G&M*, September 15, 2003, B1). See anti-globalization movement, conferences, international, organizations and publications, critical of capitalism and globalism, protectionism, trade, Qatar, Quebec City, Seattle, trade, free, World Trade Organization and links.

**capital.** Wealth that begets more wealth. See capital controls, capital flight, capital mobility, capitalism, capitalism, centres of, capitalism, finance, capitalism, national, liquidity and following entries.

**capital controls.** The free flow of capital, it is argued, destabilizes both national and the global economies. Capital controls, a classic instrument of postwar regulation, have been called for by politicians as far apart as prime ministers Mahathir of Malaysia and Jospin of France. Because both India and China retained some capital controls, both were able to weather the Asian crisis of 1997 more successfully than their neighbours. Malaysia, in the face of widespread opposition in the West, has reintroduced capital controls. The World Bank, the IMF, the *Wall Street Journal*, and the US Federal Reserve view capital controls with horror; George Soros and others are less fearful. "Asia is moving strongly in the direction of capital controls... support in Europe for the capital controls case is growing.... The US has a powerful national interest in establishing the free movement of capital worldwide—there is probably no more important foreign economic policy for the US than this" (Wade and Veneroso, 1998, 33, 35, 37, fn.55). See Attac, capital, tax, Tobin and links.

**capital flight.** Refers to the normal emigration of capital from one country to another in search of higher returns. Usually capital flows from poorer countries with unstable economies and currencies to richer ones but in 1999 the capital flight out of the Euro zone mainly to the US was $123 billion; in the first six months of 2000 it was $58 billion.

In the early 1980s capital flight undermined the economic plans of the Socialist prime minister of France, François Mitterand. Yet it is poor countries, more than rich, that suffer most acutely from capital flight. "One study of thirty sub-Saharan African countries calculated that total capital flight for the period 1970 to 1996 was in the region of $187 billion, which, when accrued interest is added, implies that Africa's ruling elites had private overseas assets equivalent to 145% of the public debts their countries owed." The authors conclude that "roughly 80 cents on every dollar borrowed by African countries flowed back as capital flight in the same year." Ferguson, 2004, 180. See capital and links.

**capital mobility.** "The theology that has driven this system [that of the US] is an undeviating faith in the unrestricted and unregulated free movement of capital. The objective of US policy has been to assure the security and mobility of that capital. That objective of US policy has overridden all other values or objectives: respect for core worker rights, environmental considerations and an equitable distribution of the burdens of adjustment that have been required to cope with the periodic financial crises afflicting the system" (Jerome Levinson, former general counsel to the Inter-American Bank and former staff director of the US Senate Subcommittee on Multinational Corporations and United States Foreign Policy, cited in Tabb, 2000, 125). See capital and links.

**capitalism.** According to Marxists, a stage in the development of Western history, following feudalism, characterized by the rule of the owners of capital, the bourgeoisie, over the producers of wealth, the workers. In this interpretation, the workers own nothing but their labour which they sell to the capitalist in order to survive and reproduce. Contemporary capitalism is marked by the ascendancy of one group of capitalists, finance capitalists, over the other main group, industrial capitalists. Imagine, if you will, then, Citibank being the single most important and influential institution in the US, towering, in its importance, over GM. England is perhaps the best example of the historic supercession of industrial capitalism by finance capitalism. See capital, capitalism and links.

**capitalism, centres of.** Europe, North America and East Asia carry on over 85% of world trade and over 90% of production of advanced sectors such as electronics. It is here that we find the headquarters of most of the top multinational corporations including banks. See capital and links.

**capitalism, finance.** Classically counterposed against industrial capitalism.

Never popular among critics of capitalism, as we see in the following from Karl Marx: "The credit system, which has its focal point in the allegedly national banks and the big money-lenders and usurers that surround them, is one enormous centralization and gives this class of parasites a fabulous power not only to decimate the industrial capitalists periodically but also to interfere in actual production in the most dangerous manner— and this crew know nothing of production and have nothing at all to do with it" (Capital, 3, 33). "Capitalism has changed in many ways in the last century [viz. the 20th]. The once dominant steel sector and the rest of old line industrial America have been eclipsed. The third industrial revolution sectors dependent on information technologies and resurgent finance capital both benefit from and are integral to the mergers that characterize this era and need global markets and an open regulatory architecture. The new leading sectors are not interested in protectionism and indeed are a dominant factor in the American state's effort to enforce a new open international economic order" (Tabb, 2000, 135).

Before 1986, the central banks of the US, the UK, Germany, Japan and Switzerland had foreign exchange reserves that were greater than the total amount of capital being traded in global markets. For instance, in 1983 these five had $139 billion in foreign exchange reserves while the turnover in foreign exchange markets was $39 billion. In 1986, the two were about even. By 1992 the central banks had $278 m. while $623 billion was involved in daily trading activities. No trader could single-handedly overwhelm governments, but when they worked together traders could. They did this by "surfing," that is, joining together on the same wave, the wave ridden, say, by George Soros. This was possible because every major trader was linked electronically for 24 hours a day; news about buy and sell orders by one trader would be passed along the line and if action looked promising, then others would duplicate the play. There were a total of 200,000 traders around the world involved in this system. See capital, market, foreign exchange, Goldman Sachs, Merrill Lynch, money, laundering of, world economy, trends since 1945 and links.

**capitalism, national.** This is the attempt by any national bourgeoisie, invariably with the help of the state that it controls, to develop and control capitalism within the frontiers of the state. It is usually defeated by the forces of international capitalism. Prime Minister Trudeau's National Energy Policy was practically the last hurrah of Canadian national capitalism. National capitalism remains central to the East Asian development model and in a different form to the Franco-German version of the European model.

"A recognition of the connections between national firms and the expansion of the national economy provided motivation for the policies of the developmental state in Brazil and also in several other countries in

Latin America, East Asia and elsewhere. In Japan, South Korea and Taiwan... governments favoured national firms precisely because they would form local supply linkages, expand the technological base and reinvest within the nation. Indeed, the governments did not rely simply on the firms' 'natural' proclivities' in the direction of national development, but, in addition to restricting foreign firms, pushed the national firms in this direction.... Foreign investment often pre-empts investment by national firms.... A broader, socio-political phenomenon of pre-emption is also associated with foreign investment in low-income countries. When foreign investors replace national capital to a significant degree, they pre-empt the social role of a national capital class. In some experiences of capitalist economic development, a capitalist class has led the process, shaping the state and obtaining its support for an economic growth agenda. In other cases, a developmental state has taken the lead, nurturing the expansion of a capitalist class along with the expansion of the economy. In general... though reality never neatly fits broad models, the class has tended to lead in the early developing models and the state has tended to lead in the later developing countries. Yet in all cases of successful development, a strong class has emerged alongside a strong state.... (W)hen foreign firms play a large role in a country, operating important industries, their presence inhibits the emergence of a strong capitalist class and undermines and perverts the essential class-state alliance...." (MacEwan, 1999, 57–59). See capital, lobbies, business, model, development, Anglo-Saxon and links.

**Captive Daughters** (www.captivedaughters.org). US charity, founded in 1997, which seeks to end the sex trafficking of children. See organizations and publications, human rights, sex, trafficking in and links.

**carbon emissions.** Refers to release of various carbon compounds into atmosphere. With only 4% of world's population, US is responsible for 20%+ of carbon emissions, or, put another way, the average American emits about 5.3 tons of carbon, the average Canadian, 4.2, the average German, 2.9, the average Mexican, 1, the average Indian 0.2% (*CCPAM*, 7,8, February 2001, 7). See organizations and publications, environmental, pollution, environmental and links.

**carbon emissions trade.** An idea, supported by the US, Canada, Australia, Japan and Russia that would allow them to pay other countries to compensate for their carbon emissions, e.g., Mexico or Russia would be paid to grow trees to compensate for US and Canadian emissions. Favoured by Liberal Party of Canada; opposed by Greenpeace and Friends of the Earth. For explication: *FT*, November 11–12, 2000, I; *ccpam*, 7, 8, February, 2001, 7. See organizations and publications, environmental, pollution, environmental, and links.

**Carnegie Endowment for International Peace (CEIP)** (www.ceip.org). Site gives access to articles on peace that have appeared in US and international press since 1992. Publishes *Foreign Policy*. See agreements, international, on arms control, organizations, peace/arms control and links.

**cartels.** Blocs of firms operating to dominate markets, manipulate governments and exclude rivals. Even Adam Smith referred to the proclivity of business to combine against the consumer: "People of the same trade seldom meet together, even for merriment and diversion, but the conversation ends in a conspiracy against the public, or in some contrivance to raise prices." Cartels exist in all areas of the economy—e.g., agriculture, cement, computers, diamonds, petrochemicals, pharmaceuticals, shipping, vitamins—and demonstrate that the idea of "free trade" is highly conditional and ultimately unattainable. Susan Strange (1996, 148): "it is as if a curtain of silence had descended over the whole subject of cartels." The last major report on the subject was published in 1977. The existence of cartels mocks the idea of "perfect markets" or "perfect competition," as celebrated in economics texts. "The conclusion seems clear that, while the rhetoric of free enterprise and open competition is necessary to the full integration of a world economy operating on a market principle, the rhetoric is often, in reality, empty of meaning. Both in the United States and in Europe, let alone Japan, the war against restrictive cartels is pretty much of a farce. In steel, in shipping, and probably in most chemicals, aluminium, electrical products, authority over the market is exercised by associations of firms organised in overt cartels to rig prices in favour of the members—'conspiracies against the public' in effect. And in political terms, since the regulators are blind, inert, or impotent, such cartels constitute 'regimes within regimes'" (Strange, 1996, 160). Although cartels are illegal within the US, former Secretary of the Treasury, Paul O'Neill, arranged for the global aluminium cartel and has worked to suppress competition within the global steel market (Stiglitz, 2002, 172). See firms, markets, theory, economic, neoclassical and links.

**catch-up developers.** States like Germany, Japan and Korea, which were in the second wave of developers, behind Britain, the US and Belgium. See Newly Industrialized Countries, world economy, trends, since 1945 and links.

**Cato Institute** (www.cato.org). Right-wing US think-tank linked to the Republican Party. Patrick Michaels, a skeptic concerning global warming and *National Post* scribe, is a senior fellow. "If the West didn't produce as much as it does, standards of living in countries like South Africa would be lower than they are today." See think-tanks for links.

**Cayman Islands.** British colony in Caribbean and leading tax and money-laundering haven. Fifth largest banking centre of world in terms of deposits, mainly by shell corporations. Deposits not subject to taxes or regulation. Other jurisdictions where tax laws are similarly lax, or non-existent, include Vanuatu (ex-New Hebrides), Luxemburg and the Channel Islands. "The billions of dollars in the Cayman Islands and other such centres are not there because those islands provide better banking services than Wall Street, London, or Frankfurt; they are there because the secrecy allows them to engage in tax evasion, money laundering, and other nefarious activities [including the financing of terrorism]" (Stiglitz, 2002, 228). See drugs, illegal, capitalism, finance, hot money and links.

**C.D. Howe Institute.** (www.cdhowe.org). Leading right-wing think-tank in Canada. Membership of 280 comprises leading corporate figures. See lobbyists, business, think-tanks and links.

**Center for Economic and Policy Research (CEPR)** (www.cepr.net). Washington-based think-tank, critical of IMF and World Bank. Paper "The Emperor Has No Growth" compares the Reagan-Thatcher period, 1980–2000, which was marked by capital deregulation, privatization and the lifting of barriers to international trade, to the previous period, 1960–1980, when most developing countries had more restrictive and inward-looking economies. "The comparison is dramatic. The researchers took all the UNDP's indicators and found that between 1980 and 2000 there was 'a very clear decline in progress.' The poorest countries went from a per capita growth rate of 1.95 annually in the 1960–1980 period to a decline of 0.5% a year between 1980 and 2000. The middle group of countries did worse, dropping from annual growth of 3.6% to growth of just under 1% after 1980. The world's richest countries also showed a slowdown" (Jonathan Steele, *GW*, August 23–29, 2001, 23). See capital mobility, globalization, theory, free trade, think-tanks, United Nations Development Program (UNDP) and links.

**Center for Global Food Issues.** A business front subsidized by Monsanto, Dupont, Novartis, ConAgra, DowElanco, The Olin Foundation and the Ag-Chem Equipment Company (*Nat*, January 7/14, 2002, 38). See biotechnology, organizations and publications, agriculture, capitalist, Monsanto and links.

**Center for International Policy** (www.ciponline.org). Liberal, democratic, Washington-based think-tank concerned with global issues such as militarization, US involvement in Columbia, embargo on Cuba, war against Iraq. See organizations, public interest and links.

**Center for Public Integrity** (www.publicintegrity.org). Washington-based centre for "public service journalism." Provides documents and discussion on contemporary US political issues, e.g., the connection between President G.W. Bush and Harken Energy Corporation. Published *The Buying of the President, 2000*. Connected to the International Consortium of Investigative Journalists. See media, alternative and links.

**Center for Responsive Politics (CRP)** (www.crp.org). Washington-based research institute researching connection between corporations and pollution. See organizations and publications, environmental, pollution, environmental and links.

**Center for Strategic and International Studies (CSIS)** (www.csis.org). Washington-based think-tank. Recent article in CSIS journal, *The Washington Quarterly* (ref. in *Nat*, December 11, 2000, 9) recommends that state of Israel detain members of Hamas and Islamic Jihad without trial and torture them. Joseph Lieberman, Democratic Vice President nominee, and major recipient of funds from reactionary Cuban-American Foundation, is a member of CSIS Middle East Task Force. See also "Canada Project" which is "dedicated to the study of Canada and the Canadian-US relationship." See think-tanks, torture, state and links.

**Centre des medias alternatifs du Québec** (www.cmaq.net). See media, alternative and links.

**Centre for Science and the Environment** (www.cseindia.org). New Delhi-based research organization. See organizations and publications, environmental.

**Centre for Social Justice** (www.socialjustice.org). Toronto-based research and educational organization with special interest in exposing excesses of neoliberals, conservatives, privatizers and CEOs of all stripes. See organizations and publications, critical of capitalism and globalism and links.

*chaebol.* South Korean conglomerate. The leading *chaebol* is Samsung, which produces a wide range of electronic goods (e.g., TVs, mobile phones). See capitalism and links.

**cheap-labour economies.** A major consequence of the search to lower costs has been the movement of capital in search of cheap labour. Examples of this are everywhere but the best example is probably in the garment industry. Garments in Canadian shops are usually produced in countries with exceptionally cheap labour costs: Sri Lanka, Vietnam, El Salvador. Chossudovsky (1997, 88–90) gives an example from Bangladesh, where female and child labour is paid around $20 per month.

These wage costs amount to less than 2% of total costs. These workers might produce a dozen shirts in 25–30 hours for which they are paid $.15–.20 per hour. The factory price of the shirts is $36–40 per dozen and they retail in the US for $266 per dozen. The mark-up ($266–$38=$228) is divided between international distributors, wholesalers, retailers, circulation costs (transport, storage) and customs. Attempts by the IMF to reduce "labour costs," that is, to drive down wages, have had the effect of impoverishing large populations and thus undermining the expansion of consumer markets. This, in turn, leads to closures and bankruptcies. As this happens in one area, new markets have to be sought elsewhere. Thus a cycle: discovery of new markets, overproduction, decline of consumer demand, collapse. See child, child labour, child poverty, International Multi-Fibre Arrangement, maquiladora, Maquila Solidarity Network, human rights, slavery, globalization, theory, free trade, textile and clothing industry, United Students Against Sweatshops and links.

**child.** Usually any young person under 14 although legal definitions vary. A minor may be a child up to 19. See cheap-labour economies, Child Labor Coalition, child labour and slavery, child poverty, Child Poverty Action Group, child slavery, organizations, for the protection of children, organizations, human rights, sex, exploitation of *Terre des Homme* and following entries.

**Child Labor Coalition** (www.stopchildlabor.org). US-based organization founded in 1989. Concerned with child labour in cocoa-producing areas of West Africa. See child, organizations, Global Exchange, human rights, slavery and links.

**child labour and slavery.** According to the ILO the total number of children in the age group five to fourteen years in developing countries is 250 million, of whom 120 million work on a full-time basis. Of these, 61% are in Asian countries, 32% in Africa and 7+% in Latin America. In India, the world's second largest country, 20% of children under 14 are labourers (*Front*, May 18, 2002, 100). In a single district (Ganjam) of the state of Orissa in India, 40,977 child labourers have been identified. Most child labourers are girls and most earn 40 to 50 rupees a day (Rs28=C$1.00). Child slavery in Côte d'Ivoire is involved in producing cocoa for chocolate. Organizations and websites: International Labour Organization (International Program on the Eradication of Child Labour), Child Labor Coalition (www.stopchildlabor.org), Human Rights Watch (www.hrw.org), iAbolish (www.iabolish.com), International Labour Organization (www.ilo.org), UNICEF (www.unicef.org) and Bhagwati, 2004, Chapter 6 for Indian sources. See child, labour, fair trade, International Labour Organization, sex, trafficking in and links.

**child poverty.** According to United Nations Children's Fund (also known as UNICEF), Canada is seventeenth among OECD nations in child poverty; 15.5% of Canadian children live in poverty; 22.4% in US; other estimates put Canadian child poverty at 19.8%. Child poverty is 2.6% in Sweden, 7.9% in France, 12.6% in Australia, 15.4% in Poland, 19.8% in Britain and 26.2% in Mexico (CCPAM, 7,4, September 2000, 23). See child, wealth, distribution of, Canadian and links.

**Child Poverty Action Group (CPAG).** UK research organization. A 1996 report showed that in pre-Thatcherite Britain one in ten persons lived below the poverty line. After two successive Conservative governments headed by Thatcher and Major (1979–1997) the ratio increased to one in four and one child in three. See child and links.

**child slavery.** Child slaves exist in the Gulf States, South Asia and West and Central Africa. See links under child.

**chloroflurocarbons (CFCs).** Ozone-depleting gases partly responsible for climate change. CFCs originate in refrigerants, foams and aerosol sprays. The first CFC, freon, was invented in 1930–1931 and was used in refrigerants, solvents and spray propellants. Other gases important to the environment are carbon dioxide, ozone and sulphur dioxide. See agreements, international, on environment, pollution, environmental, organizations and publications, environmental and links.

**Christian Aid** (www.christian-aid.org.uk). Protestant church organization founded in UK in 1945. Website offers material on child trafficking into UK. See child, organizations, human rights and links.

**Citicorp.** A US commercial bank, owned by Citigroup, which led commercial lending to Third World countries in the late 1960s. When commodity prices plummeted in the 1970s, many of these countries became deeply indebted. See capitalism. finance, debt/deficit and links.

**civil society.** According to the UNDP (1993, 1): "Civil society is, together with the state and the market, one of the three 'spheres' that interface in the making of democratic societies. Civil society is the sphere in which social movements become organized. The organizations of civil society, which represent many diverse and sometimes contradictory social interests, are shaped to fit their social base, constituency, thematic orientations (e.g., environment, gender, human rights) and types of activity. They include church-related groups, trade unions, cooperatives, service organizations, community groups and youth organizations, as well as academic institutions and others." In the Third World, NGOs form an important part of civil society. See non-governmental organizations (NGOs) and links.

**Climate Action Network** (www.climatenetwork.org/USCAN/about). US branch of global network which seeks to inform and influence government policy. See Kyoto Protocol, organizations and publications, environmental and links.

**climate change.** Normally defined as the sudden increase in temperature, especially in cold areas, caused by the depletion of the ozone layer (which insulates the earth) due to the emissions of gases, especially carbon dioxide, produced by the burning of fossil fuels. According to Princeton scientist Freeman Dyson: "The physical effects [of the release of greater amounts of carbon dioxide] ... are seen in changes in rainfall, cloudiness, wind strength, and temperature, which are customarily lumped together in the misleading phrase 'global warming.' This phrase is misleading because the warming caused by the greenhouse effect of increased carbon dioxide is not evenly distributed. In humid air, the effect of carbon dioxide on the transport of heat by radiation is less important, because it is outweighed by the much larger greenhouse effect of water vapour. The effect of carbon dioxide is more important where the air is dry, and air is usually dry only where it is cold. The warming mainly occurs where air is cold and dry, mainly in the arctic rather than in the tropics, mainly in winter rather than in summer, and mainly at night rather than in the daytime. The warming is real, but it is mostly making cold places warmer rather than making hot places hotter. To represent this local warming by a global average is misleading, because the global average is only a fraction of a degree while the local warming at high latitudes is much larger. Also, local changes in rainfall, whether they are increases or decreases, are usually more important than changes in temperature. It is better to use the phrase 'climate change' rather than 'global warming' to describe the physical effects of carbon dioxide" (*NYRB*, L, 8, May 15, 2003, 4–6, reviewing Smil, 2003). The most spectacular and alarming consequences of global warming include the melting of the polar ice caps and flooding. Conservative newspapers like the *National Post* and organizations often deny that there is a connection between pollution and global warming. For an archive on climate change, www.climateark.org, www.cru.uea.ac.uk, www.ecoequity.org, www.heatison.org, www.ipcc.ch, www.oneworld.org/cse/index. See also environment, global, Kyoto Protocol, organizations and publications, environmental, pollution, environmental and links.

**Coalition Against Trafficking in Women** (www.catinternational.org). NGO which focuses on prostitution, pornography, sex tourism and mail-order bride selling. Website contains links to World Bank and IMF policies. See Captive Daughters, International Monetary Fund, organizations and publications, human rights, sex, trafficking in, tourism, sex, women, rights of, World Bank and links.

**Coalition to Oppose the Arms Trade (COAT)** (www.ncf.ca). Produces quarterly report *Press for Conversion* and annual report monitoring Canada's arms trade. See links under agreements, international, on arms control and organizations, peace/arms control.

**colonialism.** A term now used interchangeably with imperialism, but earlier referring to the practice of direct imperial rule, i.e., of colonies such as India or Algeria, as opposed to indirect influence without rule, e.g., of the British over Argentina. In the 1950s and 1960s the term "neo-colonialism" was used to convey the idea of continued, indirect rule, either by former colonial countries (e.g., French rule over Senegal) or by the US (over Liberia or Central America). The IMF has been accused of practising a new form of colonialism. "All too often, the Fund's approach to developing countries has had the feel of a colonial ruler" (Stiglitz, 2002, 40). See foreign policy, US, International Monetary Fund, imperialism and links.

**Comité d'Accueil du Sommet des Ameriques (CASA)** (la_casa2001@hotmail.com). Anarchist group in favour of direct action; anti-capitalist, anti-patriarchy, anti-hierarchy. See anarchism, organizations, critical of capitalism and globalism and links.

**Common Frontiers** (www.web.net/comfront). Alliance of Canadian trade unions and community groups. Wants to reform FTAA by including protection for workers and of environment. Member organizations include Canadian Auto Workers (www.caw.ca), Canadian Centre for Policy Alternatives (www.policyalternatives.ca), Canadian Labour Congress (www.clc-ctc.ca), Centre of Concerned Women's Project (www.coc.org/womenspro), Communications, Energy and Paperworkers Union of Canada (www.cep.ca), Council of Canadians (www.canadians.org), Environmental Mining Council of British Columbia (www.miningwatch.org), Institute for Agriculture and Trade Policy (www.iatp.org), International Centre for Rights and Democratic Development (www.ichrdd.ca), Jubilee Campaign-Canada (www.web/net/~jubilee), Mining Watch Canada (www.miningwatch.ca), United Steelworkers of America-Canada (www.uswa.ca). See organizations and publications, critical of capitalism and globalism and links.

**companies, agribusiness/energy/tobacco/pharmaceutical/vitamin.** See firms, agribusiness/energy/pharmaceutical/ vitamin.

**companies, biotechnology.** See biotechnology and links.

**conditionalities.** A term that refers to the conditions that the World Bank insists that developing countries fulfil if they are to be given loans. These loans from the early 1980s were called "Structural Adjustment Loans" and required that borrowers shrink the state and open the economy to international transactions. Isabelle Grunberg, formerly an economist working for the UN Development Program (UNDP), writes that the defining elements of "conditionality" include an acceptance of "supply side" economics, a reduction to a strict minimum of social programs, the privatization of health and education and the abolition of food subsidies, the insistence of monetary stability (which works more for the loaners than the borrowers of capital), restrictive fiscal policies (including high rates of interest), which benefit the rich more than the poor, the stress of building up currency reserves (which puts a brake on consumption and imports), the liberalization of capital movements, and the privatization of publicly owned sectors of the economy (which means higher costs for those seeking housing). The result: the inequality of incomes has more than doubled in the world since 1960 while the gap between rich and poor countries has trebled (Grunberg, 2000, 18–19). See Fifty Years is Enough Network, IMF, inequality, development, structural adjustment, World Bank and links.

**Confederation Paysanne** (www.confederationpaysanne.fr). French small farmers coalition, led by José Bové against genetically modified crops, agro-business, McDonald's, etc. See anti-globalization movement, Bové, José, genetic engineering, McDonald's and links.

**conferences, international.** See Bonn World Climate Conference, Cancun, COP-6, Earth Summit, Group of (G) 8, Genoa, Johannesburg, Kananaskis, Kyoto Protocol, Prague, Qatar, Seattle, Windsor, World Conference Against Racism, Racial Discrimination, Xenophobia and Related Intolerance (Durban), Summit of the Americas, World Conference on Sustainable Development, World Economic Summit, World Social Summit and links.

**Convergence de lutte anti-capitalist (CLAC)** (clac@taktic.org). Popular organization of anarchist tendency originating in Montreal. Leading organizer of opposition to Free Trade Area of the Americas Conference in April 2001 since when active in campaigns on behalf of immigrants (see No One Is Illegal Campaign). See anarchism, conferences, international, migration, organizations and publications critical of capitalism and globalism and links.

**COP-6.** Sixth Conference of the Parties to the United Nations Framework Convention on Climate Change. Held in The Hague, 14–24 November 2000. Attracted 6000 participants from 160 governments plus NGOs and others. Disavowed by President George Bush in March 2001. See Canada, blocking of international protocols by, Canada, pollution, climate change, Kyoto Conference and links.

**Corporate Watch** (www.corpwatch.org). San Francisco-based watchdog group concerned with corporate malfeasance and machinations on the part of transnational firms. Presently concerned with activities of the Bush Administration and with the scramble for oil and pipelines in Central Asia. See corporations, greenwash, *Multinational Monitor*, multinational organizations, organizations and publications, critical of capitalism and globalization and links.

**corporations.** See Corporate Watch, corporations, blocking of remedial changes by, lobbyists, business and links.

**corporations, blocking of remedial changes by.** "Despite public concern and government inquiry beginning in the 1920s, General Motors and DuPont (whose joint subsidiary produced tetraethyl lead) managed to prevent regulation of lead additives in the United States until the 1970s. By then medical research showed that most Americans had elevated lead levels in their blood, and that the lead came from gasoline" (McNeill, 2001, 62). See Canada, blocking of international protocols by, Friday Group, lobbyists, business and links.

**Council for Biotechnology Information.** See Monsanto.

**Council of Canadians** (www.canadians.org). Social democratic organization active on the front of social justice and against globalization and privatization and suspicious of genetically modified foods. Headed by Maude Barlow. Claims 100,000 "members and supporters." Publishes Canadian *Perspectives*. See anti-globalization movement, genetically modified foods, North American Free Trade Agreement, organizations and publications, critical of capitalism and globalism and links.

*CovertAction Quarterly* (www.covertaction.org). Outstanding Washington-based periodical with particular interest in Third World featuring well-researched articles on contemporary events usually involving US skulduggery. Quality of research rivals *Le Monde Diplomatique*. See organizations and publications, human rights, rogue states, torture, state and links.

**crash, stockmarket.** A sudden and precipitous decline in share prices. The most famous stock market crash of the twentieth century was that of 1929 but there have been lesser crashes in 1974 and 1987. See bubble, recession, world economy, trends, since 1945 and links.

**crisis, economic, Third World.** Afflicted Mexico, 1994, East Asia, 1997–1999, Russia, 1998, Brazil, 1999, Argentina, 2001, Turkey, 2002. During the Asian financial crisis of 1997–1998, "Capital flows simply reversed course, heading towards European and US markets: for instance, in 1996 private capital flows into Malaysia, the Philippines, South Korea, Thailand and Indonesia amounted to US$93 billion. In 1997 there was an outflow of US$12 billion, and in 1998 an additional outflow of US$9 billion. This swing of US$114 billion in capital flows devalued the currencies of those countries and induced a severe recession in most of the Pacific economies... yet capital investment has continued to grow, and stock market values in the USA reached a historic height in 1999..." (Castells in Hutton and Giddens (eds.), 2000, 59–60). "The crisis now [1998] gripping East Asia bears comparison in terms of its destructive impact with the Great Depression of 1929. What started as a financial crisis has been allowed to develop into a full-fledged social and economic crisis, with devastating consequences for human development. Previously rising incomes have been reversed and unemployment and underemployment have reached alarming levels. Rising food prices and falling social spending have further aggravated the social conditions of the poorest" (Ellwood, 2001, 82–83). Former French prime minister Lionel Jospin (in Wade and Veneroso, 1998, 29): "The crises we have witnessed teach us three things; capitalism remains unstable, the economy is political, and the global economy calls for regulation." See crisis, financial, East Easian, Polanyi, Karl, predictions, slump, world, world economy, trends, since 1945 and links.

**crisis, financial, East Asian.** A financial crisis affecting five Southeast and East Asian countries in particular and lasting from 1998 to 2000. Losses to the economies of Thailand, Malaysia, South Korea, Indonesia and the Philippines are estimated at $2 trillion. The crisis led to the loss of livelihood for tens of millions, dramatically rising poverty, loss of savings, rising indebtedness, reduced health care and schooling and other costs. Western pundits claimed the crisis was due to "crony capitalism" and lack of "transparency" but it was far more than that, as Cuming (1998) has pointed out. During the crisis, the IMF at the behest of the US Treasury, blocked Japanese attempts to create a bailout fund for crippled banks and took charge of bailouts itself, on its own terms, which included structural adjustments. Incidentally, the IMF forced sales and US investors benefited hugely, especially in South Korea. While the US Treasury and the IMF worked together in US's interest; arguably, IMF management only made the crisis worse; as a result, the entire IMF orthodoxy came up for criticism and reassessment. According to Peet (2003, 81) the reputation of the IMF has never recovered. One quip by MIT economist, Rudi Dornbusch, was that the 'positive side' of the Asian crisis was that South Korea was "now owned and operated by our Treasury" (Grunberg, 2000, 18–19). In his chapter on the East Asian crisis, Stiglitz (2002, 89–90, 131) writes: "When the Thai baht collapsed on July 2, 1997, no one knew that this was the beginning of the greatest economic crisis since the Great Depression—one that would spread from Asia to Russia and Latin America and threaten the entire world.... The crisis is over now, but countries such as Indonesia will feel its effects for years. Unfortunately, the IMF policies imposed during this tumultuous time worsened the situation.... (I)n retrospect, it became clear that the IMF policies not only exacerbated the downturns but were partially responsible for the onset: excessively rapid financial and capital market liberalization was probably the single most important cause of the crisis, though mistaken policies on the part of the countries themselves played a role as well... The IMF did not learn quickly from its failures in East Asia." See capitalism, finance, crony capitalism, deregulation of capital markets, International Monetary Fund, Keynes, John Maynard, markets, transparency, model, development, East Asian, Washington Consensus and links.

**crony capitalism.** Disparaging term popularized by North American journalists at time of Asian crisis (1997–1998) and said to characterize financial dealings between Asian firms and states. Supposedly not used when Long Term Capital Management, an investment firm headed by David W. Mullins, former Harvard Business School professor and deputy to Federal Reserve Board Chairman Alan Greenspan, almost went bankrupt and was given $3.65 billion cash bailout by New York Federal Reserve Bank. "(A)s good an example of pure 'crony capitalism' as any ever attributed to the high-growth economies of East Asia" (Johnson, 2000, 208). See transparency, world economy, trends, since 1945 and links.

**David Suzuki Foundation** (www.davidsuzuki.org/climatemain). Involved in environmental education including climate change and genetically modified foods; headed by David Suzuki, host of CBC's "The Nature of Things." See genetically modified foods, organizations and publications, environmental, pollution, environmental and links.

**Davos.** See World Economic Forum.

**debt/deficit.** Lending and debt remain concentrated in middle income countries of East Asia and Latin America—in 1981, over 70% of outstanding debt was owed by just ten countries. In 1974 the total external debt of all developing nations was $135 billion. By 1981, it reached $751 billion. By the early 1990s, it was estimated to be $1,945 billion. Every major economy is deep in debt and debt is usually calculated as a % of GDP. Italy's debt is 124% of GDP, Belgium's 132%, Sweden's 95%. Up to 1997–1998 the Canadian government had run deficits for 27 years; for 14 of those years it exceeded $25 billion. In 1999–2000 the government managed a surplus of $12.3 billion. This surplus was 1.3% of GDP. It was the first surplus since 1949–1952. The latest surplus has allowed Ottawa to pay down its debt to $564.5 billion. At its peak this debt was $583.2 billion. At its highest the debt to GDP ratio was 71.2%; in 2000 it was 59.9%. The federal government has $60 billion in outstanding loans. See debt/deficit, difference between, debt, national, Canadian, debt, national, US, debt, student, Canadian, debt, developing countries, debt to GDP ratio, Jubilee 2000 and following entries.

**debt/deficit, difference between.** Countries have debts that they get by borrowing from bondholders (e.g., holders of Canada Savings Bonds), banks or international agencies such as the IMF. Deficits are the shortfall or surplus that countries have, usually calculated on an annual basis. So Canada has a relatively large debt but a budgetary surplus. See debt/deficit and links.

**debt, national, Canadian.** The Canadian federal debt as of December 2004 was $C501,493 million. For information on the Canadian economy, see www.canadianeconomy.gc.ca. See debt/deficit and links.

**debt, national, US.** The US debt as of 11 February 2005 was $7,629,245,507,947. In September 2000 it was $5,674,178,209,886. See debt/deficit and links.

**debt, developing countries.** External debt in developing countries went from $1,300 billion (one trillion, 300 billion) in 1992 to $2,100 billion (two trillion, 100 billion) by the end of 2000. Annual interest payments went from $167 million to $343 million. See debt/deficit, International Monetary Fund, Jubilee 200, Meltzer Commission, World Bank and links.

**debt, student, Canadian.** The average debt of a graduating university student in Ontario is $20,000. This is in large part a consequence of tuition doubling between 1989 and 1998. Between 1995 and 2000 tuition increased 60%. While one consequence of the increase in tuition is increased debt, another is the falling off of full and part-time enrolment. A Guelph University study that has taken account of the relationship between enrolment and background showed that whereas in 1987, 52% of entering students came from a background where parents had only a high school education, the figure shrank to 27% by 1998. A study from the University of Waterloo determined that between 1991 and 1998 the proportion of students from low income backgrounds dropped by 8.6% provincially and 14.2% at Waterloo. A study done of the background of medical students at the University of Western Ontario revealed that as a result of the 1998–1999 deregulation of fees for the medical program, which led to fees rising from C$3,500 to C$10,000, the income levels of entering students had risen dramatically. Of 80 first-year students—those hit by deregulation—24.4% reported family incomes in excess of $200,000, while just 7.7% reported family incomes of less than $40,000. Of fourth-year students (who had entered prior to deregulation), only 8.6% reported family incomes in excess of $200,000 while 17.3% reported family incomes of less than $40,000 (*Qufacts*. Queen's University Faculty Association Newsletter, March 9, 2001, 4). See students, Canadian, fees and links.

**debt-to-GDP ratio.** A normal measure of debt. World War Two drove US debt from 40+% of GDP to 110%. US debt then fell to under 25% of GDP, to rise to 50% under Reagan. It has been falling since. Under President Clinton the US had a huge budget surplus—2 percent of GDP. Bush squandered that surplus turning it to a deficit of 5 percent of GDP (*TS*, October 7, 2004, A24). See debt/deficit and links.

**Democracy Watch (Démocratie en surveillance)** (www.dwatch@web.net). Ottawa-based citizen advocacy organization founded in 1993. Headed by Duff Conacher, who formerly worked with Ralph Nader and who founded Quebec Public Interest Research Group. Has blown whistle on hidden election donations of Liberal Party and Liberal's cash-for-access scheme at FTAA meeting in Quebec. See lobbyists, business, organizations, human rights and links.

**democratization.** A euphemism. Ostensibly a process leading to more democracy, however defined, but in reality, moving in a direction approved by the US. The despotic president, Boris Yeltsin, who ruled by decree in defiance of parliament, for instance, was lauded for "democratizing" Russia. Other despots have been congratulated by Western powers, especially the US, for "restoring democracy" in the aftermath of overthrowing elected governments. See Washington Consensus and links.

**demodernization.** The effect of the Washington-led program for Russia, but includes also the bombing of Serbia and Iraq, the blockading of Cuba, the Taliban take-over of Afghanistan. See development and links.

**Demos** (www.demos.co.uk). English think-tank, launched in 1993, by ex-Marxists, produces pamphlets on wide range of issues including environment, dentistry, schools, knowledge economy and welfare reform. Third Way-ish, hence not devoid of market populist gibberish (Frank, 2000, 347–49). See Third Way and links.

**dependency, theory.** See theory, dependency.

**deregulation.** A feature of liberalization, fallen increasingly into disfavour with the stock market crash of 2002. Often involves the privatization, or at least removal from public control, of formerly publicly owned assets. Once privatization takes place, user costs rise to the advantage of investors. See deregulation, of capital markets, deregulation, of stock markets, deregulation, of utilities and following entries.

**deregulation, of capital markets.** A policy of neoliberalism, promoted by the Washington Consensus, which has as its aim greater access to markets, including financial markets. Stiglitz (2002, 100) argues that market liberalization was the single most important factor leading to the East Asian crisis and, further, that there was no basis for market liberalization "beyond serving the naked self-interest of financial markets. In the 1990s, deregulation of capital markets in Asia allowed massive inflows of short-term capital at a much faster rate than the underlying rate of growth of the economies in question. Despite maintaining favourable macroeconomic fundamentals (growth rates and savings rates were high, inflation low, government deficits under control), they then became vulnerable to destabilizing capital flight when growth slowed down." The removing of restrictions of capital mobility has been one of the main projects of the IMF: "The IMF's strategy in the 1980s and 1990s favored transnational finance at the expense of economic stability" (Tabb, 2000, 122–23). See capitalism, finance, crisis, financial, East Asian, Washington Consensus, world economy, trends, since 1945 and links.

**deregulation, of stock market.** A feature of the reign of Clinton in the US, advocated by Robert Rubin and Lawrence Summers. See bubble, Clintonomics, stock market, in the US and links.

**deregulation, of utilities.** The deregulation of water and electricity has taken place in several Western countries, with mixed reviews. In California the deregulation of power has been a disastrous. For discussion, see Public Citizen (www.citizen.org) and links.

**derivatives.** Financial instruments, essentially futures, options or swaps, used to hedge investments against adverse movements, e.g., swings in bank rates and currencies. They offer the means to speculate against movements in prices since the initial outlay is only a fraction of the notional value of a contract. Among international financial transactions, they grew dramatically in the 1980s. See capitalism, finance, stock markets and links.

**developing countries.** Also known as "Third World Countries." A few developing countries have become "Newly Industrialized Countries." See aid, developing countries, incomes of, development, development, alternatives to, development and democracy, development, interpretation of, International Monetary Fund, non-governmental organizations, protectionism, World Bank and links.

**developing countries, incomes of.** The World Bank divides developing countries into four groups: low-income economies with a per capita GNP of less than $755; lower middle at $756–$2995; upper middle at $2996–$9265; high income at $9266 or more. See debt, developing countries, development, organizations, development and links

**development.** A complex process involving a generalized improvement in the conditions which initiate and guarantee well-being, especially economic and social well-being. One mainstream approach to development favoured by the World Bank limits it to the eradication of poverty. According to Nobel Laureate Amarta Sen, "Development can be seen... as a process of expanding the real freedoms that people enjoy. Focussing on human freedoms contrasts with narrower views of development, such as identifying development with the growth of gross national product, or with the rise in personal incomes, or with industrialization, or with technological advance, or with social modernization. Growth of GNP or individual incomes can, of course, be very important as *means* to expanding the freedoms enjoyed by the members of the society. But freedoms depend also on other determinants, such as social and economic arrangements (for example, facilities for education and health care as well as political and civil rights (for example, the liberty to participate in public discussion and scrutiny)" (Sen, 1999, 3). See also Parpart and Veltmeyer, 2004, and see aid, conferences, international, demodernization, developing countries, development, alternatives to, development and democracy, development, interpretations of, developmentalism, International Monetary Fund, theories, dependency, World Bank and following entries.

**development, alternative forms of.** Since 1974 there has emerged a global movement towards an alternative form of development. Here development is viewed not simply as economic growth and modernization, as in the conventional view, but as necessarily being participatory, equitable and socially inclusive as well as being sustainable as regards the environment and people's livelihoods. Some critics who have identified themselves as "neo-Marxist" or "postdevelopment" have rejected development altogether. See, for instance, the International Network for Cultural Alternatives to Development at the Centre intercultural de montréal (www.world-culture-network-net) and the Réseau Sud/Nord cultures et développement, 172, rue Joseph-II, Bruxelles, Belgique. See development and links.

**development, and democracy.** Lee Kuan Yew, first prime minister of

Singapore and persistent critic of US foreign policy: "With few exceptions, democracy has not brought good government to new developing countries. Democracy has not led to development because the governments did not establish [the] stability and discipline necessary for development." "It should be noted," adds Chalmers Johnson (2000, 150) "that in the 1990s, Singapore, which may not be as pleasant a place for an individualist to live, nevertheless has had a higher per capita income ($23,565) than Australia ($19,960), something that lends a certain credibility in Asian eyes to what its leader has had to say." See authoritarianism, soft, development and links.

**developmentalism.** An ideology which supercededed colonialism and was itself superceded by globalism. It argued for the release of territories and their people from the sclerotic grip of European powers. Thus released they would advance economically and socially leaving behind them the cruel, distorting and above all limiting relics of their subservient past—the forced labour, plantations and mines which were so essential to the colonial powers. In their place an open economy governed by free men living in democratic republics would emerge. All this would take time and during this time the newly liberated societies would have to be vaccinated and even operated on against communism and economic nationalism for these infections of transition would distort their national developments. See development, capitalism, national and links.

**Direct Action Network (DAN)** (directactionnetwork.org/). Informal North American association of activists against WTO, IMF, World Bank. See organizations and publications, critical of capitalism and globalism and links.

**disaster, economic, predictions of.** Since the late nineteenth century, not surprisingly given the Great Depression of 1873–1896, there has been a small industry in predicting the economic collapse of capitalism. Naturally, in the long term the doomsayers are bound to be vindicated. As John Maynard Keynes said: "In the long run, we are all dead." Hence: "A new story is forming around these events within the global system, likely to become visibly disruptive within the next ten years or so" (Greider, 1997, 147). See crash, dot.com firms, downturn, economic in the G7, interest rates, Keynes, John Maynard, world economy, trends, since 1945, World Scientists' Warning to Humanity and links.

**Doctors Without Borders.** See Médecins sans Frontièrs.

**Doha.** See Qatar and links.

**dollar, US.** "Conditions in the post-war world have been especially propitious for the dollar. The uncertainty over European monetary union, Japan's zero-interest policy and the fact that much of the debt overhang of the 1980s was denominated in dollars have all contributed to the dollar's strength. So have the decade's emerging-markets financial crises, which sent floods of capital into the dollar looking for a safe haven. And, of course, so has the 'new economy' miracle and all the hype in international investor circles that it has enjoyed.... Until now, the dollar has benefitted from the fact that there was no alternative for investors to turn to in time of crisis (Schwenninger, 2000, 23). See world economy, trends, since 1945 and links.

**Donner Canada Foundation.** Right-wing US organization with endowment of $100 million, given to bankrolling conservative causes and organizations such as National Citizens' Coalition. The foundation also supports Environment Probe. See Environment Probe, lobbyists, business and links.

**dot.com firms.** Firms using the INTERNET to sell goods and services, e.g., Priceline.com which sells airline tickets, e.Bay.com which is an online auction market and Amazon.com which sells books. "In June 1999, eBay was trading for 3,991 times earnings while Amazon and Priceline had ratios that were infinite, since they had no earnings at all. And for this there was no precedent in the entire experience of the world" (Frank, 2000, 163). See bubble, stock market, crash, world economy, trends, since 1945 and links.

**Dow Jones.** US investment firm that invented "Dow Jones Industrial Average." Owns *The Wall Street Journal*, noted for its excellent journalism, reactionary views and stock market puffery, *Smart Money*, a populist and empty personal finance magazine and *Far Eastern Economic Review*, an outstanding financial weekly that deals with South and East Asia. That there is a conflict of interest here seems obvious—we get the news about the world economy via a company the primary concern of which is in selling stocks and bonds. See bubble, Dow Jones Industrial Average, Wall Street and links.

**Dow Jones Industrial Average.** A measure of the value of thirty leading US stocks, used as a gauge to measure economic well-being. In February 1995, it stood at 4000 and in March 1999 it crossed the 10,000 mark, the stock market having been "bullish" or expansionary, continuously since March 1991. On February 19, 2005, it stood at 10,785. See bear market, Dow Jones and links.

**downsizing.** Euphemism for terminating employment of working people usually in the interest of shareholder profit. An increasingly popular practice since c.1980. Often accompanied by upswing of corporate profit and handsome rewards for CEOs. "In 1996 [Levi Strauss]... paid its retiring president $126 million; in 1997 it fired 6,395 employees and closed eleven plants. Between 1988 and 1996, thirty-three BCNI [Business Council on National Interests] member corporations laid off 216,004 employees (eleven others increased employees but by just 28,073" (Dobbin, 1998, 74, 93). See Canadian Council of Chief Executives, class, wealth, Canadian, distribution of and links.

**downturn, economic, in the G7.** Associated with a fall in profitability. "Between 1970 and 1990, the manufacturing rate of profit for the G-7 economies taken together was, on average, about 40 per cent lower than between 1950 and 1970. In 1990, it remained about 27 per cent below its level in 1973 and about 45 per cent below its peak in 1965" (Brenner, 1998, 7). See bear market, Dow Jones Industrial average, crisis, economic, neoliberalism, theories, supply side, wages, repression of, world economy, trends, since 1945 and links.

**drug companies.** See firms, pharmaceutical.

**drugs, illegal.** "Illegal drugs make up 8 per cent of world trade and are worth more than the combined global market in textiles, clothing, iron and steel." Conventional attempts at stopping the drug trade are futile and a waste of money. "(A)ny economist will tell you that destroying production in one country merely raises the incentive for another to produce more. If Afghanistan wipes out its crop, Burma has a market opportunity.... The main internationally traded drugs are cocaine and heroin, both partially refined agricultural commodities—cocaine from coca leaves and heroin from opium poppies. Coca bushes are grown on a significant scale in just three South American countries; Bolivia, Columbia and Peru. Opium poppies are cultivated more widely, from Southeast Asia to central America. Yet more than 90 per cent of production is estimated to be from only two countries: Burma and Afghanistan" (*Obs*, 8 July 2001, 3, citing Donald McCarthy, "Liberalizing the Laws of Drugs," The Social Market Foundation (UK), www.smf.co.uk. According to the Organized Crime Agency of British Columbia, marijuana, most of which is exported to the US, contributes C$6 billion to the provincial economy. This makes marijuana a more valuable export than timber (*G&M*, July 17, 2001, A15). For information on the drug trade in particular countries (for instance, Columbia), type in "drugs" and then country ("Columbia"); you will get sources like the Centre for International Policy, Columbia Project (www.ciponline.org/columbia). Tom Naylor (2002, 33) argues that estimates of the world drug turnover, usually put at around $500 billion, are largely guesswork. The usual estimate for the US share is around $100 billion. A Rand Commission study suggests that the actual US drug market share might be as low as $20 billion. Afghanistan produces almost three-quarters of the world's opium (2002). "At the end of 2002, farmers could get $540 a kilo, or over $16,000 a hectare, which no other crop could rival. Last year, opium production in Afghanistan generated up to $1.2 billion, or almost 20% of GDP" *Econ*, July 26, 2003, 14). See crime, organized, Social Market Foundation and links.

**Earth First** (www.earthfirst.org). Radical, direct-action US environmental movement. Publishes *EarthFirst, the Radical Environmental Journal*, which covers US and foreign environmental issues. See organizations and publications, environmental, organizations, mining and links.

**Earth Summit.** Actually, "UN Conference on Human Development." First global conference on the protection of the biosphere, held in Stockholm, 1972. Followed by UN Conference on Human Settlements (Habitat) in 1976, first World Climate Conference in 1979 and UN Conference on Environment and Development held in Rio de Janeiro in 1992, the largest diplomatic gathering in history. See conferences, international and links.

**Earthscan** (www.earthscan.co.uk). UK-based publisher of books on environment and sustainable development. For Canadian list, see www.nextcity.com/earthscan/pubearth). See links under organizations and publications, environmental, organizations, mining and links.

**East Asian Development Model.** See model, development, East Asian and links.

**East Asian financial crisis.** See crisis, financial, East Asian and links.

**ecological overshoot.** Concept which argues that since the 1980s humans have been using Earth's resources faster than they have been replenished. See organizations and publications, environmental, Redefining Progress and links.

**ecology movement.** A popular movement particularly strong in western Europe and North America that is concerned with the protection of the environment. Leading international organizations are Greenpeace and Friends of the Earth. The political form of the ecology movement is found in the Green parties, the strongest of which is that of Germany. See ecology, deep, organizations and publications, environmental and links.

**ecology, deep.** A fringe movement within the environmental movement that rejects anthropomorphism and finds intrinsic merit in all forms of life, natural systems and natural phenomena. Deep ecologists have been known to spike trees and thus cause injury to loggers. See organizations, and publications, environmental and links.

**Economic Policy Institute** (www.epinet.org). Has produced report on NAFTA on its 7th anniversary (NAFTA *at Seven*) and on costs of invasion and occupation of Iraq. Centrist *FT* has described it as "left-leaning." See North American Free Trade Agreement (NAFTA) and links.

**economic policy, US.** "A central aim of US economic policy since the Second World War has been the worldwide acceptance of free-market ideology—the belief that the free flow of goods, services and capital is to the mutual benefit of all; that corporations should be managed for the maximization of shareholder-value; that stock-markets should be used for buying and selling corporate control; and that governments should intervene only in cases of obvious market failure. If the US can persuade powerful segments of national elites to embrace these goals for themselves, it can achieve its foreign economic policy objectives far more cheaply and effectively than through either negotiations or coercion. Once national elites accept the idea of the mutual benefits of free trade and free capital movements, they can dismiss critics of the free market as defenders of special interests, at the expense of the common good" (Wade, 2001, 126). See United States, world economy, trends, since 1945 and links.

**economic restructuring.** The practice of US capitalism and its institutions, including Wall Street, the IMF, the World Bank and the World Trade Organization with the object of expanding its control over the economies of the developing countries, including the former socialist countries. This practice had its origins in the mid-1970s. Trade and financial liberalization are fundamental to its success. Countries that succumb to it abandon autonomous development models, such as ISI, and embrace foreign investment. See economic policy, US, globalization, Import Substitution Industrialization, International Monetary Fund, World Bank, world economy, trends, since 1945 and links.

**economy, informal sector of.** That part of any economy which is unmeasured and therefore untaxed. Sometimes known as the "underground economy," or the "second economy." The institutions of certain states regularly participate in this economy, e.g., the CIA, which has had a major role in the international drugs trade, and the Chinese Peoples' Liberation Army, which has been involved in smuggling and piracy (See Nairn, 2002, Ch. 2).

**EEC.** See European Union (EU).

**Ecumenical Coalition for Social Justice (ECSJ)** (www.ecsj.org). Toronto-based ecumenical church organization favouring social justice in Third World and even in Canada. See organizations and publications, human rights and links.

**emerging markets.** Euphemism, current since the 1980s, referring to developing economies generally. Many emerging markets, those of East Asia excepted, are actually submerging, that is, in terms of GDP growth, shrinking.

**empire.** See imperialism.

**empowerment.** A process of discovering and expanding inherent human worth and skills, often from the bottom-up and through participation, as a part of the process of development. For example, advocates of the "sustainable livelihoods approach" towards development argue that development does not require the economic and political power of the dominant class. See development, alternative and links.

**Ending Child Prostitution in Asian Tourism (ECPAT)** (www.ecpat.net). International organization, formed in Thailand in 1991, concerned with child prostitution, child pornography and trafficking of children for sexual purposes. See child, organizations and publications, human rights, tourism, sex and links.

**energy.** See Energy Information Agency, energy security, gas and oil and links.

**Energy Information Agency (EIA)** (www. vizonscitec.com). US government agency for the dissemination of wildly optimistic information about oil reserves and allied matters.

**energy security.** A subject of growing concern for industrialized and industrializing economies since vital supplies of oil and gas are increasingly controlled by OPEC countries, especially in the Middle East and Venezuela. By 1946, the US was consuming more oil than it could produce domestically and by 1970 US oil production hit its peak (Roberts, 2004, 39–43). See energy, food security and links.

**enlargement.** According to US National Security Advisor Anthony Lake (1993): "the successor to a doctrine of containment [i.e., of communism] must be a strategy of enlargement, enlargement of the world's free community of market democracies. During the Cold War, even children understood America's security mission; as they looked at those maps on their schoolroom walls, they knew we were trying to contain the creeping expansion of that big, red blob. Today... we might visualize our security mission as promoting the enlargement of the 'blue areas' of market democracies" (cited in Wade, 2001, 126). See economic policy, US, Free Trade Area of the Americas, North American Free Trade Association and links.

**environment, global.** For trends regarding biodiversity, climate change, deforestation and other matters in both statistical form and in analytical essays, see *World Resources: Guide to the Global Environment.* See organizations, and publications, environmental, pollution, environmental, resources and links.

**Environment Probe** (www.environmentprobe.org). Toronto-based public interest research and advisory group founded in 1989. The organization "works to expose government policies that harm not only Canada's forests, fisheries, waterways and other natural resources but also the economy." See Donner Foundation, organizations and publications, environmental and links.

**Environmental Investigation Agency (EIA)** (www.eia-international.org). Based in London; investigates environmental criminals. First to expose billion-dollar trade in elephant and rhino horns and illegal trade in CFC gases. See organizations, environmental and links.

**environmental Malthusianism.** See Malthusianism, environmental.

**environmental security.** Control over water, resources and so on. See Green Malthusianism, environmental, food security.

**equality.** See equity, wealth, distribution of Canadian/US/world.

**equity.** A concept of justice intended to overcome bias, favouritism and inequality as well as to protect natural or intrinsic rights. Often preferred to the term "equality" as it is more sensitive to gender differences. In the context of international development and among critics of the capitalist status quo, equity is favoured over equality. See equality and links.

**Erosion, Technology and Concentration (ETC) Group.** Formerly Rural Advancement Foundation International (RAFI). Winnipeg-based group dedicated to cultural diversity and human rights. Monitors ownership and control of technology, e.g., "terminator" gene GM seeds. See organizations and publications, agricultural, organizations and publications, critical of capitalism and globalization, organizations and publications, environmental and links.

**ETC Group.** See Erosion, Technology and Concentration Group.

**Ethical Trading Action Group.** Umbrella sheltering several organizations involved in ethical wages, improved working conditions and against child labour and sweatshops. See child, Maquila Solidarity Network, organizations and publications, human rights and links.

**Euro.** Currency used by most members of European Union (but not Britain or Denmark) since 1 January 2002. "One should not be misled by the euro's current woes or by the fact that its value has fallen more than 25% since its advent. These are the natural growing pains of a new currency whose economies are exporting large sums of capital. Indeed, on the indicators that matter most to a currency's future, the euro has done extremely well. Since its creation, as much international debt has been issued or denominated in euros as in dollars, indicating an underlying confidence of the world's largest financial institutions in the currency" (Schwenninger, 2000, 23). In January 2005, the Euro/$ exchange rate was 1 Euro=$1.286. See European Union and links.

**European Network Against Arms Trade (ENAAT)** (www.antenna.nl/enaat/). Umbrella for European arms control and peace organizations. See organizations and publications, peace/arms control and links.

**European Round Table of Industrialists (ERT).** EU's most powerful lobby group representing Volvo, Nestlé, Unilever, Fiat, Philips, ICI and other large corporations favouring a single European market, privatization and trade liberalization as a condition of entry into EU (Monbiot, 2001, 11). See cartels, lobbyists, business and links.

**European Union (EU).** Economic and political association of European states including Austria, Belgium, Denmark, Finland, France, Germany, Greece, Ireland, Italy, Luxemburg, Netherlands, Portugal, Sweden, Spain, and the UK, the total population of which was 376m. In May 2004, the EU admitted Cyprus, Czech Republic, Estonia, Hungary, Latvia, Lithuania, Malta, Poland, Slovakia and Slovenia and in 2007 Bulgaria and Rumania are scheduled to be admitted. These ten countries will add a further 102 million plus to the EU total. If Turkey is admitted (date undecided), a further 65m. will be added. The states of the EU have a total GDP of $12,129,000 billion, greater than that of the US. For comparisons with the US in other respects, see Ferguson, 2004, Chapter 7. See Euro, European Union, trade policies of, North American Free Trade Association (NAFTA), Statewatch and links.

**European Union (EU), trade policies of.** European governments while ideologically committed to free trade seek to perfect their own version of the Japanese model—a purposeful system of selective protection and subsidy that relied on market leverage (Greider, 1997, 141). See European Union and links.

**exchange rates.** The term "exchange rate" refers to the price of one currency in relation to others. One of the two main reasons for the founding of the IMF was the problem of exchange rates. Between 1944 and the early 1970s all Western currencies were in fixed relationships to the US dollar. Since then relationships have ceased to be fixed and thus fluctuate like the tides, much to the profit of currency speculators. The currency of China, on the other hand, is officially fixed and does not fluctuate. The euro and the Canadian dollar have risen against the US dollar since 2002, just as, in the past, the US dollar has risen against the euro and the C$. See International Monetary Fund, Plaza Accords and links.

**Export Development Corporation.** Canadian government institution the object of which is to promote exports overseas. Functions to some extent like the World Bank: many of the projects that it supports in the Third World are environmentally and socially disastrous. See *CCPAM*, November 2001, 12. See export(s) and links.

**export processing assembly factories.** Factories in an area, normally in a developing country, designated as being outside the normal national regulations regarding importing and exporting, trade unions and environmental laws. Normally such factories employ unskilled young women in repetitive assembly-line tasks. See maquiladoras and links.

**export promotion.** One of the keys to the successful growth of a number of postwar economies, such as those of Germany and Japan. Export promotion is normally at the expense of the domestic market. It was the economic strategy that followed import substitution in Latin America from the mid-1980s. See export(s) and links.

**export-led growth.** Development mantra promoted by IMF and World Bank that affirmed that economic growth could be assured by organizing production for export and not domestic market. The model for export-led growth was the newly industrialized countries of East and Southeast Asia. The theory paid scant attention to the problems of overcapacity and overproduction. See International Monetary Fund, Newly Industrialized Countries, overcapacity and overproduction, World Bank and links.

**Exxon** (properly called ExxonMobil Corporation). World's largest petroleum company and "the largest and most profitable company in the world" presently still in denial of global warming (Roberts, 2004, 265). According to *GM* (9,4, Summer 2002, 15): "Esso is doing more than any other company to stop international action to tackle climate change.... Esso has done more than any other company to undermine the Kyoto Protocol... it's largely because of Esso that President Bush has abandoned Kyoto—and Esso's fighting hard to make sure Canada does the same." Boycotted by Greenpeace and Friends of the Earth. For Greenpeace boycott, see www.stopesso.ca. Exxon funds the Competitive Enterprise Institute. The Canadian branch of Exxon is Imperial Oil. Imperial controls the network of Esso gas stations. Imperial is the country's biggest oil producer, refiner and marketer. Imperial oil and gas liquids output averaged 258,000 a day in the third quarter of 2002. Its profits for the fourth quarter of 2002 were $4.1 billion (compared to Shell's at $9 billion for the full year) (Roberts, 2004, 173). See global warming, lobbyists, business, organizations, environmental and links.

**Fabian Global Forum** (www.fabianglobalforum.net). Established by the Fabian Society (www.fabian-society.org.uk), a British social democratic think-tank of ancient pedigree, the Fabian Global Forum describes itself as UK's only "membership based left-of-centre think-tank." Concerned with abuses caused by and remedies for globalization which it favours in a modified form. See organizations and publications, critical of capitalism and globalism and links.

**fair trade.** The marketing of tropical products in an attempt to give the producers a larger share of the profits. Fair trade organizations exist right across Canada and other Western countries. The best-known fair trade commodity is coffee. The Fair Trade Federation (www.fairtradefederation.org) is an association of fair trade wholesalers, retailers and producers committed to fair wages and good employment opportunities. Other fair trade addresses: www.transfairusa.org, www.maxhavelaar.org, www.fairtrade.org/html/english and www.oxfam.org.uk. The address of the International Federation for Alternative Trade (IFAT) is http:catgen.com/ifat/EN/. See also Ransom, 2001, 136–38. A comprehensive discussion of fair trade issues may be found in Barrett Brown, 1993. See agriculture, capitalist, organizations and publications, agricultural and links.

**Fair Trade Association.** Toothless, US government-sponsored, labour watchdog, supported by firms like Nike. See fair trade, Workers' Rights Consortium and links.

**Federal Reserve.** US central bank, founded in 1913 to oversee the issue of paper money. See Greenspan, Alan and links.

**Fifty Years is Enough Network** (www.50years.org). Coalition of groups in alliance with aim of reforming or, better, dismantling IMF, World Bank and WTO. See Bretton Woods Institutions, conditionalities, lobbyists, Third World, organizations critical of capitalism and globalism, World Trade Organization.

**finance capital.** See capitalism, finance.

**firms.** See firms, agribusiness, firms, pharmaceutical, in Canada, firms, vitamin, General Agreement on Trade and Tariffs (GATT), Trade Related Intellectual Property Rights, World Trade Organization and links.

**firms, agribusiness.** There are only a handful of transnational firms dealing in grains, the largest of which is Cargill of Minneapolis, Minnesota. One executive of Cargill, Daniel Amstutz, was appointed by President Reagan as the chief negotiator of the last GATT Uruguay Round Agreement on Agriculture. "Sure enough, between our Congress and the Uruguay Round GATT negotiations, the US got the world price of grains down so low, our exports could out compete producers almost everywhere" (Dawkins, 1997, 14). Of agribusiness firms producing genetically modified seeds, the largest are Monsanto, Syngenta, Bayer Crop Science and DuPont. See agriculture, capitalist, firms, genetic engineering, genetically modified food, organizations and publications, agriculture and following entries.

**firms, energy, US.** The political contributions of US energy firms in 1998 were as follows: Mobil Oil $6.16m, Exxon $5.62 m., Texaco $4.23 m., and Shell Oil $3.72 m. The lion's share of these contributions—between 74 and 88%—went to the Republican Party. The major lobbyists of the fossil fuel industry have tried to weaken national and international climate control legislation at least since the 1980s. These lobbyists include the American Petroleum Institute, the Greening Earth Society, the Global Climate Coalition, the Information Council on the Environment and the World Coal Institute (*Alternatives* Journal, 26, 2, Spring 2000, 13). See lobbyists, business, pollution, of the environment and links.

**firms, pharmaceutical.** Four companies dominate the pharmaceutical industry, GlaxoSmithKline, Merck, Pfizer and Eli Lilly. They operate like a cartel. During the Uruguay Round of the GATT meetings they lobbied for stricter rules covering intellectual property rights. They wanted their new products covered by patent protection for twenty years. That is, they did not want them copied. Under the Trade Related Intellectual Property Rights Agreement (TRIPS) pharmaceuticals became protected. Previously medicines had not been patented. Now if one of the monopoly companies claims one of its patents has been impinged upon, it can take the impinger to the WTO disputes panel. The burden of proof is on the defender. See Aventis, cartels, firms and links.

**firms, pharmaceutical, in Canada.** "Pharmaceutical and biotechnology companies now fund 1 to 30 percent of all research at big medical schools such as McGill, Queen's and the universities of Toronto and British Columbia. The pharmaceutical industry now funds 42 per cent of medical research in Canada. Large donations from pharmaceutical and biotechnology giants and other corporations pay for new buildings and additions that carry their names and corporate logos" (*G&M*, September 8, 2001, F4). GlaxoSmithKlein is major donor to Queen's University. See cartels, firms and links.

**firms, tobacco, in Canada.** Imperial Tobacco of Montreal, a subsidiary of British American tobacco, is the industry leader. Through its lobbyists it seeks to impede legislation that restricts the sale of tobacco products. Although the Non-Smokers' Rights Association called for a royal commission to investigate tobacco firms, nothing has been done (*G&M*, September 3, 2002, A13). In mid-2004 much of its unsold stock was seized by the Quebec Government on the basis of the claim that Imperial had been involved in cigarette smuggling. See lobbyists, business, Canadian, tobacco and links.

**firms, vitamin.** Production and sales of vitamins are monopolized globally by two cartels, Hoffman-La Roche of Switzerland and BASF in Germany. These two firms, plus Aventis, control around 75% of the $6 bn. a year global vitamin business. "Vitamin industry sources across North America and in China say that Roche and BASF appear to operate in unison..." (*Nat*, 275, 2, July 8, 2002, 19–22). See cartels, firms and links.

**Focus on the Global South** (focus.web.org). Bangkok-based development organization that works with NGOs and other organizations especially in Asian Pacific countries. See development, development, alternatives to, non-governmental organizations, development, organizations and links.

**Food First** (www.foodfirst.org). An Oakland-based research institute (officially named the Institute for Food and Development Policy) concerned with Third World food issues and critical of GM foods. Founded in 1975. Walden Bello is leading light. See firms, agribusiness, organizations and publications, agriculture, organizations and publications, development, genetically modified (GM) food and links

**food, genetically modified.** See genetically modified (GM) food, organizations, agricultural and links.

**food, security of.** There exists an argument that every state should have a secure supply of food for its population. This argument runs counter to the "comparative advantage" idea at the foundation of globalization. India, Kenya and the Dominican Republic have been demanding a WTO food security clause in the interests of achieving food self-sufficiency. The US has blocked this claiming that it would "distort markets." In a 1985 letter to *Time* magazine US Senator Rudy Boschwitz of Minnesota wrote: "If we do not lower our farm prices to discourage... developing countries from aiming at self-reliance, our world-wide competitive position will continue to slide" (Dawkins, 1997, 13). "To the dismay of devotees of the principle of comparative advantage, Britain, which grew 30 percent of its grain in 1936, managed self-sufficiency in 1986." The Saudis grow wheat in the desert pumping water from underground aquifers at five times the market price also, ostensibly, for purposes of food security (McNeill, 2001, 226, 155). See agriculture, capitalist, energy security, firms, agribusiness, organizations, agriculture and links.

*Forbes 400.* A profile of the US's 400 richest people published annually by *Forbes Magazine*. Between 1995 and 1998 the net worth of the 400 grew from $357 billion to $780 billion, an increase of 107%. In 1999, the total net worth of the 400 hit $1 trillion, up 35% in a year. The minimum cut off in 1999 was $625 million. Since the 1960s, the wealth of the richest has been growing considerably faster than that of the median. Apart from the ownership of a principal residence, the bottom 90% of the population has no wealth to speak of—it owns a mere 17.8% of total stock ownership. It was during the Clinton and Gore years that the wealth of the top 1% came to exceed that of the bottom 90% (*LBO*, 94, 5). See Canadians, rich, High Net Worth Individuals, wealth, distribution of, Canadian/US/world, World Wealth Report and links.

**foreign investment.** From the early 1980s, and perhaps even earlier, the attitude on the part of many Third World states towards foreign investment shifted, and private investment, often by TNCs became more welcome. Throughout the 1970s in Latin America, for instance, nationalization and exclusion of foreign investment was common (and enshrined in the 1970 Andean Pact). By the 1980s, according to the UN Centre on Transnational Corporations (1988): "Not many developing countries would now see the activities of TNCs as impinging on their sovereignty [and] there are clear indications of a new pragmatic approach which comes from the growing belief that developing countries can negotiate agreements with the TNCs in which the benefits of foreign investments are not necessarily outweighed by the cost" (Strange, 1996, 49). See foreign policy, US, globalization, trade, free and links.

**foreign policy, US.** See American Enterprise Institute, antiglobalism, anti-internationalism, arms, production and trade, US, blowback Free Trade Area of the Americas, imperialism, International Criminal Court, International Monetary Fund, lobbies, business, new sovereigntism and links.

**foreign reserves.** Capital, often denominated in dollars, accumulated in central banks. In 1995, the US and Germany had $80 billion in foreign reserves, Japan had $240 billion, other Asian nations had more than $400 billion. "That vast store of wealth represented a new centre of power in the global system, not fully appreciated in the Old World capitals" (Greider, 1997, 256).

**forests, destruction of.** "In Africa and monsoon Asia, only about one-third of the forests of ten millennia ago still remain. In the Americas, on the other hand, roughly three-quarters still stand; in Russia two-thirds. At the end of the twentieth century, big blocks of forest stood in only three places in the world: the Amazon and Orinoco basins of South America and across northern Eurasia, from Sweden to Sakhalin. Great swatches once existed but disappeared into patchwork remnants in four places; from central India to northern China; Madagascar; Europe and Anatolia; and the Atlantic coast of Brazil. Giant blocks of forest now much shrunken and degraded stand in tropical Africa and eastern North America. Of this monumental forest clearance, perhaps half took place in the twentieth century. Nearly half of this was cleared in the tropics between 1960 and 1999" (McNeill, 2001, 229). For the destruction of African forests, see Global Witness and Indonesia, http://wrm.org.uy/deforestation/Asia/Indonesia.wtml. Otherwise, see Amazonia, organizations and publications, environmental, pollution, environmental, rainforests and links.

**fossil fuels.** Fuels derived from oil, gas and coal. The burning of fossil fuels is the main cause of air pollution in modern times. Fossil fuel consumption and industrialization go together like wind and sailing. The spread of automobiles, which depend upon fossil fuels, guarantee air pollution. A woman in Toronto was quoted as saying she even drove her air-conditioned car to the video store because the city's air quality was so poor (*G&M*, June 29, 2001, A14). See organizations and publications, environmental, pollution, environmental and links.

**Frankenfoods.** Genetically engineered foods. See genetic engineering and links.

**Fraser Institute** (www.fraserinstitute.ca). Right-wing think-tank in Vancouver offering total market fealty. The Fraser Institute was godfathered by Macmillan Bloedel, the clear-cutting champion (later bought out by the US forestry giant Weyerhaeuser) and bankrolled to the tune of C$450,000 by the right-wing American Donner Foundation. It describes itself as "largest, privately funded, public policy research organization" in Canada and, even though it is utterly bound to and dependent upon the interests of business, "an independent Canadian economic and social research and education organization." The institute campaigns for free trade, removal of interprovincial trade restrictions, and the decentralization of government programs. Its organ is *Fraser Forum*. Supported by major donations by Donner Foundation and the Bank of Nova Scotia, Imasco, Loblaws (through Garfield Weston Foundation), Royal Bank, Sterling Newspapers, Southam, Thompson Newspapers and Standard Broadcasting. David Radler, co-defendant with Lord Black in suit alleging plunder of Hollinger Corporation, is trustee and Lady (Barbara Amiel) Black, wife of Lord Black, has been. See Free Trade Area of the Americas, lobbyists, business, theory, Hayek, Friedrich von and links.

**Free the Slaves** (www.freetheslaves.net). US anti-slavery organization. See organizations and publications, human rights, slavery and links.

**free trade.** See trade, free and following entries.

**Free Trade Area of the Americas (FTAA)** (www.ftaa.-alea.orgftaa). "The Free Trade Area of the Americas (FTAA), negotiated in April 2001 by the thirty-four countries of North, Central and South America and the Caribbean (excluding Cuba), was intended by its architects to be the most far-reaching trade agreement in history. If reports coming from the "Negotiating Groups" working on the deal are correct, the FTAA will form the largest free trade zone in the world, encompassing a population of 800 million and a combined GDP of $11 trillion (US), and reach into every area of life for the citizens of the Americas. The FTAA was launched at the December 1994 Summit of the Americas in Miami, Florida, and was the focus of talks in Quebec City in April 2001. Although it is based on the model of [NAFTA], it goes far beyond NAFTA in its scope and power. As it now stands, the FTAA would introduce into the Western Hemisphere all the disciplines of the proposed services agreement of the [WTO]... with the powers of the failed [Multilateral Agreement on Investment], to create a new trade powerhouse with sweeping authority over every aspect of life in Canada and the Americas" (*CP*, Winter 2001, 11). FTAA talks are scheduled to conclude by 2005 but are presently threatened by disagreements between Brazil and the US over the matter of inclusion of investment and competition rules, which has led the Brazilians to baulk, and the insistence of deep cuts in agricultural subsidies, which has led the US to object. According to Duncan Cameron, the FTAA is less a free trade agreement than an instrument of US national policy. Accepting the FTAA means promoting and increasing US economic dominance (CCPA *Monitor*, 8,1, May 2001, 13). For the Canadian Department of Foreign Affairs position on the FTAA, see www.dfaot-maeci.gc.ca/tna-nac/ftaal-e.asp. See

Fraser Institute, Mercosur, organizations and publications, critical of capitalism and globalism, organizations for the promotion of capitalism and globalism, Quebec City and links.

**Friday Group.** Informal Canadian business lobby on environment. Its influence led to the rejection of a proposed Canadian Environmental Protection Act into which a coalition of environmental agencies had contributed and the passing of an Act which favoured the interests of business (*G&M*, April 21, 2001, F1, 8). See lobbyists, business, organizations and publications, critical of capitalism and globalism and links.

**Friedman, Milton (1912–).** Right-wing economic prophet whose ideas are usually credited with undermining Keynesianism and preparing the way for the neo-liberal wave of the next several decades. Subscribed to and promoted the idea that the lower the level of unemployment, the higher the level of inflation. For tight money and against social spending. Canadian neo-liberal governments (Liberals and Conservative alike) and the Bank of Canada have slavishly followed this prescription although there is considerable evidence that it is erroneous. See lobbies, business, neoliberalism, Nobel Prize for Economics, theory, free trade and links.

**Friends of the Earth** (www.foe.org). Amsterdam-based environmental organization with sixty-six member groups. Canadian group founded in 1978; website (www.foecanada.org). French equivalent: *Am(e)is de la Terre* (www.amisdelaterre.org/economie). A recent report by the Canadian chapter of FOE indicated that Ontario's gas is the dirtiest in Canada (*TS*, May 18, 2002, G1). According to Tony Juniper of Friends of the Earth UK: "For the past 10 years we've been locating ourselves more in the bigger economic debate and less in the 'save the whales' type debate. Talking about rainforests led us to talking about Third World debt. Talking about climate change led us to talk about transnational corporations. The more you talk about these things, the more you realise the subject isn't the environment any more, it's the economy and the pressures on countries to do things that undercut any efforts they make to deal with environmental issues. By the time we got to Seattle, we were all campaigning on the same basic trend that was undermining everybody's efforts to achieve any progressive goals. That trend is the free market and privileges for big corporations and rich people at the expense of everything else" (*Obs*, 14 July 2002, 24–25). See organizations and publications, critical of capitalism and globalism, organizations, mining, conferences, international, pollution, environmental and links.

**futures.** Agreements to trade any quantity of a product, i.e., currency, commodity, bonds, shares, etc., at an agreed future date for an agreed price. See stock markets and links.

**gas and oil.** For Alexander's Gas and Oil Connections, a website devoted to news about the politics of oil (e.g., in Central Asia), see www.gasandoil.com. See Organization of Petroleum Exporting Countries, petroleum, Canadian, exports to US, multinational corporations, oil, petroleum, world reserves, of and links.

**General Agreement on Trade and Services (GATS).** GATS was drawn up, in considerable secrecy, as part of the agreement that set up the World Trade Organization in 1994. It is a trade pact that seeks to open public services such as health care, education and water provision to private investment both nationally and internationally. If accepted, for-profit firms could claim the same rights, such as tax concessions, as municipally and provincially owned facilities. Private hospitals and water providers would thus be able to claim government subsidies. The lobbyists for transnational firms are strongly behind GATS. For strong arguments against, see Barry Coates (of World Development Movement) "Big business at your service," *GW*, March 15–21, 2001, 28. See Bretton Woods institutions, General Agreement on Trade and Tariffs (GATT), Trade-Related Aspects of Intellectual Property Rights (TRIPS, World Development Movement, World Trade Organization and links.

**General Agreement on Trade and Tariffs (GATT).** An international agreement drawn up before most colonial countries were decolonized, or the civil war in China had ended, which attempted to establish rules for the global marketplace, dominated from the outset by the US. The GATT charter was signed by twenty-three countries, eleven of which were in the Third World, and came into effect in January 1948. In its first round of talks its members managed to agree on 45,000 tariff concessions on trade in goods. With a secretariat in Geneva and a set of rules governing negotiations over tariffs, by the early 1990s GATT had 109 members, including all of the OECD as well as the majority of developing countries. Since its emergence GATT has organized eight sets of negotiations or "rounds," the most important of which were the "Tokyo Round," which took place between 1973–1979, and the "Uruguay Round," between 1986–1993. The 1995 GATT negotiations authorized the establishment of the World Trade Organization (WTO), which replaced GATT. Among other differences, whereas GATT was essentially a set of rules and was conceived of as a provisional measure, the WTO is an institution and demands a permanent commitment for its member state. See Bretton Woods organizations, General Agreement on Trade and Services, World Trade Organization and links.

**G(roup of) 7/G8/G20.** A summit of industrialized countries, originally five (Britain, France, Germany, Japan, US), then six (Italy), then, in 1976, seven (Canada) and, in 1998, eight (Russia). A further enlargement, in the form of the G20 countries, met in Montreal in October 2000. It was convened mainly to address the questions of the effects of globalization and to improve regulations of global capital markets. The G5-8 states have gone through several stages; at first the summits concentrated almost exclusively on monetary and economic issues, then, in the early 1980s they turned more to political issues. After the Cold War they turned to encouraging democracy and market economies in the former communist countries. Since 1994, they have been preoccupied with globalization and since 2001 they have become focussed on global warming. "The ability of summits to move things forward... relies on the participation of the right people. Before departing for Genoa, President George W. Bush spoke of his desire to launch a new trade round. But any hope of a breakthrough on trade is undermined by the fact that most opponents of a new round—developing and emerging market countries that are suspicious of the process—are not at the summit. And the protestors who claim to represent their interests are on the other side of the barricades" (Peel and Beattie, 2001). See conferences, international and links.

**General Electric.** Fifty-fifth largest economy in world. "GE has one of the worst pollution records in the US, with the highest number (47) of priority clean-up sites of any US company." Spends $18.8 million in lobbying, including funds given to Institute of International Economics, a corporate lobby group, Americans for Generational Equity, which lobbies for cuts in social security, and Centre for Economic Progress and Employment which lobbies to destroy product-liability laws. Leader of Business Roundtable, model for Canadian Business Council on National Issues (BCNI) (Dobbin, 1998, 43–45). See lobbyists, business and links.

**genetic engineering.** The scientific modification of the genetic composition of plants or animals by any means. Simple genetic engineering, by means of plant selection, has been practised since the Neolithic Period. Contemporary genetic engineering, usually done by transnational agribusinesses for profit, is relatively recent and is dominated by the US. Genetically engineered seeds, for instance, are normally the monopoly of one or other giant firm, e.g., Monsanto. Several dozen transgenetic plants have been developed and are commercially available: corn (the biggest GM crop), cotton (the fastest growing), squash, potatoes, canola, soybeans and sugar beets. Although the first transgenetic crops were planted commercially as recently as 1995, by 2001 more than 20 percent of maize in the US is planted in transgenetic corn (Richard Lewontin, 2001, 81): "The introduction of methods of genetic engineering into agriculture has caused a public reaction in Europe and North America that is unequalled in the history of technology.... (A)s far as anyone knows, no one has yet been harmed by any product of genetic engineering." See Aventis, Frankenfoods, Centre for Global Food Issues, Confederation Paysanne, genetic engineering/ dangers for the Third World/ Canadian government policy regarding/US government regulations affecting/popular opposition to, Genetic Engineering Alert, genetically modified food, Monsanto, Movement of Concerned Scientists for Biosafety, organic food and agriculture, organizations and publications, agricultural, Polaris Institute, Saskatchewan Organic Directorate, trade related intellectual property rights and following entries.

**Genetic Engineering Alert** (www.canadians.org/ge-alert). Website established by Guelph plant biologist Ann Clark at request of Council of Canadians to monitor GM food. "Within months of launching GE Alert, Clark... was stunned to learn that her laboratory was being arbitrarily moved to a seed-storage room that had been sprayed with pesticides over the years. The university denies the move had anything to do with her anti-GM views, but Clark says she is convinced it did" (*G&M*, September 8, 2001, F4). See genetic engineering and links.

**genetic engineering, Canadian government policy regarding.** According to Lucy Sharratt of the Polaris Institute (2002, 10), Canadian government regulation "is designed to facilitate the speedy commercialisation of genetically engineered foods and crops rather than fully assess safety risks. This model of regulation is a product of a partnership between the Canadian government and biotech and agribusiness corporations. The Canadian government is now training government scientists around the world in biotech regulations based on this model. Trade regimes and international bodies like the OECD have been used by our government to support the Canadian model thus far, but there are emerging conflicts internationally over the Canadian approach." See genetic engineering, Polaris Institute and links.

**genetic engineering, dangers for the Third World.** "Much of the agricultural economy of [Third World] countries depends on growing specialty commodities like lauric acid oils used in soaps and detergents, once found only in tropical species. Now, with recombinant DNA, these are produced by canola. Why buy palm oils from the potentially unstable Philippines, where 30 percent of the population depends on it economically, when we can grow it in Saskatchewan? Caffeine genes have been put into soybeans. Why not Nescafé from Minnesota?" (Lewontin, 2001, 83). See genetic engineering and links.

**genetic engineering, popular opposition to.** "(P)opular opposition to GM crops has little to do with whether people understand the science or not. It has a lot to do with hostility to unaccountable corporations having control over farming, an accurate hunch that scientists do not entirely know what they are doing and an attachment to an idea of 'nature' that is emotional, sentimental and irrational, and therefore cannot be proved wrong or right by scientific means. Perhaps because of their increasing dependence on private capital, too many scientists seem to have become confused about the difference between science and the practical application of science. They need to remember that a public judgment about the application of science, based on non-scientific criteria, is valid" (*LRB*, 11 July 2002, 8). A (Canadian) Ipsos-Reid poll conducted in September 2001 disclosed that:

40% of consumers view labels as a warning
25% are less likely to buy products labelled "GM"
27% would actively seek out non-GM alternatives
51% see GM products as unacceptable
87% want all GM food labelled
(www.web.net/nbon/bio/task). See genetic engineering and links.

**genetic engineering, US government regulations affecting.** "No unequivocal conclusions can be drawn about the overall effect of genetic engineering technologies. It is clear that any manipulation of organisms, whether by conventional means or by genetic engineering, poses some danger to human health, to present systems of agricultural production, and to natural environments. All of these potential effects have led to a fairly effective apparatus of government regulation whose chief deficiency is its dependence on data supplied to it by parties whose prime concern is not the public good but private interest" (Lewontin, 2001, 83). See genetic engineering and links.

**genetically modified (GM) food.** Food grown from genetically engineered seeds that have been modified in order to yield better taste or higher harvests, often because of their resistance to disease. For instance, the firm Calgene developed the "FlavrSavr" tomato which was genetically engineered to delay rotting. GM seeds are invariably patented by agribusiness giants such as Monsanto (which bought over 50% of Calgene) that have also tried to claim patents over potato and rice seeds. Under the TRIPS agreement, all members of the WTO "shall provide for the protection of plant varieties either by patents or by an effective sui generis system or by any combination thereof." Thus "anything that can be genetically manipulated can be patented and monopolized as the private property of giant transnational agricultural and pharmaceutical corporations." There has been little debate over GM foods in the US and Canada—respectively the largest and third largest producers of GM crops—but much in Western Europe. The Royal Society of Canada convened an expert panel to consider "genetically modified organisms." In its report of February 2001, it pointed out that proper testing procedures were not in place to ensure the safety of consumers or the environment. Environmental groups liked the report. The Liberal government and certain pharmaceutical and agricultural biotechnology companies such as BioteCanada, however, disliked it. The government appointed a second panel which was more industry-friendly. Its report, issued in August 2001, was less critical (Trek. The Magazine of the University of British Columbia. Summer, 2001, 23–27). Other sources: www.nuffieldbioethics.org/gmcrops/ourfindings.asp, www.greenpeace.ca and www.foodfirst.org/resources. See firms, agribusiness, Food First, genetic engineering, organizations and publications, agriculture, Trade Related Intellectual Property Rights (TRIPS) and links.

**Genoa** (www.info@genoa-g8.org and webmaster@genoa-g8.org). Site of G8 Summit during week ending July 20, 2001, at which richest countries pledged $1.2 billion to fight AIDS and other diseases in poor countries such as malaria and TB. Disagreement emerged between US and European countries in which US showed concern over drug company profits. According to a representative for Oxfam: "Unless the fund is drastically increased and used to buy cheap, generic medication, this start might only amount to lip service and corporate welfare" (*FT*, July 21–22, 2). On July 20 massive demonstrations of up to 100,000 took place during which one demonstrator was killed. This was the first fatality since protests against liberalization took place in Seattle in 1999. On the eve of the summit thirty African countries signed a declaration in Addis Ababa rejecting new powers for the WTO. See conferences, international, organizations, anarchist, organizations and publications, critical of capitalism and globalism and links.

**global capacity.** The capacity to produce autos, textiles, semiconductors, etc. for the global market. "There is excess global capacity in almost every industry" writes Jack Welch, former self-promoting CEO of GE. The consequence of global overcapacity is the downward pressure on profit per unit sold (Tabb, 2000, 106). The fact that the IMF and WB have worked to keep labour costs down has meant that domestic purchasing power as well as standards of living have been reduced in pursuit of the production of cheap exports. This had led to underconsumption. Thus, overcapacity and underconsumption march to the same neoliberal tune. See overcapacity and overproduction and links.

**global economy, great slowdown of.** This began in 1973 and had, in its origins, little to do with the oil crisis of 1974–1975, as is often claimed. After 1973 until the boom of c.1995–2000, none of the G7 economies recovered the rates of productivity and profit they had enjoyed during the postwar boom. The unemployment rate of the G7 countries averaged 6.5% as compared to 3.1% in 1960–1973. The best discussion of postwar economic trends is Brenner, 2002, summarized in Brenner, February

2003 and criticized by Arrighi, March/April 2003. See overcapacity and overproduction and links.

**Global Exchange** (www.globalexchange.org). US-based human rights organization formed in 1988 concerned with human rights issues. Has focussed in particular on the use of slaves in the cocoa-producing areas of West Africa. See Child Labor Coalition, organizations, human rights, slavery and links.

**global governance.** The idea of a set of standardized practices emerging on a world scale, as effected by some remote, invisible and perhaps disinterested world authority. Actually global *anything* is only guaranteed by the cooperation of the most powerful states, and these must include the US. Global governance is the pursuit of national interest by other means; so is any form of international order.

**Global Policy Network (GPN)** (www.globalpolicynetwork.org). Global association of policy and research organizations connected with trade unions; founded in Hamburg, March 2000. See organizations, critical of capitalism and globalism and links.

**Global Trade Watch (GTW)** (www.tradewatch.org). Established in 1993 to promote government and corporate accountability. A division of Public Citizen. See organizations and publications, critical of capitalism and globalism and links.

**Global Witness** (www.globalwitness.org). Non-affiliated research and information group based in London investigating connections between Western firms and resource pillaging in Third World, especially forests and mines, e.g., forest exploitation in Africa and Southeast Asia and the role of oil firms and banks in Angola's civil war. Recent publication: *The Usual Suspects: Liberia's Weapons and Mercenaries in Côte d'Ivoire and Sierra Leon* (London, 2003). The publications of Global Witness, on forests and other subjects such as the corruption of African governments are listed at the back of each publication. See blood diamonds, organizations and publications, environmental, organizations, mining and links.

**globalization.** "Globalization, at its simplest, refers to a shift or transformation in the scale of human organization that links distant communities and expands the reach of power relations across the world's regions. This shift can be mapped by examining the expanding scale, growing magnitude, speeding up and deepening impact of transcontinental flows and patterns of social interaction. While globalization generates dense patterns of transborder activities and networks—economic, political, legal, social, environmental , among others—it does not necessarily prefigure the emergence of a harmonious world society or a process of integration among nations and cultures. For not only does the awareness of growing interconnectedness create new forms of understanding, it also fuels deep animosities and conflicts. Since a substantial proportion of the world's population is largely excluded from the benefits of globalization, it can be a deeply divisive phenomenon. The unevenness of globalization ensures it is far from a universal process experienced uniformly across all countries" (Held, 2004, 1). See globalization and neoliberalism, globalization, US domination of, jobs, flight of, neoliberalism, outsourcing, overcapacity and overproduction and following entries.

**globalization and neoliberalism, advocates of.** See banks, Canadian, Friedman, Thomas, Greenspan, Alan, International Monetary Fund, Martin, Paul, press, business, lobbyists, Canadian, World Bank, world economy, trends, since 1945 and links.

**globalization, US domination of.** "In discussions of globalization at the political level, one question has predominated: that of the nation-state. Is it over and done with, or does it still have a vital role to play? Should it, perhaps, be understood as merely one pressure among many on national governments—and so on. But lurking behind these debates, I believe, is a deeper fear, a more fundamental narrative thought or fantasy. For when we talk about the spreading power and influence of globalization, aren't we really referring to the spreading economic and military might of the US? And in speaking of the weakening of the nation-state, are we not actually describing the subordination of the other nation-states to American power, either through consent and collaboration, or by the use of brute force and economic threat? Looming behind the anxieties expressed here is a new version of what used to be called imperialism... An earlier version was that of the pre-First World War colonist order, practised by a number of European countries, the US and Japan; this was replaced after the Second World War and the subsequent wave of decolonization by a Cold War form, less obvious but no less insidious in its use of economic pressure and blackmail ('advisers'; covert putsches...), now led predominantly by the US but still involving a few Western European powers.

Now perhaps we have a third stage, in which the United States pursues.... a three-pronged strategy; nuclear weapons for the US alone; human rights and American-style electoral democracy; and (less obviously) limits to immigration and the free flow of labour. One might add a fourth crucial policy here: the propagation of the free market across the globe. This latest form of imperialism will involve only the US (and such utterly subordinated satellites as the UK), who will adopt the role of the world's policemen, and enforce their rule through selected interventions (mostly bombings, from a great height) in various alleged danger zones" (Jameson, 2000, 50–51). For a view of the US as the new imperial state, see Bacevich, 2002, and as the grim dystopia at the end of history, see Grey, 1998. See Americanization, fundamentalism, globalism, imperialism, US and links.

**Goldman Sachs.** A leading US investment bank, rivals of which include Morgan Stanley. When it went public in 1999, each of its full partners got $90 million. Robert Rubin, the US Treasury Secretary, who rewrote the rules of the Korean economy after the Asian crisis of 1997, had been a partner for 30 years before joining the US government. Goldman Sachs sent its man to Korea to help reorganize the re-financing of the Korean economy in 1998. The term "conflict of interest" never seems to have arisen until c.2002 when Goldman Sachs was investigated by Securities Exchange Commission. See capitalism, finance and links.

**governance.** A neologism of the 1970s, contributing to the obscurantism of the genre, extensively used by political scientists working in the area of development. Meaning, roughly, the process or practice of governments, or what governments do minus politics. Hardly an improvement on the older term "government" as in "good government."

**green.** In most contexts, refers to environmental politics. "Greens" are thus those who see the environment as the principal political concern nationally or globally. They tend to be on the side of organic agriculture as against genetic engineering. See ecology, Green Party, Green Revolution, greenhouse, greenhouse effect, greenhouse gas, greenwash, Malthusianism, environmental, organizations and publications, environmental and following entries.

**Green Malthusianism.** See Malthusianism, environmental

**Green Party.** The political manifestation of the environmental movement, particularly powerful in Germany but also significant in Britain, the US and Canada, where it is particularly strong in BC and Ontario. See green and links.

**Green Revolution.** A technical and managerial package exported from the First to the Third World that depended on plant breeding that produced new strains of wheat, maize and rice. It had its greatest impact in the 1960s and 1970s and was hailed as being the world's best hope for self-sufficiency in food. By the 1990s three-quarters of rice grown in the Third World was of Green Revolution varieties. But it had several downsides: it created a greater dependence on pesticides, promoted monoculture, strongly favoured rich farmers over poor and contributed to the Big Dam mania of the World Bank and Third World governments, which led to massive human displacements. It had a negative effect on income distribution. In Mexico, for instance, the Green Revolution "worsened the absolute living standards of most of Mexico's poor rural population, reduced domestic production of food crops, and raised the price of food, resulting in *increased* hunger and greater concentration of poverty in the countryside. Most benefits were deflected to the cities. Traditional Indian communities such as the Yaqui in northwest Mexico were 'underdeveloped' by the whole process; local traditions of economic and social democracy in the formerly self-governing communities were destroyed as they were reduced to greater dependency on the outside and suffered increasing poverty and marginalization" (Rich, 1994, 91, footnote). See green, World Bank and links.

**greenhouse.** See green, greenhouse effect, greenhouse gas, Alberta, pollution, environmental and links.

**greenhouse effect.** The effect caused by carbon dioxide ($CO_2$) and other industrial gases that prevent the sun's radiation from reflecting back into space from the earth's surface. The trapped heat increases global temperatures. Because $CO_2$ mixes in the air globally, regions which produce little gas suffer all of its effects. In fact the US, which produces the most industrial gases, is likely to suffer less than those tropical regions which produce little. See greenhouse, pollution, environmental and links.

**greenhouse gas (GHG).** All industrial gases, including carbon dioxide, ozone, sulphur dioxide and chloroflurocarbons, that contribute to global warming. See greenhouse and links.

**Greenpeace** (www.greenpeace.org). Premier global environmental organization, founded in BC in 1960s. Numerous campaigns—e.g., against whaling (greenpeace.ca/e/campaign/oceans), against genetically modified foods (greenpeace.ca/e/campaign/gmo/gmoguide), against Esso (Exxon), (www.stopesso.ca). For environmental information, see www.greenpeace.ca. The Greenpeace website provides links in English and French to a number of organizations and campaigns related to the organization's work, including climate and energy links, forest links and genetic engineering. See organizations and publications, environmental and links.

**Greenspan, Alan.** Head of US Federal Reserve Bank ("the Fed"). In 1970s an undistinguished economist and advocate of thoughts of right-wing crank Ayn Rand, from whose works "you could order the opinion you needed" (Henwood, 1998, 89). Elected head of Fed and elevated to deity during stock market boom in the 1990s. Promoted technology, media and telecommunications (TMT) revolution: "It is safe to say that we are witnessing, in this decade in the United States, history's most compelling demonstration of the productive capacity of free peoples operating in free markets" (Brenner, 2002, 218). By 2002 with stock market in free fall, his feet of clay became more apparent but by 2004 his immaculate status had been restored. See bear market, crisis, economic, advanced capitalist world, Federal Reserve, globalization and neoliberalism, advocates of, trust and links.

**greenwash.** As "whitewash" but to give the impression of concern for the environment. Widely practised by multinational corporations and the World Bank, especially under president Barber Conable (1986–1990): "Behind its long, self-proclaimed mission of banker to the poor, and behind the new green façade, the Bank continued to do what it had always done: move larger and larger amounts of money to developing-country government agencies for capital-intensive, exported-oriented projects" (Rich, 1994, 149 and Greer and Bruno, 1996); for petroleum greenwashers, see Bruno, 2001). See Corporate Watch, World Bank and links.

**Gross Criminal Product.** A figure, of doubtful accuracy, referring to the total product of all criminal activities. It was estimated in 1996 to be $1.1 trillion (Nairn, 2002, 7). See organized crime and links.

**Gross Domestic Product (GDP).** Total of goods and services produced within a country. See Gross National Product (GNP).

**Gross National Product (GNP).** Total of goods, services and "invisibles" (e.g., banking, insurance, shipping) by a national economy, not necessarily within borders of that country. The GDP growth rate is a measure of national economic wellness. Canada's GDP growth rate at the end of 2004 was 3.2%. See Gross Domestic Product (GDP).

**Groupe de recherche et d'information sur la paix et la sécurité (GRIP).** An independent Belgian organization that studies, in particular, the role of Europe in international security. See organizations, peace and links.

**Group of 8.** Consortium of the world's leading economies including Canada. See conferences, international and links.

**Groupe Oppose à la Mondialisation des Marches (GOMM)** (www.lagauche.com/gauche/lghebdo/2000-48-10). Montreal anti-globalist coalition. See organizations and publications, critical of capitalism and globalism and links.

**growth.** Economic expansion. "Median unweighted GDP per capita growth in 1960–1979 was 3.4 percent for developed countries, 2.5 percent for developing countries; in 1980–1998, 1.8 percent and 6 percent respectively" (Wade, 2001, 135, fn.14). See growth, long term, in major industrialized countries, world economy, trends, since 1945 and links.

**growth, long term, in major industrialized countries.** Up to the early 1970s the long-term growth in the major industrialized countries had been as high as 5% a year. Thereafter it fell to about 2.5%. US GDP growth in the late 1990s stood at 4.6%. It is predicted that in the early 2000s that it may stick at around 1%. See growth and links.

**guest workers.** Foreign workers, often without civic rights, imported to work for cheap wages. The classic case is probably the German *gastarbeiter*, who came especially from Turkey in the early 1970s when German productivity was losing its lead to France and Italy. In Canada, guest workers from Jamaica and Mexico may be found in the fields of southern Ontario planting and harvesting field crops including tobacco. See labour, organizations, migration and links.

**Hague Conference.** Environmental conference held 13–14 November 2000. Progress blocked by Canada and other US allies (*G&M*, November 14, 2000, A25). See Canada, blocking of international protocols by, conferences, international and links.

**Hayek, Friedrich von.** Austrian economist and contemporary in Vienna of Karl Polanyi. Hayek hated socialism and communism in any form and explained in his *The Road to Serfdom* (1944) that the free market economy, not the state, should govern the affairs of humans. Up to early 1960s, Hayek was not taken seriously except by the few including Milton Friedman of the University of Chicago who, as the world capitalist economy entered a period of slower growth, led a highly successful campaign to rehabilitate Hayek's ideas. Most writers, researchers, journalists, politicians within the liberalization/globalization camp can therefore claim to be the children of Hayek and the apostles of the god of the market. "They have spent hundreds of millions of dollars, but the result has been worth every penny to them because they have made neo-liberalism seem as if it were the natural and normal condition of humanity. No matter how many disasters of all kinds the neo-liberal system has visibly created, no matter how many losers and outcasts it may create, it is still made to seem inevitable, like an act of God, the only possible economic and social order available to us" (George, 2001, 5). See neoliberalism, Polanyi, Karl, theory, economic, neoclassical and links.

**health care.** Publicly funded health care was one of the major achievements of most Western governments in the postwar period. From c.1980 the publicly funded system came under attack by right-wing governments. In Britain under the Conservatives it suffered considerable damage and remains, due to the commitment of the Labour Government to privatization, on life-support. See health care, Canada, lobbyists, business, organizations, health and welfare and following entries.

**health care, Canada.** According to Dave Barrett, former Premier of BC: "Prior to the introduction of universal health-care insurance, the private sector accounted for about 57 per cent of the total health-care expenditures. After full medicare implementation, by 1975 the public sector share had increased to about 75 per cent with the private share at 24 per cent. Their respective shares remained relatively constant until 1985. Then there was a levelling off of public expenditures with the public sector share amount reduced to 70 per cent and the private sector share increasing to 30 per cent. In comparison with other OECD countries, Canadian public sector health spending in 1998 accounted for 69.6 per cent of total health-care expenditures compared to an average of 73.6 per cent for the OECD countries. Accordingly, Canada placed among the lowest level of public sector health-care financing for these countries" (TS, June 11, 2001). Presently public health care is under assault by the private sector, which hopes to see its most profitable elements privatized. This assault is led by right-wing advocacy groups such as the Fraser and C.D. Howe Institutes. According to Money, Politics and Health Care: Reconstructing the Federal-Provincial Partnership (2004), a publication of the National Health Council, the federal share of health-care funding declined gradually in the 1980s and precipitously in the 1990s. Around 1974, the federal share of medicare was around 43%; after the cuts imposed by Paul Martin it dropped to around 16% (G&M, January 28, 2004, A17). See C.D. Howe Institute, Fraser Institute, health care and links.

**health, public expenditure on, as a% of GDP (1999).**
| | | |
|---|---|---|
| Australia 5.5 | Greece 5.3 | Sweden 7.3 |
| Belgium 6.8 | India 0.6 | Switzerland 7.1 |
| Canada 6.4 | Israel 7.0 | UK 5.9 |
| Denmark 6.7 | Italy 5.3 | US 6.5 |

See health care and links.

**Heavily Indebted Poor Countries (HIPC).** In 1996 the IMF, in concert with the World Bank, undertook a project to deal with 41 of the world's most heavily indebted poor countries, most of which were in Africa. In these countries debt servicing consumed a large part of export earnings and half of their total population of 615 million lived on less than $1 a day. By 2001, 22 countries (of which 18 were in Africa) qualified for debt relief under the HIPC initiative. However, according to one critic cited by

Peet (2003, 95–100) this was merely a question of old IMF wine in new bottles, as the conditions applied by the IMF, which included structural adjustment, resulted in little or no amelioration. See International Monetary Fund, structural adjustment and links.

**hegemony.** Unquestioned, consensual dominance of an idea, theory or practice. The concept was refined by the Italian communist thinker, Antonio Gramsci. The idea that the earth, not the sun, was the centre of the solar system was hegemonic until it was displaced by the heliocentric view which was persuasive because it could be verified scientifically. The idea that globalization is both natural and beneficial to humankind seeks hegemonic status, while the idea that capitalism and democracy are the only viable forms of human economic and social activity is presently hegemonic in most of the world. See ideology, theory, economic, neoclassical, globalization, neoliberalism, Washington Consensus and links.

**Heritage Foundation.** Right-wing and therefore pro-business US think-tank. Furious about the UN: "The war against economic freedom, the free-enterprise system and multinational corporations permeates the UN structure.... This structure is antithetical to US interests and policies" (*NI*, July 2002, 20–22). See think-tanks and links.

**High Net Worth Individuals (HNWI).** Persons with liquid financial assets of $1 million or more as defined by Merrill Lynch and Cap Gemini Ernst & Young, publishers of *World Wealth Report*. There are 7.3 million HNWIs in the world. In monetary terms, their average wealth is $3-5 million, although Latin American HNWI's are worth about $17 million each. Their collective assets in 2000 totalled $27 trillion. This elite of 0.1% of the world's population holds about 7.5–10% of its wealth (by comparison, 1.2 billion people live on $1 a day). A third of HNWIs live in North America, a quarter in Western Europe, a fifth in Asia, an eighth in Latin America, and the remaining tenth in the Middle East, Eastern Europe and Africa (*LBO*, 97, May 24, 2001, 8). See wealth and links.

HIV/AIDS. Human immunodeficiency virus/acquired immunodeficiency syndrome are a part of an epidemic which first emerged in the late 1970s. No region is worse affected than Africa, which has only 10% of the world's population but 70% of the cases, i.e., 23.3 million cases at the end of 1999. South Africa's is the deadliest AIDS epidemic in the world. Currently, 4.1 million people, or one in nine, are living with AIDS in South Africa. See organizations, health and welfare and links.

**hot money.** Usually money moved by currency speculators in the very short term from one economy to another. See capitalism, finance, Cayman Islands and links.

**Human Development Index (HDI).** A statistical construction undertaken by the United Nations and published annually in the *Human Development Report* which attempts to measure the average achievements in basic human development in one simple composite index and produces a ranking of countries from 1 to 175. The index measures per capita GDP, life expectancy, adult literacy and primary, secondary and tertiary educational enrolment. In the 2003 *Human Development Report*, 53 are in the "High Human Development" category, 76 in the "Medium" and 34 in the "Low." Of these 34, all except Nepal, Pakistan, Yemen and Haiti are in Africa. From the inception of the HDI until 2000 Canada was in first place; in 2001 it fell to third where it remained in the 2002 index. By 2003 it had dropped to eighth. See Human Development Report.

*Human Development Report.* Annual report produced by the UN Development Program (UNDP). The Human Development Report for 2001 was subtitled "Making New Technologies Work for Human Development." It noted (9–10): "Of the 4.6 billion people in developing countries, more than 850 million are illiterate, nearly a billion lack access to improved water sources, and 2.4 billion lack access to basic sanitation. Nearly 325 million boys and girls are out of school. And 11 million children under age five die each year from preventable causes—equivalent to more than 30,000 a day. Around 1.2 billion people live on less than $1 a day (1993 PPP US$), and 2.8 billion on less than $2 a day. Such deprivations are not limited to developing countries. In OECD countries, more than 130 million people are income poor, 34 million are unemployed and adult functional illiteracy rates average 15%." See Human Development Index, United Nations Development Program and links.

**human rights.** Defined by United Nations Human Rights Committee sub-Commission on Human Rights (see below); see also organizations and publications, human rights and links.

**Human Rights Watch** (www.hrw.org). International organization dedicated to monitoring human rights abuses, e.g., trafficking in humans, conditions of captives from Afghanistan in Guantanamo (for which www.hrw.org/press/2002/05/guantanamo). See iAbolish, organizations and publications, human rights, torture and links.

**iAbolish** (www.iabolish.com). Boston-based anti-slavery organization, part of American Anti-Slavery Group. Website refers to a CIA report which claims that there are 100,000 slaves inside the US. See organizations and publications, human rights, slavery and links.

**ideology.** Any set of beliefs held by a social group or organization usually but not necessarily either reasonable or consistent. We can speak of the ideology of Communists, Catholics or even vegetarians—as being Communism, Catholicism, vegetarianism (most ideologies end in "-ism"). Ideological shifts take place when one ideology is superceded by another: for instance, the 19th century saw a shift from creationism to evolutionism. Such shifts are invariably the work of minority intellectuals (in the case of Evolution, Darwinists). Most ideologies strive for the status of "common sense." When they achieve this status they become "consensual." To the extent that they become consensual and eclipse other ideologies, they may be said to be "hegemonic." According to Adam Harmes (2001, 117): "For mutual funds have had a direct role to play in the hegemonizing strategies of finance capital...." When Tom D'Aquino of the Canadian Council of Chief Executives (formerly the Business Council of National Interests) said that he wanted to "reconstruct" Canada ("And by reconstruction we mean fundamental change in some of the attitudes, some of the structures and some of the laws that shape our lives") he was spouting neoliberal ideology (i.e., "neoliberalism"). He was seeking to install it as "common sense" in the minds of Canadians. It was already common sense in the minds of his employers, the leading CEOs who finance the CCCE (Dobbin, 1998, 165–78). See Canadian Council of Chief Executives, capitalism, finance, hegemony, market fundamentalism, mutual funds, neoliberalism and links.

**IFIAC Report.** See Meltzer Commission.

**IMF riots.** Riots caused by the introduction of measures by the IMF which led to widespread immiseration, e.g., removal of subsidies for food and kerosene in Indonesia. See International Monetary Fund and links.

**immigration.** See migration.

**imperialism.** Usually defined as the practice of creating terrestrial empires. Lieven (2000, 17) refers to the principles defining the European colonial empires from the 17th to the 20th centuries as including "autarchy, protectionism and the unblushing and consistent exploitation of the colonial economy in the cause of metropolitan prosperity and Power." In the early 20th century, imperialism was thought by some Marxists to be the highest form of capitalism, but after decolonization (c.1945–1980) empires were regarded as having become, more or less, extinct. By c.2000, however, this assumption was being reversed. "The global income distribution facts are certainly consistent with the argument that 'globalization' is simply a new term for imperialism, allowing those in the advanced countries more effective access to, control over and benefit from the world's human and natural resources" (MacEwan, 1999, 72). Chalmers Johnson's amazingly prescient Blowback (2000) is subtitled "The Costs and Consequences of American Empire." Brenner (2001,

144) refers to IMF policies towards South Korea as "imperialist." He stresses that the IMF acted "as an instrument of US foreign policy." Since the invasion of Iraq (March 2003), the old meaning of the term has gained new popularity (see "The New Imperialism," Nat, February 17, 2003, 5–6). Andrew Bacevich's American Empire (2002) sketches the outline of the current phase of US imperialism, arguing that imperialism has been central to US foreign policy throughout the whole of the 20th century. Clyde Prestowitz (2003, Ch.2) discusses "The Unacknowledged Empire." Niall Ferguson and Michael Ignatieff (see below) are liberal imperialists. They think that the US should put rogue nations right through invading them and establishing liberal democracy. They ignore the fact that the US record of interventions is mainly on the side of dictators for whom human rights abuses are normal. See foreign policy, US, globalism, imperialism, US and links.

**imperialism, US.** "The decline of US hegemony is a myth—powerful, no doubt, but still a myth. In every important respect the United States still has the predominant power to shape frameworks and thus influence outcomes. This implies that it can draw the limits within which others choose from a restricted list of options, the restrictions being a large part a result of US decisions.... What is emerging... is a non-territorial empire with its imperial capital in Washington, D.C." (Strange in Panitch, 2000, 16–17). "(A)s the Cold War has receded into the past, the conceit that America is by its very nature innocent of imperial pretensions has become not only untenable but also counterproductive; it impedes efforts to gauge realistically the challenges facing the United States as a liberal democracy intent on presiding over a global order in which American values and American power enjoy pride of place (Bacevich, 2002, 243). See America First, colonialism, foreign policy, US, imperialism, US, isolationism, US and links.

**Import Substitution Industrialization (ISI).** In Latin America, import substitution industrialization (ISI), a variant of Keynesianism, originated with the problems of the Depression wherein the larger economies of the continent, unable to export in order to pay for their imports, turned to producing their own manufactured goods. ISI thus became the dominant economic strategy in Argentina, Brazil, Chile and Mexico from the 1930s to the 1970s. It was characterized economically by the erection of protectionist barriers and the payment of subsidies to domestic producers. It was finished off by the forces of international financial capitalism in league with their local delegates, although it was fatally weakened by local problems and especially the debt crisis. Among the other problems of ISI was that of the limitations of the domestic market. Import substituting manufacture operates at relatively inefficient levels and can survive only through import restrictions and income redistribution. The structure of politics often prevents this. Export promotion, its opposite, and the most favoured doctrine of the IMF, on the other hand, increases income inequality through the suppression of wages. Inability to import foreign goods has stimulated Russian domestic production—and revived import substitution as a development strategy. Import substitution in South Korea was quite successful (Cassells in Hutton and Giddens (eds.), 2000, 71). See export promotion, Keynes, John Maynard and links.

**income distribution.** See wealth and links.

**income gap.** See wealth and links.

**income inequality.** See wealth, distribution of, Canadian/US/world and links.

**income tax, personal.** Introduced in England in 1909 and the US in 1913. Conceived of as progressive, suggesting that the richer be taxed at a higher rate than the poorer. In most Western countries income taxes have become less progressive since the 1980s, indeed, there has been an almost universal tendency towards redistribution of wealth towards the wealthy. See wealth, distribution of, Canadian/US/world and links.

**Independent Media Centre (IMC).** On-line news centre reporting news excluded from conventional media. Has numerous centres, e.g., Ontario (www.Ontario.indymedia.org) and international (www.indymedia.org). See media, alternative and links.

*Index on Censorship* (www.indexoncensorship.org). Leading UK bi-monthly. Specializes in analysis of censorship and repression of writers on part of Western and other states but also concerned with civil liberties in general. See organizations and publications, human rights and links.

**inequality.** For data, see UN *Human Development Reports,* annually. See High Net Worth Individuals, equity, wealth, distribution of and links.

**inflation.** Increase, usually in prices and values. Regarded by Wall Street and subordinate institutions like the Bank of Canada as "the worst thing in the world" (Stiglitz, 2002, 172). See banks, Canadian, capitalism, finance, Wall Street and links.

**informal sector.** A term that refers to the part of the economy that is small-scale and informally organized and usually found in urban areas. Charac-teristically, the activities of the informal sector provide services and are precarious and unprotected by law. The *World Employment Reports* of the International Labour Organization suggests that the informal sector accounts for as much as 40% of urban activity in many developing societies and accounts for up to 90% of all employment growth over the past two decades.

**information technology.** This was at the heart of the New Economy which was based on technology, media and telecommunications (TMT). See technology, media, telecommunications world economy, trends, since 1945 and links.

**Initiative for Policy Dialogue** (www.gsb.columbia.edu/ipd). Non-profit organization established at Columbia University by Nobel-prizewinner Joseph Stiglitz "through which he hopes to do nothing less than end the World Bank and IMF's fifty-year monopoly on development policy. The IPD will, among other things, bring together task forces of economists to outline alternative approaches to a range of policy questions (trade, macroeconomic policy, pension reform). It will also oversee country dialogues, in which economists, policy-makers and members of civil society from developing countries will debate strategies and ideas" (*Nat*, June 10, 2002, 14). See organizations critical of capitalism and globalization, Stiglitz, Joseph, think-tanks, World Bank and links.

**Institute for Food and Development Policy.** See Food First.

**Institute for Public Accuracy** (www.accuracy.org). Consortium of independent journalists, provides news and contact information for analysis. Links to Public-Policy.org (www.public-policy.org), which has US and Canadian government policy links. See media, alternative and links.

**Institute for Trade and Agricultural Policy** (www.iatp.org). Minneapolis-based organization concerned with sustainable agriculture and trade policy. See lobbyists, Third World, organizations, agriculture and links.

**Institute for War and Peace Reporting** (www.iwpr.net). Independent London-based journalists' organization. Reports through a network of contributors on military activities in Afghanistan, Balkans, Caucasus, Central Asia and elsewhere. Updates on regular basis. See organizations and publications, peace/arms control, media, alternative and links.

**Intellectual Property Committee.** A lobby group comprising corporate giants such as Bristol Myers, Du Pont, General Electric, General Motors, Hewlett Packard, IBM, Johnson and Johnson, Merck, Monsanto, Pfizer, Rockwell and Time-Warner, which proposed to the GATT secretariat the fashioning of an intellectual property agreement that would guarantee the control by giants of certain ideas and the technologies which were related to them. See cartels, lobbies, business and links.

**intellectual property rights (IPR).** Conventionally, intellectual property rights have fallen within the domain of national law. National law guarantees protection of trade marks, patents and copyrights, usually for finite periods such as 20 years. Intellectual property rights vary from country to country and are regularly ignored: you can buy garment and CD knock-offs in Vietnam for less than $1. Recently, attempts have been made to guarantee the IPR of giant entertainment, pharmaceutical and agribusiness firms internationally, using the courts of the WTO. In an economy dominated by knowledge, intellectual property rights "are increasingly what makes capitalism tick" (Hutton in Hutton and Giddens (eds.), 2000, 25). See Intellectual Property Committee, intellectual property rights, Qatar, Trade Related Intellectual Property Rights and links.

**Intergovernmental Panel on Climate Change (IPCC)** (www.ipcc.ch). UN organization established in 1988 by World Meteorological Organization (WMO) and United Nations Environmental Program (UNEP). "The role of the IPCC is to assess the scientific and technical socio-economic information relevant to the understanding of the risk of human-induced climate change." In early 2001 IPCC presented a report authored by 426 scientists and reviewed by 440 government and expert reviewers which "found widespread evidence of climate change, ranging from the thawing of permafrost, longer growing seasons in certain latitudes, decline of some plant and animal populations, earlier flowering of trees and egg-laying in birds. But the changes that have already happened pale in comparison with those that could take place this century. In the 20th century, the planet heated up by about 0.6 degrees. This century, the IPCC predicts, temperatures will rise 1.4–5.8 degrees C., the fastest rate of change for 10,000 years... [and] predicts spreading deserts and a decline in agricultural production in Africa, floods and droughts in Latin America, storm surges and coastal erosion off the eastern seaboard of the US and water shortages in Australia and New Zealand. Europe will suffer widespread flooding... because of heat waves and unreliable snow conditions. In southern Europe more droughts could reduce agricultural productivity. Much of Asia will suffer a decline in agricultural productivity, while sea level rises and an increases in the intensity of tropical cyclones could displace tens of millions of people in low-lying coastal areas. The small island states, which are particularly vulnerable to increase in sea levels and storms, will suffer the worst effects of all. In April 2002, Dr. Robert Watson, chair of the IPCC, was voted out of his job in a secret ballot, with the US State Department opposing his re-election. Watson, a plain speaking and highly regarded scientist, had fallen foul of the fossil fuel industry. Environmental groups uncovered a memo from ExxonMobil, who were major contributors to Bush's election campaign, asking for the removal of Watson who they felt had an 'aggressive agenda'" (Godrej, 2001, 114). See Exxon, Kyoto Agreement, lobbyists, business and links.

**Intermediate Technology Development Group.** UK-based NGO seeking to find technological answers to Third World poverty. Urged negotiations by International Undertaking on Plant Genetic Resources for Food and Agriculture (IU) to be concluded quickly but blocked by Canada and other states (US, Australia, NZ). See climate change, lobbyists, business, organizations, agriculture, food and fisheries and links.

**International Action Network on Small Arms (IANSA)** (www.iansa.org). See organizations and publications, peace/arms control and links.

**International Bank for Reconstruction and Development (IBRD).** A.k.a. "World Bank." See international financial institutions, International Monetary Fund, World Bank and links.

**International Campaign to Ban Landmines** (www.icbl.org). See organizations and publications, peace/arms control and links.

**International Centre for Human Rights and Democratic Development (ICHRDD)** (www.ichrdd.ca). Sometimes known as "Rights and Democracy." Independent Montreal-based centre with publications list focussing on such subjects as free trade and democratic rights. Ed Broadbent, former leader of federal NDP, was first head. Organized cross-Canada tour of Dr. Sima Samar, one of two women in Afghani government formed in December 2001, to whom it awarded its 2001 John Humphrey Freedom Award (*G&M*, December 6, 2001, A3). See organizations and publications, human rights and links.

**international community.** Euphemism for G8 countries and their allies and subordinates. The international community is invariably in favour of world peace, equality, prosperity, protection of the environment, endangered species, the UN, transnationals, US leadership, the World Bank, the IMF, the WTO, globalization, the use of fossil fuels, monopoly, the militarization of space and against rogue states, terrorism, anarchy. The "will of the international community" usually equals US foreign policy. "Humanitarianism" is the justification of the actions of the international community. There is no word for its inaction. See foreign policy, US, G8 countries, International Criminal Court, Washington Consensus and links.

**International Criminal Court.** Newest international institution, born on 1 July 2002 and joined by all major nations except the US. According to Lloyd Axworthy, former Canadian Minister of Foreign Affairs: "The disdain of the Americans is palpable; they'll resort to crude means to wreck any form of international architecture with which they disagree" (*G&M*, July 17, 2002, A13). See foreign policy, US, isolationism, US, organizations and publications, human rights and links.

**International Development and Research Council (IDRC).** Official Canadian agency which funds research in and about Third World. Sometimes funds dubious projects such as Monsanto's growing of genetically modified crops in China. See aid, genetic engineering, Monsanto and links.

**international development studies.** Usually an interdisciplinary program of studies that focuses on the question of economic, social and political change in developing countries ("emerging economies"). Particularly popular in the UK (at Sussex and East Anglia Universities) and the Netherlands (at the Institute of Social Studies) but also in Canada (at, among others, Queen's, McGill, Trent, Saint Mary's and Dalhousie universities).

**international financial institutions.** The leaders are the World Bank and the International Monetary Fund. Besides these are the three regional multilateral development banks (MDBS), the Inter-American Development Bank, the Asian Development Bank and the European Bank for Reconstruction and Development. The latter was founded in 1990 to lend money to the newly emergent capitalist economies of Eastern Europe and the former Soviet Union. See Bretton Woods institutions and links.

**International Forum on Globalization** (www.ifg.org). An alliance of 60 anti-globalization organizations in 25 countries which grew out of the Battle of Seattle, including Council of Canadians and Polaris Institute in Canada. Main concern is effect of global capitalism and particularly role of IMF, World Bank and WTO. See organizations and publications, critical of capitalism and globalization and links.

**International Governmental Organizations (IGOs).** Organizations such as the International Labor Organization (created in 1919) and the International Court of Justice (created in July 2002). In 1909 there were 37, by mid-1990s, 260. This increase is taken as further proof of globalization. The US routinely denounces these organizations as impeding its sovereignty. See imperialism, isolationism, US and links.

**International Institute for Economics.** Washington think-tank. See think-tanks, Washington Consensus and links.

**International Institute for Strategic Studies** (www.iiss.uk). Founded in 1958, the IISS claims to be "the world's most prestigious private not-for-profit membership organization for the study of political risk, international relations, military strategy, arms control, regional security and conflict resolution." Publishes *The Military Balance*, an inventory of the world's armed forces as well as other papers annually. See organizations and publications, peace/arms control and links.

**International Institute for Sustainable Development (IISG)** (www.iisd.org). Winnipeg-based research institution with offices in Calgary, Ottawa, New York and Geneva. Funded by governments of Canada and Manitoba as well as grants from UN. Main concern is sustainable development of Third World and also sustainable agricultural development in Canada, WTO reform, MEAS, trade related intellectual property rights, investment rules, international environment management and western hemispheric integration. See aid, development, non-governmental organizations and links.

**International Labour Organization (ILO)** (www.ilo.org). Founded in 1919 at the same time as the League of Nations (superceded by the UN) the ILO became a specialized agency of the UN in 1946. Its main concerns are international labour standards, including child labour, slavery and human rights. See labour, United Nations, organizations and publications, human rights and links.

**International Monetary Fund (IMF)** (www.imf.org). Founded, with World Bank, at conference in Bretton Woods in 1944, where it was conceived as bulwark against return of cycle of depression and war. Meant to manage world's currency system by fixing national currencies to US dollar, which was fixed to gold (until 1971, at least). It helped create stability in capitalist world in 1950s and 1960s but in the 1980s and 1990s by its advocacy of the deregulation of capital markets contributed to economic instability. Though ostensibly a multilateral institution like the World Bank, and customarily headed by a European, the IMF is essentially run by the US Treasury. Historian of Asia, Chalmers Johnson has called it "an institutional surrogate of the United States government" and "a covert arm of the US Treasury" (Johnson, 2000, 5, 210). William Greider (1997, 281–82) has called it "paternalistic agent of global capital... enforcing debt collection, supervising the financial accounts of poor nations, promoting wage suppression and other policy nostrums, preparing the poorer countries for eventual acceptance by the global trading system. The two agencies (i.e., the IMF and the World Bank) behave like righteous gatekeepers, instructing and scolding aspirants on the principles of neoclassical economics. If a nation learns well, it may become eligible for loans and projects. If it refuses to conform, it will continue to dwell in the outer circles of backward poverty." The *Globe and Mail*, on the other hand, is defensive of the IMF, reminding readers that it has been unfairly treated as a "convenient whipping boy" and is part of a "blame game [which] serves no one's interests" (January 15 2004, A22).

The IMF specialized in short-term lending to countries facing economic crises, at least until the debt crisis that began in 1982. Then it began to make loans conditional upon massive structural reforms. By 2000, there were 55 countries under at least one IMF program. In the 1990s the IMF served as a life jacket for international investors, ensuring that the people of developing countries would pay the price for bad investments. Otherwise, the IMF has been called "the debt police." In September 2000 the IMF had 182 members and employed 2700 persons, as compared to the World Bank's 8000. Its managing director from May 2000 has been Horst Kohler, who replaced Michel Camdessus, who was blamed for the "transition" fiasco in Russia (Bernard Cassen, "Dans l'ombre de Washington," *LMD*, September, 2000, 18; Tabb, 2000, 7). See Bretton Woods, institutions, capitalism, finance, conditionalities, crisis, Asian, export-led growth, imperialism, international financial institutions, market fundamentalism, transition, World Bank and links.

**International Multi-Fibre Arrangement.** Agreement made in 1973, at the behest of the US, restricting textile and clothing imports from developing countries. See development, protectionism, Voluntary Export Restraints and links.

**international strategic alliances.** Rival corporations driven together by mutual fear. See overcapacity and overproduction and links.

**investor-state rights.** "The investor-state rights provision, Chapter 11, of the North American free-trade agreement, permits corporations to challenge governments' sovereignty to make policy regarding public health, the environment, labour standards and other public services. Chapter 11 permits corporations to sue a foreign government—claiming compensation for lost and future business on the grounds they have been denied fair and equitable treatment by government policy alleged to be tantamount to expropriation of their investment. The disputes are decided upon by tribunals that conduct their proceedings in camera. While the Canadian government has stated its intention to oppose the inclusion of similar language in the proposed Free Trade Area of the Americas, it is the fear of critics that Canadian objections will be hollow... Here is how Chapter 11 works: The US Ethyl Corporation sued the Canadian government for $250 million... and obtained, in 1998, a settlement of $13 million for the government's ban on the gasoline additive mmt, labelled a known nerve toxin by reputed (sic) scientists. The ban was reversed.... California-based Sun Belt Water Incorporated, is suing Canada for the decision of the British Columbia government to refuse consent for the company to export bulk water. Sun Belt's president, Jack Lindsay, has declared: 'Because of NAFTA, we are now stakeholders in the national water policy of Canada'" (*G&M*, April 9, 2001, A7). See globalization and links.

**isolationism, US.** A constant if usually subordinate tendency in US foreign policy debates. From the late 1990s emerged in the mutant form of "new sovereigntism." The new sovereigntists' argument is that globalism impinges on US sovereignty as guaranteed by Constitution and is therefore anti-constitutional. This justifies a refusal to participate in international regimes, even those which are otherwise universally accepted, thus US Senate rejection of Comprehensive Test Ban Treaty, refusal to sign Land Mines Convention, or Rome treaty establishing an international criminal court, or to submit Kyoto Protocol for Senate approval, or ban on chemical and bacteriological weapons. The United States, along with only Somalia have not acceded to the Convention on the Rights of the Child. It also continues to defy prohibition of International Covenant on Civil and Political Rights in the matter of execution of juvenile offenders. In the latter case it stands together with Iran, Nigeria, Pakistan and Saudi Arabia. New Sovereigntists are particularly influential in conservative think-tanks such as the American Enterprise Institute (Spiro, 2000, Leyro and Moravcsik, 2001). See America First, foreign policy, US, imperialism, US and links.

**jobs, flight of.** An example: when Boeing 707 launched in late 1950s it was 100% "Made in America"; the 727 which followed had only 2% foreign content; the 737 was 10% foreign-made; 767 reached 15%; 777 was 30% foreign made; 21% made in Japan; tail sections for Boeing 737 usually produced in Wichita, Kansas, are now made in China; China and Indonesia also got some fuselage work for 767 and 777 at the behest of Boeing's Japanese partner; so jobs moved from Seattle to Nagoya to Shenyang; China is the fastest-growing aircraft market in the world; although Boeing had the most advanced workforce; thousands of Boeing workers lost their jobs, many permanently; the US had too many skilled aircraft workers; increasingly, Boeing has come to rely on overseas sales and overseas buyers demand jobs and production (known as "offsets") and technological autonomy; sales of 727 were 75% domestic; 777 is 60% international; the Xian Aircraft Company (XAC) makes tail fins, stabilizers, cargo doors and trailing-edge wing parts for the 737 and 747 at Xian. McDonnell Douglas, DASA and Aérospatial (partners in Airbus) and Canadair, also XAC, do component work; XAC has almost the manufacturing level to produce one whole aircraft of the level of the 737 (Greider, 1997, 131–32). See globalization and links.

**jobs, security of.** From the 1930s to the 1960s, it was widely assumed that one of the major responsibilities of the state was protection of its workers, both from national employers and international competition. One strategy for this was corporatism, that is, a triangular form of discussions involving the state, representatives of the working class and capital. From the 1970s, during the period of neoliberalism, this concern was abandoned in most Western states, which accepted that profitability could only return through raising unemployment and dampening wages (as well as redistributing wealth to capital through reduced taxes on corporations and diminished social spending). See globalization, neoliberalism and links.

**Johannesburg.** Site of 2002 World Conference Against Racism, Racial Discrimination, Xenophobia and Related Intolerance and World Summit on Sustainable Development. See conferences, international and links.

**Jubilee 2000** (www.jubilee2000uk.org). Influential coalition of organizations seeking Third World debt relief. Present at most international meetings such as WTO in Seattle. Successful within the terms of its mandate. See debt/deficit, lobbyists, Third World and links.

**Kananaskis.** Village in Alberta foothills, site of meeting of Group of Eight (G8) on 26–27 June 2002. Leaders discussed world poverty and health, particularly of Africa, making a number of promises, none of which were novel. Canadian newspapers published during the conference carried ads from firms (e.g., International Federation of Pharmaceutical Manufactures Associations in *G&M*, June 25, 2002, A9) who saw these promises as a potential source of profit. See conferences, international and links.

**Keynes, John Maynard (1883–1946).** Alongside Adam Smith and Karl Marx, one of the most influential thinkers in the field of economics over the last two centuries. Leading figure at both the Paris Peace Conference in 1919 and the Bretton Woods conference of 1944 (alongside the American Harry Dexter White) during the latter of which the IMF and World Bank were conceived. During the Depression, Keynes argued against free-market orthodoxy. He explained that markets could not extract themselves from permanent stagnation, high unemployment and underutilized capacity without the artificial demand stimulus of government spending. (In response to the claim that markets are self-correcting "in the long run," he replied: "In the long run, we are all dead.") This new spending, even though it increased debt, would create market demand for goods and labour. Governments should also redistribute incomes downwards to those who would spend money. Keynes' idea is usually said to be "counter cyclical" and is referred to as being a form of "demand stimulation." In similar forms it worked in all countries in the 1930s from Roosevelt's US to Hitler's Germany. The idea of government intervention was popular in the postwar era, too, but came under attack by the neo-liberals who argued that it inhibited prosperity. One of the last 20th-century attempts to use it in a Western country came in France under the Socialist prime minister, François Mitterand c1982. It led to massive capital flow out of the country and had to be abandoned. This flow of capital suggests, among other things, that states no longer have the capacity to manage their own economies, as they once had. Keynes most important books are The Economic Consequences of the Peace (1919) and The General Theory of Employment, Interest and Money (1935). See Bretton Woods Institutions, Keynesianism, neoliberalism, welfare state and links.

**Keynesianism.** The practice of the ideas of John Maynard Keynes. Keynes' ideas were a reaction to the Great Depression and were a rejection of the earlier orthodoxy of *laissez-faire* economics. The Depression raised questions about the long-term stability of capitalism; Keynesianism seemed to provide answers. It called for a managed economy that would assure national development and the improvement of national living standards through a limit of foreign ownership and capital controls. In Latin America especially, Import Substitution Industrialization (ISI) was the leading avatar of Keynesianism. The leading economic doctrine of the period 1945–1975, it was superceded by neoliberalism, which was, in the case of Latin America, implemented during debt crises and at gunpoint. A mutant form of Keynesianism is military Keynesianism (see below). See Import Substitution Industrialization (ISI), International Monetary Fund, Keynes, John Maynard, Keynesianism, military, liberalization, of trade, Reaganism-Thatcherism and links.

**Keynesianism, military.** A perversion of Keynesianism. The practice of stimulating the economy during a downturn through lavish arms contracts and providing fat profits to military contractors. Practised in Reagan-Bush era in the US c.1980–1992. The contemporary US project involving an anti-missile shield is a prime example. See aircraft, production and trade of Canadian/US, arms, production and trade of/Canadian/US, Keynesianism and links.

**Kyoto Protocol.** Vague agreement proposing Clean Development Mechanism (CDM)) reached in Kyoto, Japan in 1997 between 160 states (including the US) to cut greenhouse gas (GHG) emissions by 6% below 1990 levels by 2012. Ratified, in a compromised version in Bonn on July 23, 2001, by 178 countries (of the 189 countries in the UN). These included Canada but excluded the US, whose president, George W. Bush, denounced the treaty earlier in the year. Although Canadian federal government committed C$700 m. over the 5 years from 1997, Canada's emissions were 13% greater in 1998 than in 1990. Ontario, the major Canadian producer of GHG emissions, has committed virtually nothing.

"By the Bonn Agreement, Canada has agreed to cut its emissions to an average of 6% below its 1990 level over the 2008–2012 period. Canada produces 2.5% of global greenhouse gas emissions; the US, 25%. Canadians are the world's second-largest consumer of energy on a per capita basis. "Cabinet documents obtained by *The Globe and Mail* last year identified meeting Canada's Kyoto commitments as the biggest economic challenge since the Second World War" (*G&M*, July 24, 2001, A4). Despite the opposition efforts of a cabal of energy executives, led by Gwyn Morgan the CEO of EnCana Corp., the Kyoto Agreement was ratified. See Godrej, 2001, 94–116. See Bonn Conference, Canada, pollution, carbon emissions trade, chloroflurocarbons, Climate Action Network, climate change, COP-6, crisis, ecological, aversion of, greenhouse gases, Hague conference, Kyoto Protocol, opposition to, Kyoto Protocol, Industry Growth Opportunities, Intergovernmental Panel on Climate Change, lobbyists, business, Montreal Protocol, organizations and publications, environmental and following entries.

**Kyoto Protocol, Industry Growth Opportunities.** An Industry Canada report *The Kyoto Protocol and Industry Growth Opportunities* estimates that implementation of the protocol will cut growth by 1–2% by 2010. Meeting Kyoto's targets, on the other hand, could create C$90 in new activities and investments (*TS*, September 7, 2002, E10, 14). Such figures suggest that no one really knows what will happen if the Kyoto targets are met or what will happen to industry if they are not. See Kyoto Protocol and links.

**Kyoto Protocol, opposition to.** The US is the only major state which is opposed the Kyoto Protocol. In Canada, Alberta Premier Ralph Klein called on the federal government to delay ratification on the grounds that it would lead to disaster in Alberta. The Canadian Association of Petroleum Producers also opposes ratification saying that it would put Canadian firms at a competitive disadvantage with US firms (*G&M*, July 24, 2001, A4). See greenhouse gas, Alberta, Kyoto Protocol, lobbyists, business and links.

**labour.** See entries below and cheap labour economies, child labour, child slavery, export processing assembly factories, guest workers, International Labour Organization, jobs, security of, maquiladoras, migration, slavery, trade unions, wages, repression of and links.

**labour, child.** See child labour, child slavery, labour and following entries.

**labour, organizations.** "Advanced nations like the United States ostensibly support the idea of free labor, but, in practice, they are on the other side. Major governments like the United States take their cues from the multinationals and are unwilling to press the labor issue against even the most abusive cases" (Greider, 1997, 11). See labour and links.

**labour, women's.** In Asia and other developing regions foreign-owned factories, from electronics to textiles, were "manned" by employees which were 80–90% female; companies deliberately recruited younger women for "the sense of discipline that women have acquired through subjection to patriarchal domination in the household" (Greider, 1997, 98). See labour and links.

*laissez faire.* An 18th century economic doctrine that suggested that the state should not interfere in the economic realm. Adam Smith thought that the invisible hand of God was the surest guide. See theory, economic, neoclassical, theory, free trade and links.

**leadership.** "What the Clinton Administration never could bring itself to acknowledge openly was that *leadership* was really a codeword, one whose use honoured the cherished American tradition according to which the United states is not and cannot be an empire, but that obfuscates more than it explains. Leadership has become a euphemism" (Bacevich, 2002, 218–19). See imperialism, US and links.

*Liber.* French journal that militates against neoliberalism and Americanization. It was born out of the confrontation between students and the state in 1995 that saw the emergence of "the left of the left"; the sociologist Pierre Bourdieu is the publisher. See organizations and publications, critical of capitalism and globalism and links.

**liberalization, of trade.** Since the mid-1980s trade liberalization has been undertaken universally among developing countries. Liberalization has taken the form of opening up markets (i.e., removing protectionist impediments), privatizing public enterprises and welcoming foreign firms. See globalization, theory, economic, neoclassical and links.

**liquidity.** Capital which is investable. Poor people and countries have little or no liquidity. The liquidity of rich countries ideally flows towards poor countries in the form of investment and purchases. See capital and links.

**Living Oceans Society** (www.livingoceans.org). Non-profit organization, located in Sointula on Malcomson Island off the north-east coast of Vancouver Island, committed to marine biological diversity and creation. Presently concerned with offshore gas and oil industry and fish farming. See organizations and publications, environmental and links.

**lobbyists.** See following entries.

**lobbyists, business.** Organized business lobbyists seek, usually successfully, to influence government policy. The statement by Tom Kent, former leading Canadian civil servant, that "For years now the agendas of governments have been similar to corporate agendas" (*TS*, October 2, 2002, A21) does more than hint at the dominant role of the private sector nationally and internationally. See lobbyists, business, Canadian, lobbyists, business, international, lobbyists, business, US and links.

**lobbyists, business, Canadian.** "It is the job of ideological agencies to scorch the cultural earth to prepare it for the assault on government services, employees, and the environment. The terminology used to describe this ideology is often confusing, as the terms *neo-liberal, neoconservative*, and *new right* often seem to be used interchangeably" (Dobbin, 1998, 184–85). The main lobbyists of the ever-reigning Liberal Party of Canada are all, coincidentally, Montreal-based, namely, Bombardier, Power Corporation and the Bank of Montreal. The main professional lobbyists in Canada are Global Public Affairs, GPC Canada, the Capital Hill Group and the Wellington Strategy Group. All have given five-digit sums to the Liberal Party of Canada. The main industry lobby groups are the Canadian Bankers Association, the Canadian Association of Petroleum Producers, Canada's Research-Based Pharmaceutical Companies, the Canadian Medical Association and the Canadian Drug Manufacturers Association (*HT*, 8 July 2002). See Bombardier, Canadian Council of Chief Executives, C.D. Howe Institute, Donner Canadian Foundation, Fraser Institute, Friday Group, Intellectual Property Committee, lobbyists, business, Canadian, tobacco, National Citizens Coalition, Task Force on Food from Biotechnology and following entries.

**lobbyists, business, Canadian, tobacco.** The president of the Canadian Bar Association, Simon Potter, a partner in the Montreal law firm, Ogilvy Renault, is a listed lobbyist for Imperial Tobacco Ltd. and the Canadian Tobacco Manufacturing Council. "(I)t was revealed in 1998 that Mr. Potter shredded key internal documents on behalf of British American Tobacco... the parent firm of Imperial Tobacco, Canada's market leader" (*G&M*, September 3, 2002, A13). See lobbyists, business, Canadian and links.

**lobbyists, business, international.** According to the *New Internationalist* (July 2003, 14–15), the Translantic Business Dialogue, representing over 150 large corporations, strives to eliminate any regulation of EU-US trade. The International Chamber of Commerce, the largest of the international lobbyists, has succeeded in "weaken[ing] international environmental treaties, including the Kyoto Protocol..., the Convention on Biodiversity, and the Basel Convention against trade in toxic waste." See American Enterprise Institute for Public Policy Research, Council for

Biotechnology Information, Donner Foundation, Pharmaceutical Research and Manufacturers of America and links.

**lobbyists, critical of business.** See organizations and publications, critical of capitalism and globalism and links.

**lobbyists, environmental.** See organizations and publications, environmental and links.

**lobbyists, police, Canadian.** The RCMP regularly lobbies the Canadian government on law-and-order issues. The Mounties were successful in having the C$1000 note withdrawn, on the dubious claim that it was used by criminals (Nairn, 2002, 146). The RCMP lobby is presently engaged, shoulder-to-shoulder with other right-wing groups, in the struggle against the legalization of marijuana. See lobbyists and links.

**lobbyists, Third World.** See Action Aid, Attac, Canadian Centre for Policy Alternatives, Fifty Years is Enough Network, Institute for Trade and Agricultural Policy, Jubilee 2000, North-South Institute, Oxfam, Third World Network, War on Want, World Development Movement and links.

**Loka Institute** (www.Loka.org). "(A) non-profit organization dedicated to making research, science and technology responsive to social and environmental concerns." See organizations and publications, critical of capitalism and globalization, organizations and publications, environmental and links.

**Luddism.** Movement of early 19th century workers in England against the introduction into factories of new machinery that led to their unemployment and immiseration. By extension, any political movement against technological change, e.g., against genetically modified foods. See genetically modified foods, organizations and publications, critical of capitalism and globalism and links.

**macroeconomic stability.** This is what structural adjustment programs were supposed to guarantee. It includes, especially, currency stability. See structural adjustment, International Monetary Fund and links.

**Malthusianism, environmental.** The theory which stresses that parts of the world are likely to suffer crisis ("anarchy") due to the depletion of natural resources in relation to rising populations. Examples are to be found in Africa and Chiapas. Popularized by US journalist Robert Kaplan in *The Coming Anarchy* (New York, 2000) and U. of T. professor Tad Homer-Dixon in *Environment, Scarcity and Violence*. The phrase "eco-demographic pressure" and "environmental security" are included in the lexicon of the Green Malthusians. The terms "class," "appropriation" and "exploitation" are not (Watts, 2001). For a more recent example, see Klare, 2001. See links under green.

**Maquila Solidarity Network** (www.maquilasolidarity.org). Toronto-based network promoting solidarity with groups in Mexico, Central America and Asia concerned with work in maquiladoras and export processing zones. Archive of discussion papers from 1997 to present. See "Lessons from Mexico's Maquilas: Dispelling the Myths of Free Trade." See maquiladora.

**maquiladora.** Assembly plants located on north (US) side US-Mexican frontier but mainly employing Mexicans subject to Mexican, not US, labour and environmental laws. The object of maquiladoras is to take advantage of Mexico's lower labour costs and standards (in econospeak: "cost reduction benefits of the international division of labour"). Most maquiladora firms are American but some are Canadian, Japanese, Korean and Taiwanese. Half of maquila production is related to electronics. First introduced in 1965 and known as the "Border Industrialization Program," by 1966 there were 12 maquiladoras employing 3,000 workers and by 1989, 1500, employing 350,000. Canadian firms moved to the border region with the signing of NAFTA. At their peak, maquiladoras employed around 1.2 million but during 2001 employment in maquiladoras fell by 12%, partly due to the US recession but more importantly due to factories moving to countries where labour is cheaper, e.g., China in the case of the big three US auto manufacturers and General Electric. See export-led growth, export-processing assembly factories, globalization, labour, Maquila Solidarity Network, neoliberalism and links.

**market.** A site where goods are bought and sold. Normally constructed and protected by states and other organizations. Markets never exist in Nature. "The road to the free market was opened and kept open by an enormous increase in continuous, centrally organized and controlled interventionism" (Polanyi, 1944, 139–40.). Property rights lie at the foundation of any market; law and order shaped them. In the 1970s and 1980s neoliberals argued that a "return to markets," that is, to *laissez faire*, which diminished the role of the state, would revive lagging Third World economies. They were wickedly wrong. Here is a writer for the *Financial Times*, writing on the morrow of the G7 meeting in Genoa: "(T)here is a deeper objection [to the trust in market forces] one that is hard to articulate but that stands behind most protests against globalization. This is that global capitalism in its present form would be far from ideal even if the economic gains were fairly distributed. The reason is that although markets are often (but not always) efficient in strictly economic terms, they have other less attractive features. They encourage individualism, selfishness and materialism. They reward people for acting instrumentally, for treating others as means to their ends rather than as ends in themselves. They are inherently dynamic and so result in continual change, even though many people value stability, history and tradition for their own sakes. Worse, markets give us the illusion of being in control. Every individual is notionally free to choose what to buy, where to work and how to invest. And yet none of us controls the aggregate result of these decisions, which are each taken with an eye to an individual's personal benefit. Sadly, the unco-ordinated pursuit of personal gain often seems to result in a tawdry social existence.... Globalization is alarming because it threatens to eliminate [our] freedom of choice. Because capital can flow freely, and tends to depart from places that impose social constraints on business, there is a levelling down tendency: everyone is under pressure to give profit its head. Yet it is far from clear that this is what a majority of the world's voters actually want. The anger of the anti-globalization protesters is thus partially justified. Reforms such as the lifting of barriers to trade and investment were sold on narrow technical grounds. Yet by unifying markets while politics remained largely a national pastime, they leached power from democracies, leaving ordinary people more helpless than at any time since the mid-19th century, not surprisingly, this was the era when protests against capitalism first gathered momentum" (Prowse, 2001, 77). See civil society, crisis, financial, East Asian, globalization, *laissez faire*, Polanyi, Karl, Smith, Adam, welfare state and following entries.

**market, bear.** See bear market.

**market, bull.** See bull market.

**market deregulation.** See deregulation of capital markets and links.

**market, foreign exchange.** The largest international markets of any sort, financial or otherwise. In 1979 turnover was $17.5 trillion; in 1995, $300 trillion. Most foreign exchange business is conducted in London, Tokyo and New York, with London dominating. The leading banks involved in foreign exchange markets, by rank and estimated market share, are:
1. Citigroup (7.75%)
2. Deutsche Bank (7.12%)
3. Chase Manhattan (7.09%)
4. Warburg Dillon Read (6.44%)
5. Goldman Sachs (4.86%)
6. Bank of America (4.39%)
7. JP Morgan (4.00%)

8. HSBC (3.75%)
9. ABN Amro (3.37%)
10. Merril Lynch (3.27%)
11. Crédit Suisse First Boston (3.11%)
12. SEB (2.68%)
13. Nat West Global Financial Markets (2.63%)
14. Royal Bank of Canada (2.60%)
15. Morgan Stanley Dean Witter (2.29%)

(Ellwood, 2001, 82). See bubble, capitalism, finance, market, Tobin tax and links.

**market friendly.** Term coined by Lawrence Summers and used by World Bank for its preferred development dogma, i.e., an environment which maximizes private-sector growth through macroeconomic stability, free trade and private-sector investment. Not quite, or completely, *laissez-faire*. See *laissez faire*, market, World Bank and links.

**market fundamentalism.** Variant of neoclassical economic theory associated with the International Monetary Fund, whereby it is assumed that markets work perfectly and if they don't then it is not the fault of the markets. Unemployment is therefore the fault of greedy trade unions which drive up wages; to reduce unemployment, therefore, wages must be lowered. Elements of market fundamentalism are accepted by most business lobbyists. See ideology, lobbyists, business, theory, economic, neoclassical, market and links.

**market, global.** "Today's *Utopia* of a single global market assumes that the economic life of every nation can be refashioned in the image of the American free market. Yet in the United States the free market has ruptured the liberal capitalist civilization, founded on Roosevelt's New Deal, on which its post-war prosperity rested" (Gray, 1998, 4). See market.

**market populism.** Term popularized by Thomas Frank (2000) that refers to the ideology, especially powerful in the US, that people are completely rational actors and the market is the ultimate means and guarantee of democracy. See market and links.

**market-access regime.** All major countries seek a larger share of the world's industrial base by trying to secure a greater share of the global market for their industrial producers. Certain American writers claim that the US does not do this; it simply adjusts by reducing production capacity and employment (Greider, 1997, 141–42): "Americans, schooled in the rhetorical idealism of free trade, frequently expressed righteous indignation at the irregular practices of others, but the outrage was mostly sustained by ignorance. Their belief system was unable to incorporate the new facts of global commerce. Or even the historic truth that nations and enterprises, if they have the power, will do what they need to do in pursuit of their self-interest. Some of them would be mistaken and fail, but in the end their actions would be judged by the tangible results, not according to the abstract moral pretensions of free-market economics.... Many ambitious nations have pondered the American model and then chosen to follow the Japanese model, mainly because it seemed to work." China and other major developing countries use market leverage in reverse, granting controlled access to their home markets in order to gain for themselves a share of the world's advanced industrial base. If these efforts succeeded, they might someday be at a stage where they too could export surplus production into other, unprotected markets. See market, theory, free trade, ideology and links.

**markets, common.** Refers to situation where groups of countries agree, for purposes of economic benefit, to reduce tariffs among themselves, standardize currency, accept trade arbitration and so on in order to expand trade, reduce conflict and improve living standards. The largest common market is the European Union (EU), which includes most of Western and Southern Europe and will in 2005 encompass states in Eastern Europe (for a total of 450 m. people) and, later, possibly even Turkey. The North American Free Trade Agreement (NAFTA) aims at creating a common market between the US, Mexico and Canada. See Association of South East Asian Nations, European Union, Mercosur, North American Free Trade Agreement and links.

**markets, distortion of.** A major tenet of neoclassical economics is that which suggests that markets should be allowed to fix price and demand. Since, however, markets are political creations, price and demand are normally created and upheld by political means. See market and links.

**McDonald's.** US restaurant chain, anatomized by Schlosser (2001) and stigmatized as representing contemporary globalism and Americanization as did Coke in earlier decades. According to Jean-Michel Normand in *Le Monde*: "McDonald's... commercial hegemony threatens our agriculture and its cultural hegemony insidiously ruins alimentary behaviour—both sacred reflections of the French identity." And Allan Rollat: "Resistance to the hegemonic pretences of hamburgers is, above all, a cultural imperative" (cited in Bhagwati, 2004, 106). See Americanization, Bové, José, globalization and links.

**media, alternative.** Usually comprises periodicals and INTERNET sources which are critical of politics of conventional media. See Center for Public Integrity, Centre des medias alternatifs du Québec, Independent Media

Centre, Institute for War and Peace Reporting, Institute for Public Accuracy, organizations critical of capitalism and globalism and links.

**Médicins Sans Frontièrs** (www.doctorswithout borders.org). International organization, founded in France, concerned with medical aid in areas of famine and conflict and public awareness. Has world and national offices (Canadian office: www.msf.ca). Médicins du Monde is a spin off. See organizations, health and welfare and links.

**Meltzer Commission.** Commission of US Congress (officially known as the International Financial Institutions Advisory Commission (IFIAC)), formed 1998 under conservative economist Allan Meltzer to consider seven international institutions (including the IMF, the World Bank, the WTO) The commission submitted its report (see www.house.gov/jec/imf/ifiac.htm) in February 2000. It noted that the IMF had become "responsible for monitoring and setting conditions for virtually all aspects of the developing countries' social and economic policies." Among its recommendations was the writing off of the debts of the most heavily indebted poor countries, on the condition that they "implement an effective economic development strategy.... (T)he Commission came up with the devastating conclusion that, with most of its resources going to the better-off countries of the developing world and with the astounding 65–70% failure rate of its projects in the poorest countries, the World Bank was irrelevant to the achievement of its avowed mission of global poverty alleviation" (Walden Bello, "Turning the tide against corporate-driven globalization," *LBO*, #94, 1–2, 7; *CCPAM*, 7,7, December 2000/January 2001, 18; see also Peet, 2003, 213–14). See debt, developing countries, International Monetary Fund, Washington Consensus, World Bank and links.

**menace.** Unofficial US State Department category, less threatening than "rogue state." According to former US National Security Advisor, Condoleezza Rice, Russia constitutes a "menace" (Gorce, 2001, 4). See foreign policy, US, rogue states and links.

**Mercosur (Mercado Commun del Cono Sur).** "Common Market of the South." Members include Brazil, Argentina, Uruguay and Paraguay. The Mercosur region deteriorated in 1999 and 2000 but was expected to enjoy accelerated growth by 2001. It didn't. In 1999, Chile's economy, which had been growing uninterruptedly since 1984, saw its GDP contract by 1%. In 2000, Argentina's GDP contracted 0.5%, in 2001 it is expected to contract around 1%. In response, and in contradiction to the common market ideal, Argentina put tariffs on Chilean goods. These tariffs were expected to cost the Chilean economy $212 million. The head of Mercosur is Eduardo Duhalde, the former president of Argentina. The President of Brazil, Luiz Inacio Lula da Silva, sees Mercosur as the centre of his aggressive export policy which hopes to expand Brazil's role as a regional superpower (*G&M,* December 2, 2003, A20). See markets, common and links.

**Merrill Lynch.** The leading Wall Street brokerage firm. Owns *Wall Street Journal* and *Far Eastern Economic Review.* Fined $100 million for defrauding its customers. See capitalism, finance, press, business and links.

**migration.** An ubiquitous form of globalization, evident from earliest historic period. In recent decades has shown some decided shifts, e.g., Mediterranean states that were once exporters have become importers of migrants. Since 1980s, Western European countries have tried to shut the doors to migrants, but with limited success. As a result migration has formed an important plank in most national politics and especially for right-wing parties. Anti-migration parties are often strongest in jurisdictions where migrants are more numerous (e.g., Provence, California). Among other things, migrants provide cheap and often unprotected labour in areas which locals shun, e.g., fruit picking in Niagara. Most states are complicit in illegal migrant labour. According to *Le Monde* (30 Mai 2002, 1), "Immigration has now become at the heart of the European political debate [my trans.]." Organizations concerned with migration include the International Organization for Migration (www.iom.int), the International Labour Organization (www.ilo.org), Migrant Rights International (www.migrantsrights.org), the United Nations High Commissioner for Refugees (www.unhcr.ch), the Canadian Council for Refugees (www.web.net/~ccr/) and the Ontario Council of Agencies Serving Immigrants (www.ocasi.org). For other addresses, see Stalker, 2001, 134–35. See Convergence des lutes anticapitalist (CLAC), globalization, labour, refugees and asylum seekers, Statewatch and links.

**military expenditure, US.** In 1985 the budget of the Pentagon equalled 6.5% of GDP. By 1998 it was only 3.2%. Of global military expenditure, US spends 36%, China 2% (*FT,* February 2–3, 2002, IV, citing SIPRI military expenditure database "The Military Balance, 2000–2001"). See arms, production and sale by US, foreign policy, US, imperialism, organizations, peace/arms control and following entry.

**military training programs, US.** According to the World Policy Institute, during the Cold War (1950–1989) the US spent $1.5 billion on arms and military training in Africa. From 1991–1995 US arms sales and military training totalled more than $227 million. The US has provided arms and/or military training for 11 out of the 12 wars in Africa since World War Two. Between 1986–1991, the US spent $250 m. arming the rebel UNITA group in Angola. After the withdrawal of US aid, UNITA turned to exporting blood diamonds (*CCPAM*, 9, 5, October 2002, 15). See arms, production and sale of, US, blood diamonds, School of the Americas Watch, World Policy Institute and links.

**Mining Watch Canada/Mines Alerte** (www.miningwatch.ca). Provides technical and advocacy information about threats to public health, water and air quality, fish and so on, in French and Spanish. Shares infrastructure with Canadian Parks and Wilderness Society. Issue no.5, Winter 2001 contains articles such as "Tribal People in India Confront Alcan Investment" and "Report Links Canadian Business to Paramilitary Violence in Columbia." See organizations and publications, environmental, organizations, mining, organizations concerned with and links.

**model, development, Anglo-Saxon.** Model promoted by US government and institutions such as IMF and World Bank as well as most OECD states (with partial exception of Ireland, Norway, Netherlands). Emphasizes that global economic expansion, which leads to increased goods and services available to all and low unemployment, requires trade liberalization and deregulation, low profile states, low taxation, etc. Limited concern with social and environmental costs. See globalization, Reaganism-Thatcherism, neoliberalism, Washington Consensus and following entries.

**model, development, East Asian.** Most economists assume that there are two models, the Western model, and the East Asian model, of which Japan is the prototype and South Korea, Taiwan and Singapore are regional variants. In the East Asian model the state intervenes to protect domestic enterprises from foreign competition and provides them with low cost capital while preventing funds which are needed for domestic investment from flowing abroad where they might receive higher dividends or from being squandered on luxury imports. Financial systems are kept closed—foreign banks and currency speculators are kept at arms' length. It is said therefore to be more "protectionist" and "national capitalist." East Asia has followed this model and prospered. According to Oxfam, East Asian economies have achieved "the fastest reduction in poverty for the greatest number of people in history" (cited in Johnson, 2000, 199. For Oxfam policy papers, see its website). The weakness of the East Asian model is that it depends on a continuous growth of revenue from export sales. This has contributed to global overcapacity. The second weakness of the Asian model was the production of financial bubbles when productive investment opportunities could no longer be found for the vast savings generated by the adherents of this model. These funds found their way into and inflated property and stock market speculation and to unjustified loans based more on cronyism than other factors. A bubble of excess thus developed and inevitably burst. Bruce

Cumings agrees: "Today it [i.e., US hegemony and its globalist model] is eroding, if not erasing, the last formidable alternative system, the Japan-Korea model of state-directed neo-mercantilism—one undermined and made vulnerable by its inclusion in the post-war regional order" (Cumings, 1998, 71). See Asia and links, protectionism, national capitalism, Newly Industrialized Economies (NICS), Washington Consensus, World Bank and entry above.

**modernization.** A concept, often raised to the level of a master narrative, which preceded development by several centuries and referring to the copying of the institutions of the advanced capitalist West in order to assure the stability of regimes. In the 17th century the czars attempted to modernize Russia and in later centuries the Ottomans, Egyptians, Chinese, Japanese and others followed in the same path. Modernization usually led to disorder and the overthrow of the regimes that attempted to implement it. "In Russian history 'modernization' generally meant importing alien political and economic principles from the richer and more powerful West. Could an authoritarian empire rooted in very different principles import these alien conceptions and survive?" (Lieven, 2000, vii–viii). See development and links.

**mondalization maitrisée, la** ("globalization mastered"). Buzzword under French prime minister Lionel Jospin suggesting that the French state and the EU should be the masters of globalization, not be mastered by it. See globalization and links.

**money, laundering of.** The laundering of illegal gains is a massive, global business involving most banks. About one-quarter of UN members offer "secret banking" facilities to offshore customers. Such facilities are offered by the Canadian banks in the Caribbean, for instance, Bank of Nova Scotia and the Royal Bank of Canada. In Canada, the question of money laundering is dealt with by the Financial Transactions and Reports Analysis Centre (FINTRAC). "In an evaluation made several months ago by the Paris-based international Financial Action Task Force on Money Laundering, Canada ranked 27th out of 29 countries rated for their compliance with 40 recommendations on combating money laundering that this task force made in 1989. "Canada did not come out with a good mark," Inspector Mair [of the RCMP] said (*G&M*, October 16, 2001, B8). See capitalism, finance and links.

**Monsanto.** St. Louis-based giant transnational chemical firm which gained earlier notoriety for producing Agent Orange, which defoliated Vietnamese forests during the US invasion and produced high levels of deformity and cancers among the Vietnamese. Subsequently it joined with the pharmaceutical firm Pharmacia & Upjohn and has since become a major force in the sale of genetically modified seeds. Its aims here are furthered by its being a member of the Intellectual Property Committee, which conceived of TRIPs Agreement. GM seed plantings are the object of protest in UK and France although they are subsidized by the Canadian International Development Agency (CIDA) and criticized by Royal Society of Canada. Monsanto is the number one producer of herbicides, its Roundup having the greatest sales in the world ($2.6 billions in 2000). In early March 2001, the top aid of Canadian health minister Allan Rock, John Dossetor, was hired as a lobbyist for Monsanto. Mr. Dossetor was in the health department when Monsanto was conducting negotiations regarding genetically modified New Leaf potatoes. The negotiations resulted in Monsanto getting rapid approval over the objections of the Canadian Food Inspection Agency (CFIA), which had expressed concerns over "extremely poor" field tests. The CFIA said that a rapid approval would "compromise the integrity" of Canada's regulatory system. Monsanto is the co-founder of Council for Biotechnology Information, which distributes information on the benefits of biotechnology (*G&M*, February 13, 2001, A17, March 12, 2001, A6; *NI*, 335, June 2001, 8; Sinai, 2001). For Monsanto in India, see "Farmers in India are Fighting to Bar Monsanto's GM cotton (www.poptel.org.uk.com) and "Monsanto's Bullying Continues" (www.purefood.org.com). Because of opposition in the EU and Brazil Monsanto has had to postpone hopes for introducing GM foods in those areas. Washington threatens a trade war unless firms like Monsanto can sell GM grains and seeds in Europe (*GW* August 22–28, 2002, 1, 12). According to Action Aid Monsanto now controls 91% of the global GM food market (*GW* February 4–10, 2004, 10). See Action Aid, biotechnology, Centre for Global Food Issues, firms, agribusiness, organizations and publications, environmental, lobbyists, business and links.

**Montreal Protocol.** Officially the Montreal Protocol on Substances that Deplete the Ozone Layer, this is a multinational environmental agreement that was ratified by countries accounting for 82% of world consumption. It was succeeded by the Kyoto treaty in 1997. See Kyoto Protocol and links.

**Morse Commission.** Named after US Congressman and international civil servant (UN Undersecretary General and director of UNDP) Bradford Morse who was invited in 1992 to investigate World Bank operations in India. "The members of the independent review… were appalled by what they found. Their report… [released on June 19, 1992]… not only confirmed virtually all of the criticisms made by NGOs in India and abroad, it revealed a pattern of gross negligence and delinquency on the part of the World Bank and the Indian government that was much worse than anyone had imagined" (Rich, 1994, 250). See World Bank and links.

**Movement of Concerned Scientists for Biosafety** (www.icgeb.trieste.it). Scientists not on payrolls of business. Links to several biosafety websites. See organizations and publications, environmental and links.

**Multilateral Agreement on Investment (MAI).** "For years, government representatives had been negotiating a proposed multilateral agreement on investment intended to speed up and lock in the process of opening markets, removing obstacles to faster globalization. This negotiation was curtailed when a Canadian non-governmental organization (NGO) posted a leaked copy of the working document on a web site and a worldwide protest movement sprung into being, effectively stopping the agreement" (Tabb, 2000, 9). The FTAA summit was seen as a resurrection of the MAI. See Free Trade Area of the Americas, North American Free Trade Agreement, Quadrilateral Group of Ministers and links.

**multilateralism.** Conduct of foreign and trade policies by means of negotiations within international organizations such as UN, NAFTA or WTO. See unilateralism.

**multinational corporations (MNCs).** Firms with offices and production facilities in more than one country. The operations of MNCs are key to understanding economic globalization since they account for about two-thirds of world trade, with about a third of world trade being intra-firm trade between branches of the same company. In 1998 there were 53,000 worldwide (up from 35,000 in 1992) with 450,000 foreign subsidies selling $9.5 trillion of goods and services across the globe. The hundred largest MNCs control about 20% of global foreign assets and account for about 30% of total world sales of all MNCs. They employ around 6 million workers worldwide. A small number of MNCs dominate world markets for oil, minerals, foods and other agricultural products and services. By 2001, foreign multinationals owned 395 of the 500 largest firms in Latin America, up from 27% in 1991. "(T)he role of multinational firms in low-income countries is usually ambiguous and often negative" (MacEwan, 1999, 65, fn.7). The British East India Company was a MNC before its time. About 80% of UK export trade in the early 1980s was associated with multinational firms. According to Susan Strange (1996, 44), as markets have become more important in global politics than states, MNCs have become more important *politically*. But how can we tell which nation multinationals belong to? The Canadian firm Bombardier has more employees and makes more profit abroad than in Canada. It has been predicted that in the future multinationals will move their operations away from their headquarters and towards regional centres, that is, out of New York and Los Angeles and to Singapore and Bangalore. The basic source of information on the subject of the activities of multinational/transnational corporations is UN Conference on Trade and Development (UNCTAD) *World Investment Report* (annual), which has noted that between January 2002 and March 2003, 829 multinationals have moved their headquarters, about a quarter of which have gone to developing countries. See organizations and publications, critical of capitalism and globalism and following entries.

**multinational corporations, oil.** "Contrary to popular ideas, oil MNCs do not have unfettered production rights in the most lucrative petroleum fields. In Mexico and Venezuela and in the Middle East, state-owned oil companies run the show. MNCs were booted out in the mid-1970s under the then fashionable doctrine in the third world—nationalization. Oil MNCs have had more success in Central Asia and West Africa, where they have negotiated with governments what in jargon is called production sharing agreements. These have two striking features. One, governments which sign them are typically autocratic and/or politically unstable. Two, the agreements cannot be touched by any change in national tax laws, property rules or environment regulations. Effectively, oil in these countries does not remain a national resource. That is what oil MNCs plan for Iraq, which they correctly presume will have a regime too dependent on [President] Bush to say no to Bush's friends. A production sharing agreement with Iraq will give ExxonMobil, Shell, etc. virtually owner-ship rights—as opposed to service contracts which they have elsewhere in the Middle East—to nearly 350 billion barrels of oil (proven plus untapped). A new Iraqi government may get away by increasing taxes on McDonald's burgers but it will be disabled from putting an extra tax on oil. Or asking for a bigger revenue share than fixed by the skewed production sharing agreement. Or asking oil MNCs to leave" (*The Statesman*, Bhubaneswar, 22 March 2003, 6).

*Multinational Monitor* (www.essential.org). Tracks corporate activity around the globe. Bimonthly magazine (www.essential.org/monitor) tracks corporate abuses in developing countries. See Corporate Watch, multinational corporations, organizations and publications, critical of capitalism and globalism, revolving door and links.

**mutual funds.** Investment instruments which have come to serve as privatized pensions, popular among North Americans, less so among Europeans, unknown among the poor. Became generalized in 1980s and 1990s when over 50% of US households had share in stock market (up from 25% in 1987). In Canada, over half of those who contribute to RRSPs (a form of mutual funds) have annual incomes of less than C$40,000. Mutual funds might be ethical or nationalist, in the case of the fund launched by the Quebec-based Mouvement des Caisses Desjardins, or aimed at women. In one argument this has led to "investment culture" and the global dominance of finance capitalism and to "investor democracy" (Harmes, 2001). See class, pension funds, stocks, wealth, distribution of, Canada/US and links.

**N30.** Conference of World Trade Organization on November 30, 1999, in Seattle. See conferences, international and links.

**NAFTA.** See North American Free Trade Association and links.

**National Citizens Coalition (NCC).** Secretive political organization founded by insurance salesman and millionaire businessman Colin M. Brown Sr. in cahoots with millionaire religious fundamentalist, Ernest Manning, father of Preston, founder of the Reform Party. Leading light is John D. Leitch of Upper Lakes Shipping. Other supporters (known as "Patrons of Freedom") include former head of Magna International, John Stronach, and John Clyne of now extinct MacMillan Bloedel. The Bank of Montreal and Royal Trust are also patrons. NCC may be described as being Hayekite/Friedmanite in philosophy, racist in instinct and non-democratic in organization. One of its first campaigns "was a scurrilous anti-immigration campaign that focused on the Vietnamese refugees arriving in the late 1970s. Brown himself led the charge...." (Jeffrey, 1999, 408). Its successful court challenge blocked limits to third party spending in elections, thereby allowing corporate spending to determine the Canadian election of 1988. It wages a regular guerrilla struggle against the Canada Health Act, the diminution of which would be profitable for health insurance companies. Through "Ontarians for Responsible Government" NCC organized an electoral war against the NDP government in Ontario. Awarded Conservative Premier Mike Harris the Colin M. Brown Freedom Medal. Budget for 1996 was $2.6 million. Presidents of the NCC have been David Somerville and head of Conservative Party, MP Stephen Harper (Dobbin, 1998, 184, 197–207). See lobbyists, business and links.

**National Endowment for Democracy** (www.ned.org). US government backed and funded organization launched in 1980. Its purpose is to develop and cultivate pro-US "leaders" in the Third World. Affiliated organizations are Centre for International Private Enterprise, National Democratic Institute for International Affairs, National Republican Institute for International Affairs and Free Trade Union Institute. Involved in an attempted overthrow of Hugo Chavez of Venezuela and successful toppling of Jean-Bertrand Aristide of Haiti.

**National Energy Policy.** Initiative of Liberal government under Trudeau, sought to control Canadian gas and oil in national interest. Loathed by oil companies, American and Canadian, and by Albertans. Destroyed by Mulroney government. See fossil fuels, lobbyists, business and links.

**nationalism, Canadian.** "During the battles against NAFTA, there emerged the first signs of a coalition between organized labour, environmentalists, farmers and consumer groups within the countries concerned. In Canada most of us felt we were fighting to keep something distinctive about our nation from 'Americanization'" (Klein, 2000, 83). See Americanization, anti-Americanism, Council of Canadians, imperialism, US and links.

**neoliberalism.** Economic doctrine which rose to prominence in the 1970s and which repudiates the role of the state in the economy, preferring, instead, to leave the economy in the hands of the market. The greatest priests of neoliberalism were Reagan and Thatcher, its greatest theoretical advocate Milton Friedman and its saints, Fredrick von Hayek and Adam Smith. Advocates of neoliberalism support laissez-faire, free markets, the rich and are against the welfare state and therefore have all but the most limited concerns with welfare and the poor. "At the time of the [Asian] crisis I thought neo-liberalism might be dead.... It might be true that in intellectual economic and social science circles... neo-liberalism is pretty much stone dead. But it lives on in politics" (Hutton in Hutton and Giddens (eds.), 2000, 43). Neoliberals accept that the market exists outside of, that is independently of, society and history (MacEwan, 1999, 11). For a history, see Susan George Une courte histoire du néoliberalisme (www.attac.org), and George, 2001. See Friedman, Milton, Hayek, Fredrick von, jobs, security of, Reaganism-Thatcherism, social market economy, theory, laissez faire, There is No Alternative (TINA), welfare state and links.

**New Economic Foundation** (www.neweconomics.org). UK-based radical think-tank with newsletter. Concerned *inter alia* with reshaping the world economy. Publications include "An Environmental War Economy: The Lessons of Ecological Debt and Global Warming." See organizations and publications, critical of capitalism and globalism and links.

**New Economy.** The western capitalist economy that emerged in the 1980s, spread in the 1990s and by the beginning of the new millennium entered a period of uncertainty. The centre of this economy was the US, and the economic network which it dominated spread throughout the OECD countries and beyond. The central feature of the New Economy was TMT— technology, media, telecommunications. Between c.1980–2000, business spending in the US on information equipment as a share of GDP came close to tripling. Its proponents claimed that the New Economy had created a new growth paradigm that would allow US GDP to grow over 4% per year. They drew analogies to the earlier effects of the railway and electricity. Doubters argued that while computers did contribute to an increase in productivity, this was limited and that the stunning growth of the 1990s was as much to do with the business cycle as new technologies. It is true that growth of the computer sector accounted for about a quarter of US output growth in the 1990s and that the internet has affected other parts of the economy, raising productivity in both manufacturing and services. After some 20 years of annual productivity growth averaging around 1%, since 1995 productivity growth in the US increased as much as 3% per year. But in Europe and Japan, productivity growth has not accelerated. "Despite a 3 percent unemployment rate for American adults, hundreds of thousands of people are still being fired every year. As companies restructure and adapt to the New Economy, they are churning their workforces. Many operations are being sent overseas. In the 1980s, only blue-collar workers faced this problem. In the 2000s, white-collar employees are watching their jobs migrate to India and Ireland" (Tabb, 2000, 11; *Human Development Index, 2001*, 36). See globalization, stocks, Technology, Media and Telecommunications, world economy, trends, since 1945 and links.

**New International Information Order (NIIO).** Emerged in 1970s in Third World; against "free flow" of information; abjured by US and UK.

**New Politics** (www.newpolica.ca). An initiative, formulated by persons both within and without the NDP, to construct a progressive anti-globalization political group or perhaps even party. See organizations and publications, critical of capitalism and globalization and links.

**New Sovereigntism.** See foreign policy, US, imperialism, US, isolationism, US, and links.

**New World Order.** A neologism popular in Washington in the early 1990s and a precursor to the idea of political and economic globalism. See foreign policy, US.

**New York Stock Exchange (NYSE).** World's leading stock market, the hub of contemporary capitalism. For a discussion of its function, see Henwood (1998), Chapter 1. See capitalism, finance, stock markets and links.

**Newly Industrialized Economies (NIEs).** A term that refers to the economies of South and Southeast Asia, which grew rapidly from the 1960s, became crisis-ridden in 1997, and have since, for the most part, recovered. Most began by producing and exporting clothing and textiles and then switched to electronics. These economies became the models for "export-led growth" touted by the IMF and World Bank. See industries, textile and clothing, model, development, East Asian, overcapacity and overproduction, technology, media, telecommunications, world economy, trends, since 1945 and links.

**Newswatch Canada** (newswatch.cprost.sfu.ca). Independent media watch-dog at Simon Fraser University, publishes *Newswatch Monitor*. Each year students at the School of Communications undertake a series of content-analysis studies focussed on particular topics or news media. See media, alternative for links.

*Newswatch Monitor*. See Newswatch Canada.

**Nike.** Leading sportswear manufacturer. Famous for low wages paid to Third World workers (as low as $.17 per hour) and long hours. Market-ing targets youth and young adults. "A 1997 report by Hong Kong human rights groups revealed conditions at a Wellco [Nike] subcontrac-tor in Dongguan, China, employing children as young as thirteen 'that have resulted in workers losing fingers and hands; beatings by security guards... fines levied for workers who talk to each other on the job; 72 hour work weeks; and pay less than the... minimum wage of US$.24 an hour" (Dobbin, 1998, 137). See labour, child, labour, textile and clothing industry, United Students Against Sweatshops and links.

**Nobel Prize for Economics.** This is not awarded by the Swedish Nobel Prize Committee but by the Swedish Association of Bankers in honour of Alfred Nobel. The Swedish bankers consult a broad constituency of economists and bankers, of which the largest and best-organized group is in the US. See theory, economic, neoclassical and links.

**non-governmental organizations (NGOs).** First established in the 1960s and considered as part of "new social movements," NGOs serve many, contradictory, purposes, some charitable, some political. Often they are supported by governments and therefore may serve not to promote change but to sustain existing order, sometimes through poverty allevia-tion. The World Bank, in its untiring attempts at co-option, claims to favour them as instruments of "good governance." A number of them serve the World Bank and promote anti-state and pro-market policies. NGOs are mainly centred in the West and sometimes criticized as being a part of system of foreign domination. In 1989 in Honduras, for instance, NGOs spent $50 million, twice the amount spent by the government on social programs. Petras (1997, 11) is explicit on the connection between NGOs and neoliberalism: "(A)s the neoliberal regimes at the top devas-tated communities by inundating the country with cheap imports, ex-tracting external debt payment, abolishing labor legislation, and creat-ing a growing mass of low-paid and unemployed workers, the NGOs were funded to provide self-help projects, popular education, and job training, to temporarily absorb small groups of poor, to co-opt local leaders, and to undermine anti-system struggles." BONGOs are "Business Oriented NGOs" and GRINGOs are "Government Run/Initiated NGOs." Many NGOs were present at confrontations with global capitalism, e.g., Seattle, Quebec City. Typical NGOs are Alternatives (Montreal), Oxfam and Greenpeace (Ottawa). NGOs number, globally, over 10,000. See organizations and publications, critical of capitalism and globalism and links.

**North American Free Trade Agreement (NAFTA).** Signed in 1993 between US, Canada and Mexico agreeing to free trade, the NAFTA, backed by Bay Street in an expensive advertising campaign, was at the centre of the re-election campaign of the Conservative Party under Brian Mulroney in 1992. "[NAFTA's] meetings are secret. Their members are generally unknown. The decisions they reach need not be fully disclosed. Yet the way a small group of international tribunals handles disputes between investors and foreign governments has led to national laws being revoked, justice systems questioned and environmental regulations challenged. And it is all in the name of protecting the rights of foreign investors under the North American Free Trade Agreement" (*New York Times*, March 11, 2001, cited in "Private Rights, Public Problems..." 2001, vii). A report by the Economic Policy Institute concludes: "In Canada, more jobs have been destroyed by imports than have been created by exports, for a net loss of 276,000 jobs. Average per capita income in Canada fell steadily under NAFTA, only regaining its 1989 level in 1999" (CCPA *Monitor*, July/August 2001, 3). Michael Den Tandt, however, points out (*G&M*, November 14, 2002, B2): "For all its perils and pitfalls, NAFTA has been astonishingly fruitful. In the five years between 1997 and 2001, total Canadian exports grew nearly 37 per cent, to $414.6-billion. Over the same period, exports to the United States increased 45 per cent. The American market now accounts for 85 per cent of our sales beyond our borders." See also *G&M*, December 12, 2002, B2 where he points out that "Bilateral trade between Canada and the United States amounted to $569 billion in 2001, a 185 per cent increase from 1990." He makes no mention of jobs. According to Leys (2001, 19, fn. 21): "The USA was able to impose a structure [on NAFTA] in which decision-making was entrusted largely to unaccountable bodies dominated by US corporations, and the Canadian and Mexican governments do not have the influence over it that the larger EU members governments... have in EU institutions.... How far other states will be induced to surrender their sovereignty to TNCs in as wholesale and humiliating a way as Canada and Mexico have done under NAFTA remains to be seen." "(T)he Mexican economy seems to be doing pretty well out of the deal [i.e., NAFTA]" (Giddens in Hutton and Giddens (eds.), 2000, 43). See globalization, labour, lobbyists, business, trade, free and links.

**North Atlantic Treaty Alliance (NATO).** US-dominated Cold War relic uniting a dozen north European and North American countries including Britain, Canada, Germany, Turkey and, fitfully, France.

Headquartered in Paris but led and bankrolled by Washington. Formed in 1949, NATO armies fought together only twice, in Korea, 1950–1951, and Serbia, 1998. NATO is now in a state of transformation being expanded with inclusion of Eastern European members (Bulgaria, Romania, Estonia, Latvia, Lithuania, Slovakia and Slovenia in May 2004; Russia is a semi-member). Each NATO member is required to maintain defence spending at least 2%. NATO has been weakened by the formation of a EU army and disowned militarily by the US, which wants to restrict the role of NATO to that of a peacekeeping under the orders of Washington. See foreign policy, US, trade, free and links.

**North-South Institute** (www.nsi-ins.ca). Ottawa-based advocacy group dealing with development issues. President is Roy Culpepper, formerly of the Department of Finance. Supported by politicians such as Paul Martin and Joe Clark. Supports Tobin tax. See lobbyists, Third World, organizations, development, Tobin tax and links.

**Northwest Coalition for Alternatives to Pesticides (NCAP)** (www.pesticide.org). Oregon-based lobby and information group providing both popular and scientific information on use of pesticides and alternative methods of disposing of weeds, insects and rodents. Also takes position on biotechnology. See organizations and publications, environmental and links.

**Nuclear Information and Resource Service** (www.nirsnet@nirs.org). US-based lobby group with office in Amsterdam concerned with proliferation and use of nuclear power. See organizations and publications, environmental, power, nuclear and links

**nuclear power.** See power, nuclear.

**Nukewatch** (www.nukewatch.com). Peace and environmental group based in Wisconsin. See arms, production and trade, Canadian/global/US, organizations and publications, peace, organizations and publications, environmental and links.

**Olympic Games.** A publicly financed athletic entertainment held every four years to the immense profit of private firms of all sorts. Considered as having succeeded world's fairs as the biggest economic stimulus for cities. The Seoul Olympics of 1988, for instance, brought widespread attention to the prosperity of South Korea. The self-elected International Olympic Committee (IOC), which runs it, has been described as having been "a band of graft-seeking freeloaders, peddling a commercial sports festival." The British representative of the IOC was Princess Anne. The head of the IOC for 21 years was a former Falangist (Spanish fascist) banker, Juan Antonio Samarranch, under whom corruption exploded at Salt Lake City where IOC members were found to have taken bribes and other favours from the bidding city's Olympic committee. Over a four-year cycle, including one summer and one winter Olympics, revenues generated by the IOC now exceed $35 bn.

**Ontario Coalition Against Poverty (OCAP)** (ocap@tao.ca). Coalition of groups including anti-Conservatives, anti-poverty and anti-globalization. See organizations and publications, critical of capitalism and globalism and links.

**options.** An agreement which gives a holder the right to buy an agreed quantity of a product at an agreed price on an agreed date. See stock markets and links.

**organic food and agriculture.** For websites of groups see www.organicadvocates.org/links, See also genetic engineering, organizations and publications, agriculture and links.

**Organization for Economic Co-operation and Development (OECD).** Club of the advanced capitalist countries, the number of which has varied and was 30 in 2004). Japan is the only Asian country in list. There are no Latin American or African countries except Mexico. The Secretary-General is Donald Johnston, former Liberal Party MP for Westmount and failed contender for party leadership. Johnston is a nuclear power advocate (see his "Colour nuclear power green," *G&M*, November 16, 2000, A19). See organizations, for the promotion of capitalism and globalism and links.

**Organization of American States (OAS).** Association of states of the Americas including Canada and the US. Foreign ministers met in spring 2000, in Windsor, Ontario. Overwhelming police presence; demonstrators intimidated. Official propaganda suggested that protest and dissent were criminal activities. Its 2001 annual conference (called "Conference of the Americas") was held in Quebec City in April 2000. Serge Menard, Minister of Public Security, Government of Quebec: "If you want peace, prepare for war" (Klein, November 15, 2000, A15). See conferences, international, organizations for the promotion of capitalism and globalism and links.

**Organization of Petroleum Exporting Countries (OPEC).** Consortium of a dozen petroleum exporting countries the six largest of which are Kuwait, the United Arab Emirates, Iran, Iraq, Venezuela and Saudi Arabia. These together produce 28 million barrels a day and control 38% of world's supply. See multinational corporations, oil and links.

**organizations, aid.** See aid and links.

**organizations, anarchist.** See anarchism, organizations and publications, critical of capitalism and globalization and links.

**organizations and publications, agriculture, fisheries and food.** See Action Aid, Aventis, Centre for Global Food Issues, Erosion, Technology and Concentration Group, Food First, genetic engineering, genetically modified foods, Frankenfoods, Institute for Trade and Agricultural Policy, Monsanto, organic food and agriculture, Pacific Environment, Polaris Institute, Saskatchewan Organic Directorate, Trade Related Intellectual Property Rights, Movement of Concerned Scientists for Biosafety, Union of Concerned Scientists, World Health Organization and links.

**organizations and publications, critical of capitalism and globalization.** See Canadian Centre for Policy Alternatives, Center for Economic and Policy Research, Center for Social Justice, Common Frontiers, Corporate Watch, Convergence des luttes anti-capitalistes, Direct Action Network, Fabian Global Forum, *Multinational Monitor*, New Economic Foundation, New Politics, Ontario Coalition Against Poverty, Oxfam, Parkland Institute, Peoples Global Action, Polaris Institute, Public Citizen, Ruckus Society, SalAMI, Transnational Institute and links. See also www.hazelhenderson.com.

**organizations and publications, development.** See aid, development, Erosion, Technology and Concentration (ETC) Group, Focus on the Global South, Food First, North-South Institute, Transnational Institute, World Development Forum and links.

**organizations and publications, environmental.** See Basle Convention, Canadian Parks and Wilderness Society, Concerned Scientists for Biosafety, David Suzuki Foundation, Earth First, Earthscan, Environmental Investigation Agency, Environment Probe, Global Witness, Greenpeace, Kyoto Protocol, Living Oceans Society, Loka Institute, Mining Watch Canada, Northwest Coalition for Alternatives to Pesticides, Nuclear Information and Resource Service, Nukewatch, Pacific Environment, Parkland Institute, Pembina Institute, Pollution Watch, Public Citizen, Rainforest Action Network, Research Foundation for Science, Technology and Ecology, Sierra Club, Sierra Legal Defence Fund, Sustainable Energy and Economy Network, Union of Concerned Scientists, Western Canadian Wilderness Committee and links.

**organizations and publications, human rights.** See Amnesty International, Anti-Slavery International, Canadian Action for Indonesia and East Timor, Coalition Against Trafficking in Women, Democracy Watch,

Ecumenical Coalition for Social Justice, Free the Slaves, Human Rights Watch, Physicians for Human Rights, Polaris Project, Public Citizen, sex, trafficking in, Statewatch, Terre des Hommes, United Nations Human Rights Committee and links.

**organizations, for the promotion of capitalism and globalism.** See Free Trade Area of the Americas, globalization, lobbyists, business, Organization of American States, Organization for Economic Co-operation and Development, press, business, Trilateral Commission and links.

**organizations, health and welfare/relief.** See health care, Peoples' Global Action, Médicins Sans Frontièrs, Tommy Douglas Research Institute and links.

**organizations, mining and drilling.** See Union of Concerned Scientists, gas and oil, petroleum, organizations and publications, environmental and links.

**organizations, peace/arms control.** See arms, production and trade, British American Security Information Council, Canadian/global/statistics/ US, Campaign Against Depleted Uranium, Canadian Peace Alliance, Canadian Peace Building Coordinating Committee, Carnegie Endowment for International Peace, Coalition to End the Arms Trade, Groupe de recherché et d'information sur la paix et la sécurité, Institute for War and Peace Reporting, International Institute for Strategic Studies, Nukewatch, Stockholm International Peace Research Institute, Project Ploughshares, World Policy Institute, US Arms Control and Disarmament Agency and links.

**organizations, public interest.** See organizations, critical of capitalism and globalism, organizations, environmental and links.

**organized crime.** Like other organized assaults on Western civilization, largely chimerical (Nairn, 2002, Ch. 1). See drugs, illegal, Gross Criminal Product and links.

**outsourcing.** The exporting of jobs from the developed centre to the developing periphery ("lower-cost foreign jurisdictions") in the interests of profitability. Originally these jobs were in manufacturing but by the early 2000s they had come to include services. "From telemarketing to data entry to accounting, business service outsourcing is growing by leaps and bounds, with annual growth close to 10 per cent in the United States. And increasingly in today's wired world, outsourcing is going offshore, much in the same fashion and for the same reasons that so much manufacturing activity has migrated from the US economy. Pretty soon that call centre in New Brunswick will be in New Delhi. And it won't be long before data processing follows suit. Just as China is becoming the world's factory, India is rapidly becoming the world's back office, drawing on a highly educated and largely English-speaking population. Like China's advantage in goods production, India's advantage in services emanates from labour costs that are a fraction of those in North America. An MBA in India with three years working experience will make $12,000 (US) a year, compared with $100,000 in the United States" (G&M, November 10, 2003, B8). "In Canada, the average computer programmer with two or three years experience earns between $33,000 and $65,000 annually. In comparison, programmers in India earn between $8,000 and $13,000 each year..." (G&M, November 11, 2003, B7). See globalization and links.

**overcapacity and overproduction.** A term, of Leninist origins, invoked by writers such as Greider (1997) and Brenner (2002). For the global system as a whole overcapacity and overproduction are said to represent a threat to stability. Excess supply, it is universally acknowledged, leads to a downward pressure on wages; between 1980–1994, 32 car and truck assembly plants were closed in North America, wiping out 5.4 m. units of production capacity with 180,000 jobs lost (Greider, 1997, 113). The European auto industry has 22% overcapacity while global steel capacity exceeds demand by 20%; there is also overcapacity in commercial aircraft (2x market demand); consumer electronics, textiles, computers; but not advanced technologies such as semiconductors or communications. Overcapacity drives industries to move where they seek better market positions through cheaper labour, more efficient technology, avoidance of import barriers, fast-developing markets. "The central irrationality of the Great Depression years has reappeared in our times. In a depressed world of inadequate demand, each firm, industry and nation attempts to save itself by competitive deflation. Some can 'win' in this struggle by cutting their costs and boosting their efficiency the most. However, the more the winners win, the more the losers lose as this is a negative sum game"; so even in advanced economies, mass consumption is not able to keep pace with new abundance (Greider, 1997, 119–20). Between March 1988 and March 1998, 337,000 manufacturing jobs were lost in the US; automobile industry had 30% unused capacity: "The extraordinary addition of manufacturing plants in the world during the 1990s, particularly in Asia, seemed to be leading to a glut of manufactured foods, thus lowering prices, sometimes below production costs." Furthermore, commodity prices fell by 30% in 1997–1998, according to The Economist index, which reached its lowest level in 150 years. "The USA cannot go on producing and consuming an increasing share of the world's output by itself (currently standing at over a quarter of the world's GDP)—mainly because domestic consumption remains the principal factor accounting for economic growth, and household savings are reaching dangerously low levels. Productivity gains, after all, have to be realised by sale of output to someone with money to spend" (Castells in Hutton and Giddens (eds.), 2000, 53, 65). See globalization, world economy, trends, since 1945 and links.

**Oxfam** (www.oxfam.org). Pioneering charity that originated in Oxford, England, and was originally concerned with famine relief in the aftermath of World War Two. Now focussed internationally and concerned with development, the environment, global pharmaceutical monopolies and fair trade. Has branches throughout the world; in Canada (www.oxfam.ca). Oxfam pulled its pension fund monies out of arms and tobacco companies. Because of its political activism, Oxfam is sometimes denigrated by conservative NGOs. It is usually anathematized by globalizers (e.g., Bhagwati, 2004, 5, 81). For its policy papers, see (www.oneworld.org/oxfam/index). See lobbyists, Third World, organizations, critical of capitalism and globalization and links.

**ozone.** See trace gases.

**Pacific Environment** (www.pacificenvironment.org). NGO founded in 1987 concerned with Pacific Rim environmental issues including exploiting of Russian forests and North Pacific fisheries. See organizations and publications, environmental and links.

**Parkland Institute** (www.ualberta.ca/PARKLAND). Research and public awareness institute with newsletter. Concerned with Canadian public health, globalization, G8, corporate power. See organizations and publications critical of capitalism and globalization and links.

**participation.** An important aspect of alternative development. Participatory research, for instance, involves people in the investigation of their own communities and environments and their design of development objectives. Ideally, this leads to more understanding. See development, interpretations of.

**patriarchy.** An ideology, often supported by metaphysical texts (i.e., the Bible, Quran, Torah), that contends that men should naturally dominate women. A central issue for those involved in development. See development, interpretations of and links.

**pay, CEO.** Hot issue in the early 2000s. In the 1990s the pay given to the CEOs of large firms was related to the share-price of those firms. As share prices increased, usually a functioning of downsizing and de-unionizing the workforce, CEO pay rose vertiginously. According to *Business Week* (cited in Frank, 2000, 7), CEO compensation in the decade went from 85x that of an average blue collar worker to 475x. "In 1997, Jack Welch [CEO of General Electric] was paid some 1,400 times the average wage earned by his blue-collar workers in the US and 9,571 times the average wage earned by Mexican industrial workers, who made up an increasing percentage of the GE workforce as production was moved to the region just across the border" (Frank, 2000, 7). See wages, repression of, wealth, distribution of/Canadian/global/US and links.

**Pembina Institute for Appropriate Development** (www.pembina.org). Alberta-based independent environmental organization concerned with environmental education and especially climate change. A Pembina Institute study shows that Alberta is Canada's major emitter of greenhouse gas (*G&M*, September 24, 2001, A16). See organizations and publications, environmental and links.

**pension funds.** Pension funds are immense reservoirs of capital formed by the combination of savings and interest. By 1994, the worldwide value of pension funds was ten thousand billion. In the US, in one account, one-third of all corporate shares are held in workers' pension funds. In another, US pension funds accounted for 26 per cent of total equity holdings. UK pension funds controlled assets of £830 billion in 1998. In the UK, pension funds owned 27.8 percent of all shares (1994). "Pension funds own nearly half the quoted shares in British companies." In Canada, pension fund administrators manage C$360 billion (Dobbin, 1998, 67; Hutton in Hutton and Giddens (eds.), 2000, 35). See mutual funds, pension funds, Canadian, stocks and links.

**pension funds, Canadian.** The main Canadian pension funds are the Caisse de dépôt et placement du Québec, the Ontario Teachers Pension Fund, the Ontario Municipal Employees Retirement Board and the new Public Sector Pension Investment Board. These funds manage, respectively, C$125, C$72, C$36 and C$130 billion. The Public Sector Pension Investment Board was established in June 2000 to manage the pension money of 307,000 public servants including the RCMP and the Canadian Armed Forces. The Ontario Teachers' fund is one of the biggest landlords in North America, owning, through their wholly owned subsidiary Cadillac Fairview Corporation, such landmark real estate as the Toronto-Dominion Centre and the Eaton Centre in Toronto, the Pacific Centre in Vancouver and the Fairview Mall in Montreal. The Caisse de dépôt owns Pen-York Properties of Toronto which, in turn, is a subsidiary of the real estate and management firm SITQ Immobilier. SITQ Immobilier has assets of C$7 billion including 55 University Avenue in Toronto. It also has projects in Paris, London and Washington, DC (*G&M*, December 23, 2000, B1; *G&M*, June 16, 2001, B9; *G&M*, June 19, 2001, B15). See mutual funds, pension funds, stocks and links.

**Peoples' Global Action (PGA)** (www.agp.org). Network of social organizations, inspired by the grassroots democracy movement in Chiapas, launched in Geneva, in February 1998, against wTO and free trade. Its Canadian address is the headquarters of the Canadian Union of Postal Workers (CUPW). See organizations and publications, critical of capitalism and globalism and links.

**Peoples' Global Action Manifesto** (www.urban75.com). UK-based site "featuring direct action, rave, drug info, stories, photos, rants and more.... [A] new platform [which] will serve as a global instrument for communication and coordination for all those fighting against the destruction of humanity and the planet by the global market, building up local alternatives and peoples' power." See Peoples' Global Action and links.

**Peoples' Health Assembly 2000** (www.pha2000.org). A website used by health activists worldwide. See organizations, health and welfare and links.

**pepper spray** (*oleoresin capsicum*). Police weapon of choice of the 1990s. In Seattle, police used MK-46 First Defense Red Pepper manufactured by Defense Technologies (Def-Tech) in Caspar, Wyoming. Pepper spray causes choking and has been linked to fatalities. In national parks such as Banff and Waterton used against grizzly bears. See Asian Pacific Economic Cooperation (APEC) and links.

**periodicals.** See press.

**periodicals, anti-globalization.** See organizations and publications, critical of capitalization and globalization and links.

**petro dollars.** Dollars accumulated through the sale of oil and held outside of the US, often in accounts in US banks. See petroleum and links.

**petroleum.** See gas and oil and links.

**petroleum, Canadian, exports to US.** Canada is now the top supplier of oil to the US, outstripping other sources such as Saudi Arabia and Venezuela. See gas and oil, petroleum and links.

**petroleum, world reserves of.** "The world's oil companies are now finding only one barrel of oil for every four that we consume.... North Sea oil... is at its peak. Venezuela, the former USSR, Mexico and Norway are all past theirs. Saudi Arabia will peak in less than a decade... global production will start to feel the pinch around 2005 when reserves begin to dwindle by three per cent a year" (Ellwood, 2001, 12). "(S)ince 1995, the world has used 24 billion barrels of oil a year but has found, on average, just 9.6 billion barrels of new oil annually" (Roberts, 2004, 51). See gas and oil, multinational corporations, oil, petroleum and links.

**Pew Centre on Global Climate Change** (www.pewclimate.org). A top US environmental NGO that works on climate policy. See climate change and links.

**Pharmaceutical Research and Manufacturers of America** (www.pharma.org). Agitprop for Big Pharma. See lobbyists, business, US and links.

**Physicians for Human Rights** (www.phrusa.org). See organizations, human rights and links.

**Polanyi, Karl.** Deceased Hungarian economist, increasingly popular among left nationalists in the 1990s. Author of *The Great Transformation* (1944), where he explained the "double movement" of capitalist growth. The first movement was marked by *laissez faire* liberalism but this gave rise to such instability and inequality as to trigger a counter movement resulting in a move towards tighter social and political controls over markets and especially over finance. "To allow the market mechanism to be sole director of the fate of human beings and their natural environment... would result in the demolition of society," he surmised (73). Polanyi coined the term "market society." His influence is evident in Gray (1998) and Wade and Veneroso (1998). A new (2001) edition of *The Great Transformation* has a preface by Joseph Stiglitz. Discussed by McQuaig (2001, Chapter 4). See theory, economic and links.

**Polaris Institute** (www.polarisinstitute.org). Ottawa-based social democratic think-tank founded in 1997. Object is "retooling citizen movements for democratic social change in an age of corporate-driven globalization." See organizations and publications critical of capitalism and globalism and links.

**Polaris Project** (www.polarisproject.org). Washington-based NGO combating trafficking of women and children. See organizations and publications, human rights, trafficking in humans and links.

**policy, foreign, US.** See foreign policy, US and links.

**pollution, environmental.** The main source of air pollution in the 20th century has been fossil fuel combustion. "Since the 1960s, automobile tailpipes have challenged smokestacks and chimneys, and by 1990, road traffic has become the largest single source of air pollution around the world. Pollution history followed the history of industrialization and 'motorization'" (McNeill, 2001, 58). One estimate suggests that air pollution killed 20–30 million people between 1950 and 1997; roughly as many as were killed by World Wars One and Two (McNeill, 2001, 103). See acid rain, blocking of remedial environmental changes by, carbon emissions trade, chloroflurocarbons, COP-6, crisis, ecological, aversion of, firms, energy, US, gas and oil, greenhouse gas, International Panel on Climate Change, Kyoto Protocol, organizations and publications, environmental, pollution, of the environment, in Canada/Ontario, smog, trace gases and links.

**pollution, environmental, in Canada/Ontario.** Ontario is North America's 3rd worst polluter, after Texas and Pennsylvania. The worst Canadian polluters according to one measure are Dofasco in Hamilton, Co-Steel Lasco in Whitby, Inco in Sudbury and Dominion in Ajax (CCPAM, 7, 4, September 2000, 23). According to another, they are Ontario Power Generation, Nanticoke, Cabot Canada, Sarnia, Syncrude Canada, Fort McMurray, Agrium, Redwater (AB), Canadian Fertilizers, Medicine Hat, Bowater Pulp and Paper, Thunder Bay, Inco, Copper Cliff, General Chemical Canada, Amherstburg, General Motors, Oshawa, Nova Scotia Power, New Waterford, Agrium, Calgary and Bayer, Sarnia (G&M, April 18, 2001, A1). Note the remarkable coincidence between pollution and Conservative governments. In February 2001, the attorneys-general of New York and Connecticut alleged that air pollution from Ontario's coal-fired power-plants caused deaths, illnesses and extensive environmental damage in the US. The coal-fired plants at Nanticoke, Lambton, Lakeview and Atikokan, owned by Ontario Power Generation, produce more than 30% of Ontario's energy (G&M, February 5, 2001, 1; TS, September 11, 2002, A17). A single Canadian contributes as much to global warming as 190 Indonesians (Rich, 1994, 262). See agreements, international, on environment, Canada, obstruction of international protocols, organizations and publications, environmental, pollution, environmental and links.

**Pollution Watch** (www.pollutionwatch.org). An environmental information service provided by the Canadian Institute for Environmental Law and Policy, the Canadian Environmental Law Association and Canadian Environmental Defence. "PollutionWatch is your source for information about the chemicals that manufacturing facilities release in your community. Simply type in your postal code or check on the map of Canada, to get the facts on pollution in your community, in your province and in Canada. You can also find out about the health effects and regulations concerning toxic chemicals and take action to voice your concerns." See organizations and publications, environmental and links.

**polyvinyl chloride (PVC).** Production and disposal of PVCs create persistent organic pollutants (POPs), which are extremely toxic, even in small amounts. PVCs are in appearance like plastics and are used in a broad range of products including toys, flooring, waterbeds, swimming pools and hospital supplies. They are often distinguishable by being stamped with the number "3." See pollution, environmental and links.

**population, world.** The world's population in 2004 was estimated at nearly 6.4 billion. For estimates see www.geohive.com. See also boom, baby.

**Porto Alegre.** See World Social Forum.

**poverty.** Absence of wealth. According to the World Bank, the global poor are those who earn less than $1 a day. See poverty alleviation, Third World, wealth, distribution of and links.

**poverty alleviation, Third World.** The IMF, having done its fair share to increase Third World poverty, began in the early 1990s to seek ways to alleviate it. It accordingly developed a caring mask. See International Monetary Fund, non-governmental organizations (NGOs) and links.

**power, nuclear.** "(N)o nuclear power plant anywhere made commercial sense; they all survived on an 'insane' economics of massive subsidy" (McNeill, 2001, 312). See organizations and publications, environmental, pollution, environmental and links.

**Prague.** Venue for IMF/World Bank meetings in September 2000. Even though numbers on street far fewer than predicted IMF/World Bank again relaunched themselves as agencies that care for the global poor. James Wolfensohn, head of the World Bank, 1995–2005: "We live in a world scarred by inequality. Something is wrong when the richest 20 percent of the global population receive more than 80 percent of the global income." Both institutions rejected Canadian initiative on debt repayment moratorium for poorest countries. See conferences, international, and links.

**press, business.** Newspapers and journals which principally serve to encourage and inform business and which therefore, naturally, disparage criticism of any aspect of business save the most blatant of criminal practices. The emperor of business newspapers is the *Wall Street Journal*, followed at a safe distance by the *Financial Times*. There are numerous business weeklies, the best of which are *Business Week* and *The Economist*. See organizations, for the promotion of capitalism and globalism, press, non-business.

**press, non-business.** Newspapers and journals which do not principally serve business. These are rare in Canada but include the *Toronto Star* and *Le Devoir*. The *Guardian Weekly* is probably the best-known English non-business weekly, followed by *Le Monde* and *Le Monde Diplomatique*. *The Nation* tops the US list. See media, alternative, press, business and links.

**primary products/staples.** Raw materials that enter at an early stage into the production of other goods, e.g., sugar for candy production, iron for steel production, palm oil, coffee, cocoa, mangoes. Usually prices are unstable and inelastic and are subject to a long-term downward pressure e.g., palm oil, sugar, coffee, cocoa, mangoes. As income rises in the advanced countries, the demand for food rises less rapidly. So the national economies of primary products producers rise less rapidly than advanced countries. The problem of primary producers has been aggravated by the development of substitutes, e.g., corn sweeteners for sugar, artificial fibres in place of cotton, plastics in place of wood. Free trade theory takes no account of these factors. See theory, free trade and links.

**privatization.** The practice, universally supported by neoliberal regimes, of taking publicly owned assets and publicly controlled services (railways, airlines, prisons, hospitals, water supplies, road maintenance, garbage collection) and selling them off at a loss to private investors.

Although it is alleged that publicly owned assets inevitably run at a loss, many are profitable. On the whole, there is no evidence that privatized services offer better service to the public. A study by four University of Alberta academics has concluded that the privatization of the Alberta Liquor Control Board "was conceived with little thought, and implemented in haste." According to Dobbin (1998, 235): "The study reveals... (that)... (t)he government... lost $400 million in annual revenue, gaining only $40 million from the sale of the board's assets, half of what they cost originally. Thirteen hundred full-time jobs, at an average wage of $30,000, were lost. The new system pays workers between 35 and 50 per cent less, resulting in less spending in the community and a loss of tax revenue." In Ontario health services have become increasingly privatized while the privatization (sometimes called "deregulation") of university education continues to be debated. See neoliberalism and links.

**profits, untaxed, Canadian.** Corporate tax breaks and other boons have led to the steady increase of untaxed profits from C$9.9 billion (from 62,619 firms) in 1980 to C$27 billion (from 93,405 firms) in 1987. "The total exceeded $125 billion for the eight years. This was just for the corporations that managed to reduce their taxes to zero; many more billions were lost in reduced taxes" (Dobbin, 1998, 225). See wealth, distribution of, Canadian and links.

**Project for the New American Century (PNAC).** US neoconservative think-tank founded by neoconservatives in 1997. In January 1998 several members of this lobby group, including Donald Rumsfeld, wrote to President Clinton advocating that he remove Saddam Hussein (see www.newamericancentury.org/iraqclintonletter.htm). It is assumed, therefore, that the Republicans had decided to invade Iraq well before the events of September 11. See think-tanks and links.

**Project Ploughshares** (www.ploughshares.ca). Canadian organization involved in promotion of peace and critical of arms trade. Centred in Conrad Grebel College, University of Waterloo. See organizations and publications, peace and links.

**prostitution, child.** See child, organizations and publications, human rights, trafficking, sex, exploitation of and links.

**protectionism, trade.** The opposite of *laissez faire* and trade liberalism, it is deplored by proponents of globalism who have worked to see it abandoned in the Third World. Yet, since the late 1970s protectionism has been widely practised by both the US and the EU to keep Asian and other Third World imports out of their markets. Thus there are few Japanese cars in France and Italy and high US tariffs steel from South Korea. Canadian protection has largely been negotiated away in the last decade as a condition for greater access to US market. It is now impossible for Ottawa to alter the price or amount of petroleum or water exports to the US. According to Kevin Watkins (*GW*, January 18–24, 2000, 23), of Oxfam UK, "While poor countries have liberalised their markets, rich nations have remained protectionist, especially in areas such as textiles and agriculture.... Each year developing countries lose about $700 billion as a result of trade barriers in rich countries: for every $1 provided by the rich world in aid and debt relief, poor countries lose $14 because of trade barriers. Reducing those barriers would create jobs and take millions of people out of poverty.... [At Seattle] the industrialized countries promised to provide the 48 least developed countries—which account for 12% of the world's population but only .5% of trade—with improved market access. One year on, they have done nothing. Poor countries exporting to the industrialized world face tariffs four times as high as those facing rich countries. Industrialised countries have promised to withdraw restrictions on imports of textiles, the third world's biggest manufactured export. But less than 10% of the restriction has been lifted.... Poor countries are losing export markets, and rural livelihoods are being destroyed on a huge scale because millions of poor farmers in Africa, Asia and Latin America cannot compete against subsidised imports. The resulting loss of food self-reliance is good news for the giant corporate grain exporters, who dictate US trade policy, but bad news for the fight against poverty." John Ibbitson argues that George W. Bush is the most protectionist president since Herbert Hoover (*G&M*, May 3, 2002, A13). Barrie McKenna writes: "There isn't a WTO member on the planet—Canada among them—that isn't steamed by a rising tide of US protectionism" (*G&M*, May 17, 2002, B9; see also *G&M*, August 9, 2003, B2 for recent figures and the reminder: "The industrialized countries' positions, including Canada's to a degree, are riven with hypocrisy. As a rule they have preached free trade and development while doing their level best to freeze Third World farm goods off the market.") See development, International Multi-Fibre Arrangement, tariffs, trade, free, Voluntary Export Restraints, World Bank, World Trade Organization and links.

**Public Citizen** (www.citizen.org). Organization founded by Ralph Nader sometime head of US Green Party. See organizations and publications critical of capitalism and globalism, organizations and publications, environmental and links.

**purchasing power parity (PPP).** "To compare economic statistics across countries, the data must first be converted into a common currency. Unlike conventional exchange rates, PPP rates of exchange allow this conversion to take account of price differences between countries. By eliminating differences in national price levels, the method facilitates comparisons of real values for income, poverty, inequality and expenditure patterns" (*Human Development Index, 2001*, 135).

**Qatar.** Gulf state, the capital of which is Doha, site of November 2001 meeting of World Trade Organization. "Rebalancing the rules [of international trade] was the promise made by rich countries in Doha nearly two years ago. Since then, the vaunted Doha Development Agenda has gone nowhere. Not one of the deadlines for issues of importance to developing countries has been met—not on agricultural subsidies, not on special and differential treatment, not even on access to medicines" (*G&M*, 30 July 2003, A13). "The failure of rich countries to make bold concessions on agriculture has left the World Trade Organization's Doha round of talks in disarray" (*Econ*, 04, 92). See Cancun, conferences, international, intellectual property rights, World Trade Organization and links.

**Quadrilateral Group of Ministers (QUAD).** Formed in 1981, but not generally heard of before Seattle, the QUAD is an informal committee guiding the global trade regime. Its members—the US, EU, Japan and Canada—meet before the public meetings of the WTO. "Before public meetings of the WTO, members of the QUAD... meet privately, making key decisions without the participation of other representatives of the world community. Once the QUAD reaches agreement, a larger, select group of twenty to thirty countries are invited to come together in informal meetings. Only after that do the 143 members of the WTO discuss and vote on proposals that are typically, by this point, *faits accomplis*. The poor countries of the periphery are forced to fall into line by the pressure of the economic and political muscle arrayed against them.... Officials that represent the QUAD are closely linked to the corporations they serve. Personnel move back and forth between lobbyists for and leadership of giant corporations, banks, legal firms, and what is called the public service sector. The Business Roundtable in the United States, the European Roundtable of Industrialists, Canada's Business Council on National Issues, and Japan's Keidanren have an enormous influence on the decisions that are made by the QUAD. The QUAD policy-making advisory committees are headed by important CEOs. They consult closely with the officials who attend the QUAD meetings as well as the more general gatherings. Through this transmission belt, the desires of the dominant factions of the capitalist class are first negotiated and then imposed on weaker capitals and on the workers of the world. For some time, the use of this procedure had been accepted as inevitable. In Seattle, Third World delegates, perhaps emboldened by the presence of the demonstrators, publicly criticized it" (Tabb, 2000, 9–10). See lobbies, business and links.

**Quebec City.** Site of April 20–22, 2001, Summit of the Americas conference to promote hemispheric free trade. Impressive levels of state violence. See conferences, international, Convergence des lutttes anti-capitalist, Free Trade Area of the Americas and links.

**Rabble** (www.rabble.ca). A Canadian-based news analysis and comment website from a leftist perspective. Supported by a number of household names as well as such institutions as BC Teachers' Federation, Canadian Centre for Policy Alternatives, Canadian Union of Public Employees and the Public Service Alliance. See media, alternative and links.

**Rainforest Action Network** (www.ran.org). Public education and information group founded in 1985 in an attempt to protect tropical rainforests and the human rights of those living in and around them. Conducted a successful boycott of Burger King, which had been buying cheap beef from producers who destroyed rainforests for grazing. Site informs on current campaigns, e.g., "Citigroup under Fire for Lack of Environmental Standards." See Amazonia, organizations, forests, destruction of, organizations and publications, environmental and links.

**rainforests.** Forests in the tropics, as opposed to temperate areas (the largest of which are the boreal forests that stretch across North America and Eurasia). For the destruction of rainforests, see Amazonia, forests, destruction of, organizations and publications, environmental and links.

**Reaganism-Thatcherism.** The most coherent version of neoliberalism. Under its banners neoliberalism, an unprecedented attack on the wages of the US and UK working classes took place, to be followed by similar campaigns worldwide. Following the theories of supply-side economics, the two principals attacked the trade unions, which they claimed were responsible for high wages which were strangling profits. As a corollary, they reduced taxes for the rich and thus, with the reduction of wages for the working class, undermined the provision of and accessibility to social services and education. This revolution, which was on the whole successful, has been carried forward by most Canadian governments, federal and provincial, up to the present and has been one of the main causes of growing social inequality. One consequence in the US was all-time high levels of debt. In Ontario it was called the "Common-Sense Revolution." It should be noted that one of the reasons for the success of Reaganism-Thatcherism was that in both countries there had been, in the 1970s, palpable defeats. The US had been humiliated in Vietnam and Iran and the UK had suffered prolonged economic decline. Reagan's "It's morning in America" and his Hollywood cowboy talk about "walking tall" thus spoke to the need of national redress (see Anderson, 2001). See neoliberalism and links.

**recession.** A contraction in GDP for two consecutive quarters. The latest recession to affect Canada was that of 1990–1991. See bubble, crash, recessions, predictions of, world economy, trends, since 1945 and links.

**recessions, predictions of.** A recent paper by Prakash Loungani for the IMF shows that economists predicted only 2 out the 60 recessions in the 1990s. In August 1990, the chairman of the US Federal Reserve Bank, Alan Greenspan, denied there would be a recession when one was already under way. Not only are neoclassical economists, thus, hopeless at prediction, they are often quite blind to reality. William Rees-Mogg, a British Conservative whose writings appear fitfully in the *G&M*, has been predicting recession on an annual basis since the late 1990s. See bubble, stock market, in the US, Clintonomics, overcapacity/overproduction, world economy, trends, since 1945 and links.

**Redefining Progress** (info@rprogress.org). Non-profit public policy organization concerned with environment. Source of article "Tracking the Ecological Overshoot of the Human Economy" by the National Academy of Sciences. See organizations and publications, environmental and links.

**refugees and asylum seekers.** A refugee as defined by the UN as a person with "a well-founded fear of persecution for reasons of race, religion, nationality, membership of a particular social group or political opinion." An "asylum seeker" is a person seeking asylum on the basis of "refugee status." There are currently fifteen m. refugees in the world. There are about 4m. refugees and exiles from each of the following groups: Palestinians, Afghanis and Sudanese (*CCPAM*, 9, 8, February 2003, 3, 19). See migration and links.

**Research Foundation for Science, Technology and Ecology** (www.vshiva.net). Indian research institution. See organizations and publications, environmental.

**revolving door.** Used to describe process whereby retired government officials take positions with corporations in order to use their influence. Robert Rubin, the US Treasury Secretary under President Clinton, joined the government from the investment banker, Goldman Sachs. After leaving the government he returned to Citigroup, which controlled the largest US commercial bank, Citibank. The #2 person at the IMF, Stanley Fischer, went straight from the International Monetary Fund to Citigroup. According to the *Multinational Monitor*'s list of the affiliations of the Bush cabinet, Ann Veneman, Secretary of Agriculture, was previously a vice president of Monsanto and a GATT negotiator. In the US government's Environmental Protection Agency, Christine Whitman, former governor of New Jersey, has interests in Texas oil wells, household cleaning product companies, Aventis, Exxon, du Pont, and Weyerhauser. Her deputy, Linda Fisher, was previously vice president of regulatory affairs at Monsanto and ran the firm's political action committee. See Aventis, Exxon, General Agreement on Trade and Tariffs, Monsanto, *Multinational Monitor*, Rubin, Robert, Washington Consensus and links.

**Rocky Mountain Institute** (www.rmi.org). US organization concerned with efficient and restorative use of resources. "Genetically modified crops were created not because they're productive, but because they're patentable. Their economic value is oriented not toward helping subsistence farmers to feed themselves, but toward feeding more livestock for the already overfed rich." See genetically modified food, Monsanto, organizations and publications, environmental and links.

**rogue states.** Sobriquet attached to states whose activities do not conform to requirements of US State Department but which can be bullied and vilified at no great expense, e.g., Libya, North Korea, Afghanistan. Although the term "terrorism" is often attached to these states, this term is used selectively and does not apply to states that use terrorism against their own people (Chile, Guatemala, Indonesia), or their neighbours

(Israel), or who employ it against the enemies of the US (as Operation Condor), nor does it apply to the terrorism perpetrated or encouraged by the agencies of the US itself (CIA, USAID, US military). "Even though it remains a small, failed Communist regime whose people are starving and have no petroleum, North Korea is a useful whipping boy for any number of interests in Washington. If the military needs a post-Cold War opponent to justify its existence, North Korea is less risky than China. Politicians seek partisan advantage by claiming that others are 'soft' on defending the country from 'rogue regimes.' And the arms lobby has a direct interest in selling its products to each and every nation in East Asia, regardless of its political orientation" (Johnson, 2000, 133). See Blum (2002) and foreign policy, US menace and links.

**Ruckus Society** (www.rukus.org). Direct action organization with training centres founded in 1995 and based in Berkeley. Prime mover is John Sellers, formerly of Greenpeace. Ruckus was initially funded by Ted Turner, the media magnate, a proponent of free trade. Sellers was an outstanding leader of protests at Seattle. The society trains demonstrators in the arts of non-violent direct action protest: tree climbing, road blocking, dealing with police, etc. In 2000 there were training camps in Alberta, Pennsylvania, Florida and California. Differs from EarthFirst and Rainforest Action Network in that it campaigns on wider range of issues, including WTO (Sellers, 2001, 71–85). See anarchism, organizations and publications, against capitalism and globalism and links.

**Rural Advancement Foundation International (RAFI).** See Erosion, Technology and Concentration (ETC) Group, organizations and publications, environmental and links.

**Saferworld** (www.saferworld.or.uk). UK think-tank concerned with effective ways for dealing with armed conflict. See organizations and publications, peace/arms control and links.

**SalAMI (Sal Accord Multilateral sur les Investissement)** (www.alternatives-action.org/salami). Montreal anti-globalization group, active and effective in movement against MAI. Favours non-violent direct action. See organizations, anarchist, organizations, critical of capitalism and globalism and links.

**Saskatchewan Organic Directorate** (www.saskorganic.com). Umbrella organization involved in combat against genetically modified foods. See genetic engineering, organizations, agricultural and links.

**School of the Americas Watch** (www.soaw.org). Watchdog organization that monitors infamous US Army School of the Americas in Benning,

Georgia, alleged nursery of state terrorists including contras and torturers attached to militaries of Latin America. See terror, state, torture, state and links.

**Seattle.** Demonstrations against WTO in Seattle on November 30, 1999, launched global protests against WTO, IMF and World Bank. Estimated numbers 50,000 plus included large contingents of trade unionists who were absent from later demonstrations in Washington. See conferences, international, organizations and publications, critical of capitalism and globalism and links.

**semiconductors.** "Semiconductor chips, as a basic commodity in every modern industrial product, were sometimes described as the 'crude oil of the information age,' but that comparison obscured the fabulous mobility and complexity. Malaysia was but one important outpost in a dizzying network of production locations, from Scotland to California and Texas to the belt of East Asian nations that runs southward from Korea and Taiwan to Indonesia and Thailand." Movements of factories and training programs "were originally driven by a straightforward search for cheaper workers, but the rationale evolved into more sophisticated strategies as the rising complexity reduced the labor dimension and greatly multiplied the capital costs of building new semiconductor plants. Locating production elements in different regions became a hedge play for multinationals of all kinds, protecting prices and profits against the constant storm of currency changes or market shares against the growing threat of protectionism. If major consumer markets were to close access to outside producers, the semiconductor industry had already established itself as a ubiquitous insider" (Greider, 1997, 90). Originally the plan was to shift abroad to lower labour costs and keep the highest technology at home; now accumulated capability has emerged in a number of different regions. Malaysia sought to become a major export platform by offering semiconductor industry tax holidays; plants in economic zones were given "pioneer" status for 5–10 years; no taxation on earnings in the country, exemptions from import duties and state subsidies; new investments meant new exemptions; government offered semiconductor pioneers a union-free environment. See industry, world economy, trends, since 1945 and links.

**sex, trafficking in.** A universal phenomenon involving young women. Deception is commonly used in sex trafficking. "Young women and girls are told that there are opportunities for legitimate work overseas but discover on arrival that they are expected to offer sex. This happens all over the world but is particularly prevalent in Southeast Asia in the Mekong Delta—which comprises Cambodia, Laos, Burma, Thailand, Vietnam and the two southern Chinese provinces of Yunnan and Guangxi.

The International Organization for Migration estimates that up to 300,000 women and children are trapped in "'slavery-like' conditions in the Mekong Delta" (Stalker, 2001, 58–59). See Captive Daughters, organizations and publications, human rights, prostitution, child, slavery, tourism, sex, trafficking, in humans and links.

**Sierra Club** (www.sierraclub.ca). Environmental organization that coordinates the Canadian Climate Action Network, which includes over a hundred groups. See organizations and publications, environmental and links.

**Sierra Legal Defence Fund** (www.sierralegal.org). "The SLDF is a non-profit environmental law organization that provides free legal services to the environmental community in Canada." Publications include *The Lost Decade*, a report on Canada's dolorous conservation record since 1992, as well as subjects as logging, Ontario's dirty water and the destruction of wildlife habitat. See organizations and publications, environmental and links.

**slavery.** As many as 27 million people around the world are slaves. Slavery exists in several forms, included as bonded labour, and in a number of countries, most notably India, Pakistan, Thailand, Mauritania and Brazil. See Bales, 2000 and anti-slavery and human rights organizations, e.g., Anti-Slavery Society of Australia (Melbourne), Anti-Slavery International (London, formerly Anti-Slavery Society), *SOS Esclaves*, (Nouakchott) and Human Rights Watch. See www.abanet.org/irr/hr/kyslave.html (aba=Americal Bar Association). See anti-slavery, child, organizations, human rights, sex, exploitation of, trafficking, in humans and links.

**slavery, anti-.** The oldest campaign against slavery is that run by the Anti-Slavery International (formerly the Anti-Slavery Society) of London (www.antislavery.org). Its North American sister organization is Free the Slaves (www.freetheslaves.net) (*NI*, 337, August 2001). See slavery and links.

**slavery, child.** See child slavery.

**slavery, sex.** See tourism, sex and links.

**slump, world.** Regularly anticipated since the late 1990s: "We may well be on the verge of a world slump.... So even the US may succumb to the gathering slump, as may Europe" (Wade and Veneroso, 1998, 14, 19). "(A) stock market crash is easily imaginable in the next couple of years" (Cumings, 1998, 72) and "The risks ahead for the world economy"

(*Econ.*, September 11, 2004, 63–65). See crisis, recession, theory, economic, crisis, world economy, trends, since 1945 and links.

**Smith, Adam.** Clergyman, economist, moralist; author of *The Wealth of Nations* (1775). Frequently cited by economists and other writers for his suggestion that economies are directed by a "hidden hand." To Smith, this hand was God's. See theory, economic, neoclassical and links.

**social exclusion.** The notion that people especially in advanced capitalist countries are excluded from full participation in civic life because of their poverty. See poverty, unemployment and links.

**social market economy.** A national economy, like that of France, which attempts to intervene in the lives of its citizens in order to keep unemployment down (to around 4–5%) and to guarantee minimum standards of well-being for its citizens. See welfare state and links.

**Social Market Foundation** (www.smf.co.uk). Centre-left UK think-tank, concerned with rational, non-ideological solutions to economic and social problems. See organizations and publications, critical of capitalism and globalism and links.

**state, welfare.** See welfare state and links.

**states.** For the past 30 or 40 years there has been an earnest discussion surrounding the nature and viability of states. By the end of the 20th century, however, this debate has narrowed down to whether the modern state is more or less like the states of the past—that is, like the states which evolved after the Treaty of Westphalia (1648) or whether they are significantly changed. There seems to be considerable evidence of widespread and deep change over the last 20–30 years. Strange (1996, 87): "the last time that anything like this happened was in Europe when states based on a feudal system of agricultural production geared to local subsistence, gave way to states based on a capitalist system of industrial production for the market. The process of change was spread over two or three centuries at the very least...." One suggestion is that market shares, not territory, are now the dominant preoccupation of states. In any case, we have to acknowledge that the success of the modern state has in recent times varied; some states, as in sub-Saharan Africa, seem unable to fulfil the basic requirements of providing their citizens with security and prosperity so it seems that the citizens might be better without them. Other states may have been viable but seem no longer to be so: Russia, Columbia. And what are we to think of the long-term viability of such endangered states as Israel? Then there is the case, in the 20th century, of states breaking up, usually into two parts: Norway breaking off from

Sweden, the Slovak Republic breaking off from Czechoslovakia and, possibly, Scotland and Northern Ireland breaking off from England and Quebec breaking off from Canada. There is no doubt that the US state, on the other hand, is in little danger of extinction. There has never been a moment when Canadians did not fear that the Canadian state would disappear. Susan Strange argues that the powers of states have, in recent years, greatly declined while the powers of non-state authorities has increased (The one exception to this is the US, as Leo Panich also emphasizes). George explains that if you want to understand relative power and authority in the world, then you must ask four questions: who has the power to offer, or threaten, the security over others, who is in a position to offer or withhold credit, who is in a position to offer or withhold access to knowledge and information and who is in a position to define the nature of knowledge. "All of these power structures spill over those often arbitrary lines that are drawn on maps to indicate the territorial limits of the authority of one state from that of another" (Strange, 1996, ix). See globalism, world economy, trends, since 1945 and links.

**states, rogue.** See rogue states.

**Statewatch** (www.statewatch.org). London based organization that monitors the state and civil liberties in the EU. Statewatch has a database of over 25,000 entries, a bulletin, pamphlets and reports. It is especially good on questions of emigration. See European Union, organizations and publications, human rights, migration and links.

**stock.** A share of ownership in a firm, usually acquired on the stock market. Firms sell shares in order to raise capital for expansion. Speculators buy stocks in the hope that their value will increase. The payment of stocks to the managers of firms (CEOs) is usually the main source of their inflated incomes. The ownership of stocks gives shareholders voting rights. "In 1992, 16.9 percent of families owned stock directly, which number actually declined to 15.3 percent in 1995 and then rebounded to 19.2 percent in 1998. Among the wealthiest families... these trends were much more pronounced. In the income bracket $50,000–$99,999, mutual fund ownership increased from 15.3 percent in 1992 to 20.9 percent in 1995; in the income bracket $100,000 or more, mutual fund ownership increased from 30.5 percent to 38 percent" (Frank, 2000, 372, fn.7). See stock market, world economy, trends, since 1945, swap and links.

**stock market.** Site where stocks are bought and sold. The most important stock market is that of New York ("Wall Street") and after that, London ("the City"). There are several different kinds of activities carried out in a stock market besides simply buying and selling stocks—including buying futures—and a number of markets for specialized stocks. NASDAQ is the market for shares in technology and telecommunications stocks. See bubble, capitalism, finance, futures, derivatives, options, New York Stock Exchange, stock, swaps, technology, media and telecommunications, Wall Street and links.

**Stockholm International Peace Research Institute (SIPRI)** (www.sipri. se/). Research institute concerned with conflict resolution, arms control and security. Invaluable source for information on military expenditure and arms production globally. See arms production, Canadian/global/US, organizations and publications, peace and links.

**structural adjustment/structural adjustment policies (SAPs).** The practice, supported by the International Monetary Fund and the World Bank, of making loans on the basis of conditionalities which include enforced retrenchment and the opening of markets and currencies to foreign capital. By cutting wages, SAPs supposedly reduce aggregate demand and thus inflation. Following from recession, which is intentional, comes macroeconomic stability and then growth and greater equality. At least in theory. In practice, SAPs lead to greater income inequality. "There is considerable evidence that the neo-liberal programmes, and SAPs in particular, are not effective in bringing about economic development, either when economic development is defined narrowly in terms of economic growth or when it is defined more broadly to include other aspects of social well-being" (MacEwan, 1999, 146) (*CCPAM*, 7, 7, December 2000/January 2001, 17–18): "After over 15 years, there were hardly any cases of successful adjustment programs. What structural adjustment had done, instead, was to institutionalise stagnation in Africa and Latin Africa, alongside rises in the levels of absolute poverty and income inequality." "Since the early 1980s, the 'macro-economic stabilisation' and 'structural adjustment' programmes imposed by the IMF and the World Bank on developing countries (as a condition for the renegotiation of their external debt) have led to the impoverishment of hundreds of millions of people. Contrary to the spirit of the Bretton Woods agreement which was predicated on 'economic reconstruction' and the stability of major exchange rates, the structural adjustment program has contributed largely to destabilising national currencies and ruining the economies of developing countries.

"Internal purchasing power has collapsed, famines have erupted, health clinics and schools have been closed down, hundreds of millions of children have been denied the right to primary education. In several regions of the developing world, the reforms have been conducive to a resurgence of infectious diseases including tuberculosis, malaria and cholera. While the World Bank's mandate consists of 'combating poverty' and protecting the environment, its support for large-scale hydroelectric and agro-industrial projects has also speeded up the process of deforestation and the destruction of the natural environment, leading to the forced displacement and eviction of several million people" (Chossudovsky, 1997, 33). Peet (2003, 92 and 143) notes that "the number of people who die as a result of the social and economic effects of IMF austerity programmes, from the increased incidence of starvation and the concomitant reduction of health programmes, has never been reliably estimated...." For a useful chart comparing debt interest payments as% of government revenue and social services as% of government expenditure see Ellwood (2001, 50). See conditionalities, development, International Monetary Fund, macroeconomic stability, neoliberalism, World Bank and links.

**Students Against Sweatshops.** See United Students Against Sweatshops.

**students, Canadian, fees.** Canadian undergraduate university students will pay an average of C$3,733 in 2002–2003. This will be more than 135.4% than they paid in 1990–1991. Undergraduate fees in Ontario will rise from $4492 to $4634. Undergraduate fees in BC, where a Liberal government recently ousted the NDP, will increase 25.2%. Tuition fees in Quebec will be frozen at $1675, the lowest in Canada. See debt, student, Canadian and links.

**Summit of the Americas.** Meeting of hemispheric heads of state (minus Fidel Castro) held at Quebec City in April 2001. Main item on agenda: a hemispheric free trade agreement. Met with considerable resistance from NGOS, trade unionists and others. See conferences, international and links.

**supply side economics.** Prevailing global economic doctrine, of American origin, as adhered to, from the early 1980s, by the IMF and the World Bank. Supply side economics is the opposite of the economic principles of Keynesianism, which prevailed from the late 1940s to the early 1970s. It stresses the importance of market friendliness, which is not quite the same as *laissez faire*. See IMF, neoliberalism, theory, economic, neoclassical, World Bank and links.

**Survey of Consumer Finances** (www.bog.frb.fed.us/pubs/oss2/scfindex.html). A US survey that studies national income, assets and debts. See world economy, trends, since 1945 and links.

**Sustainable Energy and Economy Network** (www.seen.org). Joint project of Institute of Policy Studies in Washington and Transnational Institute in Amsterdam. Seeks to stimulate popular response to issues connected with climate change. Website links to news about campaigns against Big

Oil in Nigeria, Indonesia, Peru and elsewhere. Reproduces articles on energy issues. See organizations and publications, environmental and links.

**swap.** A transaction where agents swap the payments associated with two assets. See stock market and links.

**sweat shops.** See textile and clothing industry and links.

**Sweatshop Retailer of the Year Award.** Co-sponsored by Oxfam-Canada and the Maquila Solidarity Network. Winner in 2001: Disney, followed by Wal-Mart, Nike and Reitman's. "Disney's selection... came after a report documented sweatshop abuses in 12 Disney supply factories in China. According to the report by a Hong Kong NGO, young women making Disney clothes, toys and accessories were forced to work up to 16 hours a day, six or seven days a week, for wages as low as $90Cdn a month" (CCPA *Monitor*, 8, 4, September 2001, 3). See Maquila Solidarity Network, Oxfam, textile and clothing industry and links.

**Sweatshop Watch** (www.sweatshopwatch.org). Oakland-based coalition of labour, community, civil rights and other groups committed to eliminating sweatshops in global garment industry. See textile and clothing industry and links.

**tariffs.** Taxes on imported goods, usually to protect native industries. See protectionism, tariffs, Third World countries, US and links.

**tariffs, Third World countries.** Although most discussion about tariffs (for instance at the WTO talks) is focussed on the tariffs of the G7 countries that exclude agriculture and industrial products from the developing economies, Third World countries themselves impose significant tariffs against one another. Under WTO rules the allowable Brazilian tariff on industrial goods is 30% and the Indian 40%, as compared to the US 4%. See tariffs and links.

**tariffs, US.** "The steel tariffs [imposed by the Bush Administration in March 2001]... are just temporary aberrations from the norm; they will be lifted in a couple of years. But for dozens of other products—sneakers, spoons, bicycles, underwear, suitcases, drinking glasses, T-shirts, plates, and more—tariffs of 8–30 percent are neither aberrant nor temporary. In fact, they are normal and permanent parts of US trade policy. Barring a deliberate change in policy, they will never be lifted...." Shoe manufacturing which employs a mere 2000 US workers (down 90% from 1992) is a good example of high tariffs having almost no relation to job preservation. "Cheap sneakers valued at $3 or less per pair carry tariffs of 48 per cent.... Virtually none of these shoes is made in the United States. Last year, the United States imported 16 million pairs of these sneakers, at a total cost of $35 million.... (T)he average price at the border was $2.20 per pair. The Treasury Department then collected $17 million in tariffs, adding another $1.06 to the buyers' cost. The extra dollar and change is then magnified by retail markups of around 40 percent and state sales taxes of about 5 percent to raise the final consumer price of the sneakers from about $3.25 (without tariffs) to $4.80 per pair (with tariffs).... For Bangladesh, Cambodia, Nepal, Mongolia, and a few [other countries] clothes make up 90 percent of all exports to the United States. So they face average tariff rates of 14.6 percent—nearly 10 times the world average, and 15 times the rate for wealthy Western countries.... (T)he US now collects more tariff revenue from Bangladeshi goods than from French goods, even though Bangladesh exports $2 billion in goods a year to the United states and France $30 billion." (Gresser, 2002, 12–13). See tariffs and links.

**Task Force on Food from Biotechnology.** Lobby group of Canadian agri-food industry (Canadian Council of Grocery Distributors, Canadian Federation of Independent Grocers, Canadian Federation of Agriculture, Food and Consumer Products Manufacturers of Canada) which has sought, so far successfully, to prevent labelling of GM food in spite of evidence that substantial proportion of Canadians are concerned about the effects of genetic engineering (51% of consumers polled by Ipsos-Reid in September 2001 see GM products as unacceptable). See Canadian Biotechnology Advisory Committee, genetic engineering, popular opposition to, lobbyists, Canadian, business and links.

**tax havens.** Defined as countries with banking secrecy laws and few or no taxes. The main havens for Canadian tax avoiders are the Bahamas, Barbados, Bermuda, Cayman Islands and Panama. In 1988, C$80 billion were sent tax havens, in 2001, C$44.6 billion, an increase of 891% (*G&M*, June 9, 2003, B1, B6).

**tax, Tobin.** Named after US Nobel-prize-winning economist who proposed it in 1972, this is a tax on all transactions on foreign exchange markets, which has the dual purpose of stabilizing the markets and raising money to mitigate poverty. At the rate of 0.1%, the Tobin tax would obtain an annual sum of $166 billion (1998) and, if imposed, would have eradicated extreme poverty by 2000. A UN conference of experts examined the feasibility of the tax and recommended that it be studied further by governments—advice that has been ignored since with the imposition of the tax the banks would lose a major source of profits. For discussion, see Ellwood, 2001, 124–30; McQuaig, 1998, 150–54, 164–67. See Attac, North-South Institute and links.

**taxes, lower, leading inevitably to faster economic growth.** A truth universally acknowledged by neoclassical economists and persons of that ilk. But Andrew Jackson, director of Canadian Council on Social Development, says it isn't so, i.e., that the correlation between taxes and growth is not evident (*G&M*, December 11, 2000, B8). See Canadian Council on Social Development, theory, economic, neoclassical and links.

**technology, media, telecommunications (TMT).** Areas of capitalist growth that formed the basis of the New Economy, now ruinous. See dot.com firms, information technology, markets, bear, New Economy, stocks, world economy, trends, since 1945 and links.

**Terre des Hommes** (www.terredeshommes.org). A network of ten international organizations working for children's rights. See child and links.

**terror, state.** Terror has two different meanings; first, the activities of terrorists, defined narrowly as those who victimize civilians in pursuit of their political objectives (such as the IRA, the PLO, the Tamil Tigers). Defined more broadly, terrorism includes "state terrorism," the activities of death squads, government hit men and so on, not excluding the activities of the CIA. Terrorism is the ideology appropriated by the US government to justify global interventions, as in "War on Terrorism." By pointing to this or that group alleged to be terrorists, the US and allied governments justify their own interventions, as in Afghanistan. "The average American is several times more likely to be felled by lightning than to be killed by a foreign terrorist" (*FP*, July–August, 2001, 9). "One man's terrorist is... another man's freedom fighter, and what US officials denounce as unprovoked terrorist attacks on its innocent citizens are often meant as retaliation for previous American imperial actions. Terrorists attack innocent and undefended American targets precisely because American soldiers and sailors firing cruise missiles from ships at sea or sitting in B-52 bombers at extremely high altitudes or supporting brutal and repressive regimes from Washington seem invulnerable" (Johnson, 2000, 9). For the US State Department view, see "Report on Foreign Terrorist Organizations" (www.state.gov/s/ct/rls/rpt/fto/2001/5258). See globalization, reaction to, rogue states, School of the Americas Watch and links.

**textile and clothing industry.** Among the most widespread across the globe since production technology is easy to acquire and operate. Important to developing countries where it is often subcontracted to independent firms. East Asia, especially China, has become a key global supplier. Most workers in these industries are young women. Ross (1997) provides a comprehensive discussion and the Canadian Labour Congress (November 2000) has produced a useful pamphlet. See industries, Sweatshop

Retailer of the Year Award, Sweatshop Watch, United Students Against Sweatshops (USAS) and links.

**theory, dependency.** A theory first articulated by Latin American economists in the early postwar period, which had as a central tenet the impossibility of development of the "periphery" (i.e., the Third World) due to the dominance of the "metropole," i.e., the OECD countries. A central tenet of the theory was that "integration into the international economy leads to disintegration of the national economy." While the Argentinian economist, Raul Prebisch, first developed the theory, and the Brazilian Fernando Henrique Cordoso further articulated it, it was the American, André Gunder Frank who popularized it. Dependency theory was applied to Africa by Colin Leys, Canada by Kari Levitt and to Atlantic Canada by Brym and Sacouman. By the 1990s the theory had only antiquarian interest. See development, interpretations of and links.

**theory, economic.** See theory, economic, comparative advantage, theory, economic, crisis, theory, economic, neoclassical, theory, economic, free trade and links.

**theory, economic, comparative advantage.** First articulated by David Ricardo, who used the argument for trade between England and Portugal. But Adam Smith had shown how the cloth-for-wine exchange was not the result of free trade but rather the Treaty of Methuen (1703). Smith showed that through this treaty the English consumers got bad wine so that the English cloth exporters could get a monopoly of the Portuguese market. Thus this was not free trade, it was trade regulated by politics, a politics that was dependent on British political power. The theory of comparative advantage was the ideological cornerstone of 19th century British trade expansion but free trade was not advocated until British trade had grown secure behind tariff walls. See theory, economic, neoclassical and links.

**theory, economic, crisis.** Theories that capitalism was bound to enter a period of crisis from which it might exit with difficulty, or not at all, have become common currency since the late 19th century. The world depression of the 1930s gave them credence. A contemporary variant of economic crisis theory is ecological crisis theory. Of course, just because political writers say something is true, it isn't necessarily false. See slump, world and links.

**theory, economic, neoclassical.** Sometimes known as "bourgeois economic theory," this is the mainstream interpretation and explication of economics as taught in all Canadian post-secondary institutions. Neoclassical economic theory, usually associated with Adam Smith, has as its central dogma the view that their exists a disembodied set of laws (perhaps like gravity) called "the market" that exists naturally and is best left to work on its own. "Freedom" in this theory is the freedom of an unfettered market. Neoclassical theory asserts that, under conditions of perfect competition, markets balance (or "equilibriate") the supplies and demands for each commodity. Under certain, ideal conditions, the market forces of supply and demand will allocate resources efficiently, at least in the long run, and consumers will be left satisfied. And of huge importance, all participants in production receive incomes commensurate with their skills and efforts. Capitalism is not only the best system, according to neoclassical theory, it is the only sane system. Interfering with the markets can only bring heartache and sorrow, not to mention serfdom. Man, according to neoclassical theory, is one-dimensional and that one dimension is essentially economic, a being in a perpetual state of yearning to possess more goods. His thinking is mainly about satisfying this yearning by rational means, if possible. All this is why free traders in the Liberal and Conservative parties have promoted NAFTA, that is, to satisfy economic man (*Homo Economicus*), to promote human happiness and liberate people from the shackles of statism. It is universally acknowledged that neoclassical economic theory has in the last couple of decades become highly abstract and certifiably divorced from reality. In June 2000, French students demonstrated against the teaching of neoclassical economics. Their demand for more pluralism was supported by leading economics professors and by *Le Monde*. By November 2000, a student petition against neoclassical economics had 800 signatures (*CCPAM*, 7, 6, November 200, 12, *Adbusters*, 34, Mar/Apr 2001, 40). Chalmers Johnson (2000, 180): "[One] aspect of the ideological challenge to the Soviet Union was the development and propagation of an American economic ideology that might counter the promise of Marxism—what today we call "neoclassical economics," which has gained an intellectual status in American economic activities and governmental affairs similar to that of Marxism-Leninism in the former USSR... Americans like to think... that their economics is a branch of science, not a fighting doctrine to defend and advance their interests against those of others. They may consider most economists to be untrustworthy witch doctors, but they regard the tenets of a laissez-faire economy—with its cutthroat competition, casino stock exchange, massive inequalities of wealth, and a minor, regulatory role for government—as self-evident truths." See market fundamentalism, neoliberalism, Nobel Prize for Economics, Smith, Adam, theory, free trade and links.

**theory, free trade (*laissez faire*/liberal).** This is no more than a refinement and reassertion of neoclassical economic theory. It became increasingly popular in the advanced capitalist economies during the crisis of the early 1970s "The essence of the neo-liberal position on international commerce is the proposition that economic growth will be most rapid when the movement of goods, services and capital is unimpeded by government regulations" (MacEwan, 1999, 31). "In the orthodox theory guiding the US government's economic policy, these shifts of production were regarded as beneficial to the US, despite the job losses, because they strengthened the companies and would presumably stimulate US exports. By establishing elements of production in other nations, the global manufactures would increase their intra-firm trade and thus support the jobs back home.

"That was the theory promoting greater globalization. For the US, the theory was not supported by the trade statistics; Asian economies absorbing new US investments were also running persistent, substantial trade surpluses with the US. Malaysia, for instance, bought $4.4 billion in trade goods from the US in 1992 and sold it $8.3 billion. When the trade flows from all of Asia's developing countries, included China, were combined, they represented a US trade deficit rivalling the one with Japan" (Greider, 1997, 9–10); so given wage differences, it is unlikely that jobs will return to the US: "globalization strategies meant the dispersal of more high-end engineering jobs as software design centres were located in Malaysia, India and elsewhere"; further, as production is exported, multinationals help to create further competitors. "In sum, despite the reigning pieties, the global system could not properly be called a free-trade regime. When all of the contradictions, exceptions and purposeful evasions were taken into account, most of the world's trade was not a free exchange based on market prices. One way or the other, trade was massaged and regulated, managed explicitly by governments or internally by multinational corporations or often by both in discrete collaboration"; different estimates have argued that free trade accounts only for 15–30% of trade. Multinationals manage about $405 billion of global trade through the intra-firm trade among their own subsidiaries; 22% of world trade is accounted for by sectors like aircraft and petroleum which is managed by governments or concentrated firms; instead of free trade we have a market-access trade regime where market-access bargaining has become standard; as enforceable law GATT was largely fictional, a bargaining tool; hence the WTO was created; but if the WTO should ever intrude on America's sovereign decision-making, the US-government promised to withdraw (*op. cit.*, 1997, 137–39); the political management of trade and foreign industrial investment is not gradually receding but is actually expanding and refining its dimensions; thus the global system is not one of "free trade" but should be described as a "market-access" regime; firms globalize and jobs are exported so that greater market access can be assured; "Corporate alliances are... the antithesis of free-market dogma and the supposed liberalization of free trade. One the one hand, multinationals preach free-market competition and aggressively promote the dismantling of governments' legal controls over commerce and finance. On the other hand, the same firms are busily forging territorial compacts with each other—collaborative mechanisms that may be used to manage trade privately, on their own terms, above and beyond the reach of national governments" *(op. cit.,* 1997, 172). MacEwan (1999, 64–65, fn.6) adds his criticism of free trade theory: "During the 1980s, even when the ideology of free trade was solidifying its hegemony among economists, a major theoretical challenge appeared under the name of the 'new international economics.' Working well within the framework of mainstream, orthodox economic theory, a number of economists demonstrated that when certain crucial and unrealistic assumptions of the traditional trade theory were altered to correspond more closely to reality, there was no theoretical foundation for the conclusion that free trade was necessarily the optimal economic policy. Once such realities as economies of scale, technological externalities and monopolistic competition were introduced into the analysis, there was simply no foundation for the simplistic traditional claim that economic theory supported the principle that the state should not intervene in a country's foreign commerce.... The economic arguments for free trade remain the doctrine of basic English-language textbooks." A signal that neo-liberal ideology had reached a high point came in the World Bank's *World Development Report* of 1991, which argued taxes and protection produced inequality in Latin America and that open markets would end this: "When markets work well, greater equity often comes naturally." Thus the central tenet of neoliberalism: incomes are low when the state plays an excessive role in the economy. See Free Trade Area of the Americas, market-access regime, North American Free Trade Agreement, primary products, theory, economic, neoclassical, There Is No Alternative, Hayek, World Bank and links.

**theory, Keynesian.** See Keynes, John Maynard and links.

**theory, supply side.** A family of theories, collectively hegemonic since the 1970s, which contend that the downturn and failure of recovery of the US economy is due to the pressure on wages by workers. See theory, economic and links.

**theory, trickle down.** Economic theory favoured by IMF and development agencies that holds that by making the rich richer the poor, too, will benefit. The origins of this theory are with such writers as Arthur Lewis and Simon Kuznets, both winners of the Nobel Prize for Economics. Trickle down theory is not now widely accepted, as such, although Joseph Stiglitz (2002, 80) says that it has merely changed its clothes. Trickle down theory has recently been used by Ontario's Housing Supply Working Group to explain how the poor, too, would benefit from the provision of high-cost rental housing. "Interesting theory, but the real world doesn't work that way" (TS, August 1, 2002, A21). See International Monetary Fund, theory, economic and links.

**There Is No Alternative (TINA).** Thatcherite mantra of 1980s taken up by neoliberals, globalizers, transitionologists, the World Bank and even some vulgar Marxists since. Supposes that options are stark, a simple choice between capitalist, free-market civilization or autarky and barbarism. In Russia, it was argued that there was no choice but to destroy the communist system in place, nor were there alternatives to the program proposed by Washington. The World Bank view was articulated by President Barber Conable: "A... basic truth is that development cannot be halted, only directed" (Rich, 1994, 147). See neoliberalism, Reaganism-Thatcherism and links.

**think-tanks.** Sometimes referred to as "policy institutes" these institutions of political advocacy provide ammunition for lobbyists. Their recent history dates from the 1970s. Most are very right wing and are funded by corporations that seek to sway politicians; the US defence giants (Lockheed Martin, Boeing and Rayethon) spend millions on think-tanks which, in return, advocate increased military spending. The Fabian Society is the oldest of the left wing think-tanks. See Adam Smith Institute, American Enterprise Institute, Brookings Institute, Cato Institute, C.D. Howe Institute, Demos, Fabian Global Forum, Fraser Institute, lobbyists, business, Canada/US, Pembina Institute, Project for the New American Century, Tommy Douglas Institute, World Policy Institute and links.

**Third Way.** A rhetorical device whose time came with the New Labour victory in Britain in May 1997 but which had largely disappeared from use by the time of the second Labour victory in June 2001. Promoted by Tony Blair, the sociologist Anthony Giddens and New Labourites in UK, Bill Clinton, Jorge Haider in Austria, Fernando Cardoso in Brazil and one faction within the Canadian NDP, the "Third Way" called for a political ceasefire and a surrender to a caring capitalism (sometimes known as "caring conservatism"), a capitalism, supposedly occupying a no-man's-land between brutish conservatism and ineffectual social democracy. In fact, what it called for was an acceptance of the victory of the market and US global hegemony. The World Bank, as its web page attests, moved in the direction of the "Third Way" in the late 1990s by hiring more women, "people of colour," regional experts and ostensibly showing a more earnest concern for poverty. Symptomatically, the cover of the World Bank's annual report for 2000 is decorated by a Third World artist. See Clintonomics, wealth, distribution of, Canada/global/US, World Bank and links.

**Third World Network** (www.twnside.org). A research and information network based in Penang, Malasia. See lobbyists, Third World, organizations and publications, development and links.

**TMT**. See technology, media and telecommunications.

**Tobin tax**. See Attac, tax, Tobin and links.

**Tommy Douglas Research Institute** (www.tommydouglas.ca). Left-leaning research institute with offices in Vancouver and Toronto, headed by former NDP Premier of BC, Dave Barrett. Mainly concerned with health and welfare. See, for instance, Barrett's article on health care in TS, June 11, 2001. See organizations, health and welfare and links.

**torture, state**. Practised systematically by most regimes including the US and Israel but outlawed in others such as Canada, the EU and even Turkey. Recently Harvard law professor, Alan Dershowitz (Why Terrorism Works, 2002), has advocated the use of torture on Palestinians and, presumably, other Muslims. Whether he and those of his ilk feel that it might justifiably have been used against Christians (e.g., the IRA, ETA, FLQ) or Jewish terrorists (Haganah, Stern Gang) is unclear. For US, see CAQ, 73, Summer 2002; Nat, March, 31, 2003, 11–16; NYRB, LI, 12, July 15, 2004. See imperialism, organizations and publications, human rights and links.

**tourism, sex**. Widely practised in Southeast Asia, especially Thailand and the Philippines. "Until the withdrawal of US forces from the Philippines in 1992, the town of Olongapo, adjacent to the US naval base at Subic Bay, had no industry except for the "entertainment business, which supported approximately 55,000 prostitutes and a total of 2,182 registered establishments offering 'rest and recreation' to American servicemen" (Johnson, 2000, 35–36 and Thanh-Dam Troung, 1990). As many as 35,000 girls have been sold into sex slavery in Thailand, where two-thirds of the tourists in the 1990s were unaccompanied men (Nat, April 23, 2003, 36–37). See organizations, human rights, sex, trafficking in and links.

**trace gases**. The major trace gases in the atmosphere are carbon dioxide, ozone and sulphur dioxide. Carbon dioxide is a "greenhouse gas." It keeps the planet warm. Without it the earth would be frozen and lifeless. Humans increase carbon dioxide by burning fossil fuels and by deforestation. Ozone is a second greenhouse gas and a major component of urban smog. In the stratosphere it absorbs ultraviolet radiation from the sun and protects plants and animals from harmful radiation. Between 1960–1995 the ozone shield over the Northern Hemisphere thinned about 10%. Sulphur dioxide is the main ingredient in acid rain, which destroys lakes and aquatic life as well as stone. Its main human sources are fossil fuel burning and the smelting of metallic ores. See pollution, environmental and links.

**trade, arms.** See arms, production and trade, Canadian/US/global and links.

**trade balance.** The relationship between imports and exports of two trading partners. China's trade surplus with the US was more than $160 billion in 2004 and Canada's was more than $65 billion.

**trade, free.** "Free trade was the doctrine of economically powerful states which flourished without protection, but would be fatal to weak states. This came as a revelation to me, and was doubly significant because of the part played by free trade in my intellectual upbringing. If free trade went, the whole liberal outlook went with it" E.H. Carr, 1930, at the League of Nations in Geneva (Haslam, 1999, 50). "Few politicians are actually swayed by free trade arguments. They are generally used when convenient and ignored when interests dictate.... The United States, like other countries, is opportunistically a free trader when it serves the purposes of its most powerful economic interests...." (Tabb, 2000, 135). William Finnegan (HM, May 2003, 41–54) notes that free trade "has been the main American ideological export since anti-Communism lost strategic relevance. It is promulgated directly through US foreign policy and indirectly through multilateral institutions such as the World Bank, the International Monetary Fund, and the World Trade Organization." See cartels, economics, neo-liberal, capitalism, finance, Free Trade Area of the Americas, ideology, International Monetary Fund, North American Free Trade Agreement, protectionism, trade, managed, Washington Consensus, World Bank, World Trade Organization and links.

**trade, intra-firm.** In the early 1980s, more than a third of US international trade (exports and imports) and about one-quarter of Japanese trade was intra-firm trade.

**trade, managed.** Opposite and antidote to free trade. See trade, free and links.

**Trade Related Intellectual Property Rights (TRIPs).** An agreement at the Uruguay Round of the General Agreement on Trade and Tariffs, and thus binding the signatories of the World Trade Organization, which seeks to protect patents, including the patents on genetically modified plants and pharmaceuticals. Almost invariably these patents are held by leading Western firms. The protection of these patents means that copying by poorer companies becomes illegal. The Indian parliament has resisted changing its laws to conform with TRIPs. In retaliation the US ambassador to India has announced that "certain areas of research and training will be closed to cooperation" if India fails to mend its ways. Furthermore, 130 scientific projects supported by the US-Indian Fund will be closed. "In April 1997, completely ignoring the WTO process for dispute settlement, the United States unilaterally cancelled $260 million worth of Argentina's trade on grounds that Argentina's intellectual property laws did not comply with 'international standards.' The US has brought similar pressure against Pakistan, Ecuador, Thailand, Ethiopia and other countries whose intellectual property regimes fail to satisfy transnational agricultural and pharmaceutical interests" (Dawkins, 1997, 28–29). See firms, pharmaceutical, General Agreement on Trade and Tariffs, firms, genetic engineering, genetically modified foods, globalization, neoliberalism and links.

**trade unions, in Canada**. In 1999, 3.6 million or 29.8% of employees belonged to unions. In May, 2004, this figure was 435,000 out of 13,635,600 (31%). Employees in the public sector are four times as likely to be unionized than in the private sector; this partly explains why right-wing governments want to privatize public services. Public sector workers often belong to the Canadian Union of Public Employees (CUPE). University of Toronto non-teaching staff belong to the United Steelworkers of America and UQAM teaching staff belong to the Confédération des Syndicaux Nationale (CSN) (G&M, December 23, 2000, B6). See pension funds, unemployment, wealth, distribution of, Canadian and links.

**trade, world**. For statistics on international trade and investment, see United Nations, Direction of Trade Statistics and International Trade Statistics Yearbook (from 1955 onwards).

**trafficking, in humans**. Trade in humans, sometimes as slaves, for various purposes including labour and sex. It is the third largest criminal industry in the world, after arms and drug dealing. Trafficked people are often moved far from their homes, for instance, from Thailand to Canada. The UN has addressed the question in its Protocol to Prevent, Suppress, and Punish Trafficking in Persons, Especially Women and Children (2000). According GW (July 18–24, 3) "Every year more than 6,000 children between 12 and 16 are smuggled into western Europe to work as prostitutes and drug traffickers or to beg.... About 2 million juveniles worldwide fall victim to people-smugglers every year." "An estimated 400,000 children are trafficked in India every year" (GW, February 13–19, 2003, 21). See organizations and publications, human rights, slavery, antislavery, child, trafficking, in sex and links.

**trafficking, in sex**. See sex, trafficking in, tourism, sex, trafficking, in humans and links.

**transition.** In 1970s used with reference to Third World countries, often in Africa (Tanzania, Mozambique, South Africa), which, it was argued, were making a transition towards socialism. Since the 1990s the term has referred to ex-Soviet Bloc countries supposedly moving towards capitalism. Hence Pulitzer Prize winning editor of the New Yorker: "While it is undoubtedly true that daily life in Russia today suffers from a painful economic, political and social transition, the Russian prospect over the coming years and decades is more promising than ever before in its history." Other views stress that transition in the former Soviet bloc has been calamitous. "We want to remind the world that transition can kill," wrote the head of Red Cross in former Soviet Georgia, 1996 (cited in Cohen, 2000, 33, 3). A recent book on Russia by Lawrence R Klein and Marshall Pomer (see below) has been called The New Russia: Transition Gone Awry (2001). Joseph Stiglitz (2002, 151, 214) stresses: "Seldom has the gap between expectations and reality been greater than in the case of the transition from communism to the market." He notes (153): "In 1989 [when the transition to capitalism began], only 2 percent of those living in Russia were living in poverty. By late 1998, that number had soared to 23.8 percent, using the $2 a day standard." His conclusion: "The transition from communism to a market economy has been so badly managed that, with the exception of China, Vietnam, and a few Eastern European countries, poverty has soared as incomes have plummeted" (Stiglitz' source is the World Bank's World Development Indicator, 2001). John Mueller (in FA, July/August 2004, 150–51) notes that since 1998, when most experts agree Russia's economic rebound began: "the Russian population decline has approached one million people per year—935,000 in 2002, for example, as opposed to a loss of 697,000 in 1998 and a robust gain of 580,000 in 1989. These dramatic figures represent the largest peacetime rate of population loss in Europe since the plagues." A former US Secretary of State argued against the extradition of Chilean mass-murderer Augusto Pinochet on the grounds that countries like Chile undertaking a "transition to democracy" must allow former human rights offenders immunity from prosecution if they are to "move forward" (Johnson, 2000, 18–19). See neoliberalism, transitionology, International Monetary Fund and links.

**transitionology.** In US Sovietological circles, the study of the political epoch which followed "totalitarianism," as in "the transition from communism to free-market capitalism and democracy." One of the assumptions of transitionology was universalistic, that is, that Russia's transition would follow pathways blazed by the West. See transition and links.

**transnational corporations** (TNC). See multinational corporations (MNCs).

**Transnational Institute** (www.tni.org). An independent global research institute founded in 1984. Interests include Israel-Palestine conflict, Kashmir conflict, nuclear abolition, Enron scandal. Associated with other groups such as Focus on the Global South and the Alternative Information and Development Centre. See organizations and publications, development, organizations and publications, human rights and links.

**transparency.** Visible probity, usually as a result of free access to information. Demanded by World Bank etc. of clients but visibly not practised in its own purleis. Stiglitz accuses the IMF of lack of transparency (2002, 33–34, 51–52). Lack of transparency has been associated with major corporate failures especially since the collapse of Enron. See crony capitalism, International Monetary Fund, World Bank, World Development Report, world economy, trends, since 1945 and links.

**Transparency International** (www.transparency.org). An international NGO founded in Berlin in 1993 dedicated to combating corruption. In its annual report, it offers a "Corruption Perceptions Index" that ranks states in ascending order from least (Finland) to most corrupt (Nigeria and Bangladesh). France, surprisingly, ranks only slightly above Namibia. Its "Bribe Payers' Index" puts Australia at the top (i.e., as the cleanest) and Russia at the bottom. The 2002 Report emphasizes: "It is estimated that the official arms trade accounts for 50 per cent of all corrupt international transactions. A conservative estimate of the level of commissions paid is 10 per cent in an industry worth USD 40 billion a year." See arms and following entries.

**trickle down theory.** See theory, trickle down and links.

**Trilateral Commission.** Formed in 1973 in response to fears of big transnational finance capital. This was the year that Republican President Richard Nixon unilaterally decoupled the US dollar from gold, imposed a ten% tariff on many goods entering the US, and gold and world oil prices began their vertiginous rise. Both the Second and the Third Worlds were moving out of control. Above all else, "trilateralism" was the ideological argument against national and in favour of transnational capital. The first trilateralist capos were Zbigniew Brzezinski and David Rockefeller. It was their interpretation of globalism which ultimately became the "Washington Consensus" of the mid-1990s and which is, under Republican President George Bush Jr., giving way to US unilateralism. Financing for the Trilateral Commission came from major corporations (GM, Coke, Exxon) and from the Ford and Rockefeller foundations. Canadian commissioners have included Conrad Black, Jacques Bougie of Alcan, Mickey Cohen of Molsons, Paul Desmarais of Power Corp. and Alan Gottlieb. See organizations, for the promotion of capitalism and globalization and links.

**trust.** This word was resurrected from the archives of business jargon in mid-July 2002, when Alan Greenspan announced that the "market system depends critically on trust—trust in the word of our colleagues and trust in the word of those with whom we do business." Alas, he noted, "Lawyers, internal and external auditors, corporate boards, Wall Street security analysts, rating agencies, and large institutional holders of stock "all failed for one reason or another to detect and blow the whistle on those who breached the level of trust essential to well-functioning markets" (G&M, July 19, 2002, B8). The message here seems to be that personal failure, not problems inherent in the market or capitalism, generally has led to the bubbles bursting. See bubble, stock market, in the 1990s, in the US, Greenspan, Alan, theory, economic, neoclassical, world economy, trends, since 1945 and links.

**underemployment.** Partial employment, usually effecting the young and especially chronic in Third World countries. See unemployment.

**unemployment.** Usually a statistical measure of people seeking jobs but unable to find them. Seldom takes into account people who stop looking. Unemployment rates vary according to country and age group with the US usually having the lowest unemployment rates among the G7 countries and Germany having an unusually high rate. In France the unemployment rate among persons under 30 is unusually high (around 30%). See unemployment, in Canada, unemployment, long term, underemployment.

**unemployment, in Canada.** Usually, Canada's main economic problem (i.e., as opposed to inflation or debt, which the likes of Paul Martin and the Bank of Canada stress). The unemployment rate in Canada as of February 2005 was 7%. In reality, it is considerably higher. Those most affected by unemployment in Canada are people in the Atlantic provinces, those with little education, blue-collar workers, women, youth and the newly married. See trade unions, wages, wealth, distribution of, Canadian and links.

**unemployment, long term.** Unemployment for more than one year. See unemployment.

**unilateralism.** Foreign policy of abjuring international organizations in favour of pursuit of narrow national goals, as practised by US and North Korea. For criticism of US unilateralism, see Prestowitz, 2003.

**Union of Concerned Scientists** (www.ucsusa.org). Experts on health and environment-related issues including climate change, GE foods and biotechnology. See under these subjects and links.

**United Nations (UN).** International organization founded at San Francisco in 1944. Descended from League of Nations, founded in aftermath of World War I. Remains dominated by Great Powers as they existed c.1945: China, Russia, US, Britain, France. See United Nations, agencies and publications and links.

**United Nations, agencies and publications.** See United Nations Conference on Human Development, United Nations Conference on Trade and Development, United Nations Framework Convention on Climate Change, United Nations Human Rights Committee, United Nations Intrergovernmental Panel on Climate Change, United Nations Development Program, United Nations Millennium Summit, United Nations World Development Report, United Nations World Economic and Social Survey and links.

**United Nations Conference on Human Development.** See Earth Summit.

**United Nations Conference on Trade and Development (UNCTAD)** (www.unctad.org). Statistics-generating UN agency which provides turgid material on trade growth. Annual Trade and Development Report has valuable analysis. See United Nations and links.

**United Nations Development Program (UNDP)** (www.undp.org.in). UN organization working internationally on development issues. See United Nations, agencies and publications.

**United Nations Framework Convention on Climate Change (UNFCCC).** Result of 1992 Earth Summit in Rio de Janeiro. Expressed concern over effects of climate change. See Canada, blocking of international protocols by, carbon emissions trade, COP-6, greenhouse gases, International Panel on Climate Change, Kyoto Protocol.

**United Nations Human Rights Committee (HRC)** (www.unhchr.ch). Sub-Commission on Human Rights (SCHR). Mother of all human rights organizations. Recent report has declared the WTO "a nightmare" for developing countries (CCPAM, 7, 6, November 2000, 19). See World Trade Organization and links.

**United Nations Intergovernmental Panel on Climate Change (IPCC).** See Intergovernmental Panel on Climate Change.

**United Nations Millennium Summit.** Held in September 2000 and led to the adoption of "Millennium Declaration." Signed by 189 countries, which set out eight economic and social goals. See Millennium Development Goals.

**United Nations World Development Report.** See *Human Development Report*, Human Development Index and links.

**United Nations World Economic and Social Survey.** Annual survey of global trends with headings such as "economies in transition" and "developing countries." Good on such matters as hydrocarbon reserves in Caspian Sea area.

**United States.** See America, economic policy, foreign policy, US, globalization, US, imperialism, US, and following entries.

**United States Agency for International Development (USAID).** Aid organization which funds globalization and supports military regimes. Its most famous employee was Dan Mitrone, who trained Uruguayan police in methods of torture. He was kidnapped and shot by Tupamaro guerrillas in July 1970 (Blum, 1995). See aid, Canadian International Development Agency (CIDA), development, Harvard Institute for International Development and links.

**United States Arms Control and Disarmament Agency** (www.state.gov/ www/global/arms/98_amiextoc and www.state.gov/www/global/arms/99/ _amiextoc). Source of data on global arms production and sales. See organizations, peace/arms control and links.

**United States government.** See United States above and links.

**United States government, environmental policy.** The environmental policy of the Bush regime is laid out in the National Energy Policy: Report of the National Energy Policy Development Group. This document was drawn up in the first months of the Bush administration and more or less dismisses the recommendations of the Intergovernmental Panel on Climate Change (IPCC). "The effect of the [National Energy Policy] would clearly be to obliterate any serious attempt to restrain carbon dioxide emissions in the nation that produces a quarter of those emissions globally, and hence must take the leading role in controlling them. The National Energy Policy is based instead on the administration's projections of energy needs, which it says will rise by 32 percent by 2020. It chooses vastly increased production of coal, gas, and oil as the primary means of dealing with these needs, and in so doing would effectively pre-empt the possibility of any of the reductions in $CO_2$ emissions envisioned by the IPCC scientists. That is to say, it treats the energy problem essentially on its own, and argues that the problem could be solved by increasing supply." The US President, George W. Bush, and his family have considerable interests in the oil industry. The US Vice President was the CEO of a major oil drilling company and the President's chief of staff, Andrew

Card, was an auto industry lobbyist. Oil and gas lobbyists contributed $14 million to the major political parties in the presidential election of November 2000; $10 million went to the Republicans (McKibben, 2001, 36–37). See Intergovernmental Panel on Climate Change (IPCC), organizations and publications, environmental, theory, environmental and links.

**United States government, foreign policy.** See foreign policy, US.

**United States military.** Nothing has ever existed like the disparity of power between the US and the rest of the world. The US annual military budget is $350 billion, about the same as India's entire national income. This equals the defence spending of the next 14 highest countries combined. The US accounts for around 40% of global military spending and has the capacity to spend much more. At present the US spends less than 3.5% of its GDP on the military; in the 1980s it spent 6.5%. "(The) unique combination of economic and military might permits the US to take an extraordinarily arrogant, imperious, unilateralist stand, defining 'threats' and riposts, as it pleases—ignoring the United Nations and the rest of the world when it likes" (*Front*, 19, 12, June 8–21, 2002, 109–10). See foreign policy, US and links.

**United Students Against Sweatshops (USAS)** (www.students againstsweatshops.org). US and Canadian organization founded in 1998 which agitates against Third World sweatshops in general and their links to universities in particular. In 2000 Canadian groups attacked U. of T. for selling sweatshop goods. Attacked by pro-globalization economists who formed Academic Consortium on International Trade (ACIT) (Featherstone and Henwood, 2001, 27–33). See Maquila Solidarity Network, Nike, Sweatshop Retailer of the Year Award, textile and clothing industry and links.

**Voluntary Export Restraints.** Agreement between the US and other states aiming to restrict imports into the US. Such restraints followed from the US Trade Act of 1974, which authorized the US to take punitive action against countries that were found guilty of "unfair" trading. See protectionism, trade and links.

**wages, repression of.** One of the leading characteristics of developed economies since the 1970s and especially since the 1980s. Lower wages combined with a lower dollar were key elements in the US strategy to gain ground from its German and Japanese competitors. Thus the US working class has been one of the main victims, not beneficiaries, of the US economic miracle. Brenner (1998, 30) says that wage repression in the US since 1973 has been without precedent in the 20th century and perhaps since the Civil War. See labour and links.

**wages, US.** "Between 1979 and 1995, average annual real wage growth for the bottom 40 per cent of the labour force fell by almost 12 per cent, for the bottom 60 per cent by 9.8 per cent (Even workers in the 80th percentile saw their wages fall by 0.4 per cent between 1979 and 1995). Put another way, over the course of this sixteen-year period, the bottom 60 per cent of the US labour force worked for progressively lower real wages and, by the end of the period, was working for real wages that were, on average, 10 per cent lower than they had been at the start" (Brenner, 1998, 205). "Between 1947 and 1973, economic growth averaged 4 per cent and non-managerial wages—that's the pay of more than 80 per cent of American workers—rose 63 per cent, in real dollars. Since 1973, with international trade soaring, real wages have fallen 4 per cent, while economic growth has averaged 3 per cent" (*HM*, May 2003, 48). While in most advanced economies CEOs earn between 5 and 20 times more than workers, in the US this can reach as high as 475 times. See free trade, Reagan-Thatcher revolution, wages, repression of and links.

**Wall Street.** A street in Manhattan on which the New York Stock Exchange stands; metaphorical centre of US and therefore global financial capitalism. Example of use: "The Democratic Party and the Clinton administration badly need Wall Street to contribute generously to the campaign costs of their candidates in the 1998 election" (Wade and Veneroso, 1998, 38). See stock markets and links.

**War on Want** (www.wow@gn.apc.org). UK-based advocacy group concerned with poverty and campaigning for global currency transaction tax. See lobbyists, Third World and links.

**Washington Consensus.** A consensus of the US Treasury, the International Monetary Fund (of which the Treasury is the largest shareholder), the World Bank and US investment bankers and the source of the dogma that minimum government and free markets are achievable and desirable throughout the world and that finance capital should be globalized. This consensus reflects the most powerful segment of the US ruling class. The Washington Consensus was codified by John Williamson of the International Institute for Economics in 1989 and was meant to apply to Latin America. According to him, the 10 areas of consensus involved governments agreeing to enforce the following reforms: (1) a guarantee of fiscal discipline, and a curb to budget deficits; (2) a reduction in public expenditure, particularly in the military and in public administration; (3) tax reform, aiming at the creation of a system with a broad base and with effective enforcement; (4) financial liberation, with interest rates determined by the market; (5) competitive exchange rates, to assist export-led growth; (6) trade liberalization, coupled with the abolition of import licensing and a reduction of tariffs; (7) promotion of foreign direct investment (8) privatization of state enterprises, leading to efficient management and improved performance; (9) deregulation of the economy; (10) protection of property rights.

"(T)his gospel [i.e., the Washington Consensus] has been the main American ideological export since anti-Communism (to which it is related) lost strategic relevance. It is promulgated directly through US foreign policy and indirectly through multilateral institutions such as the World Bank, the International Monetary Fund, and the World Trade Organization. Its core tenets are deregulation, privatisation, 'openness' (to foreign investment, to imports), unrestricted movement of capital, and lower taxes. Presented with special force to developing countries as a formula for economic management, it is also, in its fullness, a theory of how the world should be run, under American supervision. Attacking America is, therefore, attacking the theory, and attacking the theory is attacking America" (Finnegan, May 2003, 41–42).

The member states of the EU might be in a position to challenge the "Washington Consensus" within the World Bank since they contribute 22.66% of World Bank funds, as compared to 17.87% contributed by the US. But it never seems to have occurred to them to do so. It seems likely that sometime before 2000, the Washington Consensus had actually outlived its usefulness and no longer enjoyed a hegemonic role among economists. That it has been sustained is in part because the World Bank has yet to find a way out from it and in part because it still has utility for US foreign policy purposes. Joseph Stiglitz (2002, 53) says that "(f)iscal austerity, privatisation and market liberalization were the three pillars of Washington Consensus advice throughout the 1980s and 1990s." The term later became synonymous with market fundamentalism." See Bretton Woods institutions, crisis, Asian, deregulation of capital markets, free trade, hegemony, international community, International Institute for Economics, market fundamentalism, models, development/East Asian, revolving door, wages, US and links.

**Washington (DC), demonstrations.** In April 16–18, 2000, at meeting of IMF and World Bank. Attracted around 10,000 demonstrators, compared to 50,000 plus at Seattle, leading to theories that Seattle was an isolated political episode. Notably absent at Washington were trade unionists and President Clinton. See conferences, international and links.

**water, Canadian.** Canada's annual renewable volume of fresh water is 6.4% of the world's total, fifth after Brazil (12.7%), Russia (10.2%), China (8.3%) and Indonesia. Depletion of Canadian water is a question that has been largely ignored by the government which seems satisfied with the erroneous notion that Canadian water supplies are infinite, or at least, renewable (*G&M*, 25 June 2002, A19). See Canada, blocking of international protocols by, Canada, pollution, Canadian Centre for Policy Alternatives, World Resources Institute, World Scientists' Warning to Humanity and links.

**water, world.** Increasingly in short supply and the object of privatization. The largest private water dealers are Vivendi Universal and Suez, both of France. These and other private water firms "are aided by the World Bank and the IMF, which are increasingly forcing Third World countries to abandon their public water delivery systems and contract with the water giants to be eligible for debt relief. The performance of these companies in Europe and the developing world has been well documented: huge profits, higher prices for water, cutoffs to customers who cannot pay, no transparency in their dealings, reduced water quality, bribery and corruption" (Barlow and Clarke, 2002, 12).

**wealth.** Accumulated income. See following entries and bourgeoisie, bubble, stockmarket, of the 1990s, in the US, Clintonomics, debt, Forbes, High Net Worth Individuals, Human Development Reports, mutual funds, Reagan-Thatcher Revolution, Third Way, World Wealth Report, organizations, for the promotion of capitalism and globalism and links.

**wealth, distribution of, Canadian.** "The income gap between rich and poor in Canada has now reached its widest point since Statistics Canada first started calculating it 28 years ago. From 1994 to 1998, the degree of income disparity increased by 7.9%." The top 20% of Canadians now own 68% of the country's wealth (*TS*, Editorial, cited in *CCPAM*, September 2000, 2; see also CCPA *Monitor*, 9, 1, May 2002, 3, 9, 5, November 2002, 1, 7 and Kerstetter, 2003). The World Bank tabulation of income distribution (1994) is:

| lowest 10% | lowest 20% | second 20% | third 20% | fourth 20% | highest 20% | highest 10% |
|---|---|---|---|---|---|---|
| 2.8% | 7.5% | 12.9% | 17.2% | 23.0% | 39.3% | 23.8% |

(World Bank, *World Development Report 2000/2001*, Table 5, 282–83). Ken Thompson, the richest Canadian, was richer than ever with $23.7 billion. Other rich Canadians include Galen Weston (Loblaws) at $8.61 billion, the Irving family (New Brunswick) at $4 billion and la famille Bombardier at $3.97 million (*G&M*, 11 December 2001, B8). As for the rest: "Between 1970 and 1977, most groups gained a bit of ground at the expense of the richest 10 per cent of family units. But the shift was temporary. The richest 10 per cent increased its share of the wealth slightly in 1977 and 1984. Between 1984 and 1999, the richest group made substantial gains, and the other nine groups lost ground" (Kerstetter, 2003, 13). See also *Statistics Canada, Income after Tax, Distribution by Size in Canada; Income in Canada, 1998*. See wealth and links.

**wealth, distribution of, US.** The US is probably the most noted case of the tendency towards income inequality among advanced countries. Between 1950 and 1970, the ratio of income going to the top 20% of families to that of the bottom 20% fell from 9.5 to 7.6. After 1970, this ratio rose to 9.6 in 1990 and to 11.1 in 1996. Another way of putting this is to say that between the mid-1960s and early 1970s the top 5% of households received 16.6% of national income; by 1998, their share was 21.4%). The trend continued in the 1990 during the Clinton Administration: "(D)uring the first two years of the Clinton Administration, the share of national income earned by the top 5 per cent grew at a faster rate than during the eight years of the Reagan administration. Between 1992 and 1996, the share of income going to the top one-fifth of the population increased from 46 per cent to 49 per cent" (Brenner, 1998, 211–12). The US is not typical of Europe or Japan, although the UK has moved in a direction similar to the US. During the 1980s, the total financial wealth of the bottom 80% of Americans fell from 9 to 6%. The top 1% increased from 43 to 48%. See wealth and links.

**wealth, distribution of.** Here we have the central question in the whole debate about globalization—have more of the world's poor people got richer, that is, have their living standards risen in the recent belle epoque of globalization, c.1980–2004? If there are fewer poor people now than before, globally, that is, there is a strong argument in favour of globalization. On the other hand, to the extent that increased poverty or even stagnation can be traced to the globalizers' recipes, then the case for globalization is undermined. Alas, it is not easy to arrive at a clear conclusion because, of course, the debate about globalization is, in essence, a debate about modern capitalism. Thus, to oversimplify only slightly, the arguments about globalization are part of the older debate about change with various nationalists (especially the French), conservationists, leftists and students in the arts on one side and businesspersons, neoliberals and commerce students on the other. In between are various conservatives and protectionists. To make matters more opaque, both sides caricature their opponents, mock their arguments as being either ill-informed or dishonest and distrust any statistics that cannot be used as ammunition for their own guns. Take the figures generated by the World Bank, for instance. Anti-globalizers regard the Bank as part of the "unholy trinity" of institutions that work in the interests of the rich against the poor. They therefore distrust Bank statistics utterly. Yet even globalizers are critical of Bank statistics if they don't support their arguments. (Or if a particular statistical sample is not representative and measures "exceptional" not "typical" time periods.)

Consider Martin Wolf, associate editor of the *Financial Times* and highly regarded exponent of globalization by *The Economist*. Wolf argues forcefully that globalization has led to such demonstrable improvements for the whole of humanity that no open-minded person could possibly think otherwise. In his own words: "China [which] alone contains more people than Latin America and sub-Saharan Africa together has achieved a rise of real incomes per head of over 400 per cent between 1980–2000 [i.e., during the heyday of globalization]." Citing the UN's *Human Development Report* for 2003, he notes that between 1975 and 2001, GDP per head rose at 5.9% a year in East Asian countries (with 31 per cent of the world's population in 2000) and 2.4% a year in South Asian countries (where 22% of the world's people live). His conclusion: "Never before have so many people—or so large a proportion of the world's population—enjoyed such large rises in their standards of living" (2004, 141).

Yet his opponents seem immoveable. They argue that: 1. in large parts of the globalized world, as we shall see below, poverty is actually increasing; 2. in other parts, there is slow or no growth; 3. everywhere, even where the poor are becoming a little less poor, the rich are becoming monstrously rich, that is, inequality is expanding, and inequality, as much as absolute poverty, is politically explosive; and 4. the cost of growth, most conspicuously in China, is unsustainable environmentally. And even the World Bank itself has moments of doubt about the globalization to which it is apparently devoted. According to a recent Bank report (2000/2001, 3): "The world has deep poverty amid plenty. Of the world's 6 billion people, 2.8 billion... live on less than $2 a day, and $1.2 billion... live on less than $1 a day, with 44% living in South Asia.... In East Asia the number of people living on less than $1 a day fell from around 420 million to around 280 million between 1987–1998. Yet in Latin America, South Asia, and Sub-Saharan Africa the numbers of poor people have been rising. And in the countries of Europe and Central Asia in transition to market economies, the number of people living on less than $1 a day rose by more than twentyfold." See wealth and links.

**welfare state.** Name given to certain Western governments that rose after World War Two and sought to use the state, through interventions in the areas of taxation and social reform, to reduce wealth, to promote economic and social equality especially in the areas of health, education and security. In Canada, this object has been associated with the CCF/NDP and in Britain with the Labour Party before "New Labour." In France and Germany the welfare state is accepted by all parties. The idea of the welfare state came under attack by the advocates of neoliberalism in the 1970s. They demonized it as being corrupt, inefficient and, in some places, even anti-Christian. Since the late 1970s there has been a generalized crusade against the state on the part of almost all political formations in Anglo-Saxon countries. The IMF has sought to carry this crusade to the Third World. See International Monetary Fund (IMF), Keynes, John Maynard, neoliberalism, social market economy, structural adjustment programs, unemployment and links.

**Western Canada Wilderness Committee (WCWC)** (www. wildernesscommittee.org). Founded in 1980, "Canada's largest membership-based citizen-funded wilderness preservation organization." For Alberta, www.wcwc.ab.ca. See organizations and publications, environmental and links

**Windsor.** Meeting on 4–6 June, 2000 of OAS/FTAA. Protestors overwhelmed by police. See conferences, international and links.

**women, ill-treatment and abuse of.** See report by Amnesty International "Broken bodies, shattered minds. Torture and ill-treatment of women" (French version: <Torture: ces femmes qe l'on détruit> Amnestie international section francaise) and Paringaux for women in India and Pakistan. See organizations, human rights, torture, trafficking, in humans and links.

**women, rights of.** Codification of the rights of women are to be found in the 1952 UN Convention on the Political Rights of Women and the 1979 Convention on the Elimination of All Forms of Discrimination against Women. See sex, trafficking in and links.

**Workers' Rights Consortium** (www.workersrights.org). Non-profit organization created by college and university administrators, students and labour rights experts. "The WRC's purpose is to assist in the enforcement of manufacturing Codes of Conduct adopted by colleges and universities; these codes are designed to ensure that factories producing clothing and other goods bearing college and university names respect the basic rights of workers; there are more then 80 colleges and universities affiliated with the WRC." See Fair Trade Association, labour, organized, Students Against Sweatshops and links.

**World Bank** (www.worldbank.org). Motto: "Our dream is a world without poverty." "For fifty years the World Bank has been the arbiter of all questions of development. Its annual publication, *World Development Report*, establishes the priorities, the terminology, the concepts and the questions around which all questions of development are formulated" (my trans.) (Guilhot, 2000, 20). "(T)he most important development institution in the world" (Peet, 2003, 111). Created, with the IMF, at a conference in Bretton Woods in 1944, the World Bank had as its original mission the financing of the reconstruction of Western Europe and Japan; implicit here was the maintenance of a structure of global hierarchy at which the Bank and IMF had succeeded brilliantly. When the fixed exchange rate system fell apart in the early 1970s—with markets, not governments, now setting exchange rate values, it began writing economic prescriptions for the Third World. Between 1968–1981, under

Robert McNamara, former US Secretary of Defence ("the Butcher of Vietnam"), the World Bank was "a sanctuary of Keynesian thought and a temple of state modernization" (my trans.) (Guilhot, 2000, 20). Under McNamara, the volume of loans went from one to three billion dollars. From the 1960s to the early 1980s, the Bank organized long-term loans for major infrastructural projects—roads, ports, power plants, to support an export-oriented economic model. "Until 1987 the development banks [including the World Bank] paid virtually no attention to the ecological consequences of their lending programs, even those with far-reaching effects such as road building and settlement in Amazonia" (McNeill, 2001, 323). It was at a joint World Bank-IMF meeting in Bangkok in October 1991, the incoming president of the World Bank, Lewis Preston, announced: "Poverty reduction, to which I personally am fully committed, remains the World Bank Group's overarching objective." The Bank would "articulate the interests of developing countries" in countless international meetings and negotiations, and "help coordinate the efforts" of innumerable government agencies and nongovernmental organizations around the world. At 50th anniversary celebrations in 1994, critics organized around slogan "Fifty years is enough." The next year the World Bank got a new president, James Wolfensohn. "The bank was created as an internationally financed development program for the poor nations, but, critics charged, it now did grave harm to the very people it was supposed to help. Shut it down. These critics were not right-wing libertarians but activists from the non-governmental organizations committed to social and environmental justice in the developing world. The bank listened politely, promised to consider their complaints and then went on with business in the usual manner" (Greider, 1997, 281). "The World Bank remains faithful to the Washington Consensus in treating differences between cultures, regimes and kinds of capitalism as of marginal importance in determining the economic role of the state. In fact these differences are decisive. It has not accepted—or, perhaps, fully perceived—the diversity of contemporary capitalism" (Gray, 1998, 203). "Policies seen to be inconsistent with neo-classical normative theory are excluded from the start.... The art of paradigm maintenance begins with the choice of staff. [A]bout 80 per cent of Bank economists are North American or British trained, and all but a few share the preconceptions of mainstream Anglo-American economics. If they were to show sympathy for other ideas... they would be unlikely to be selected for the Bank, on the grounds of incompetence" (Wade, 2001, 16, 31). In March 2000 a commission appointed by the US Congress issued a report on the Bank and the IMF. The World Bank group comprises the original IBRD, the International Development Association (created in 1960), the International Finance Association (created in 1956 as the Bank's soft loan facility) and the Multilateral Agency for Investment Guarantees (1988). In early 2001, according to a report in *The Observer* (Business

Focus, 3, 4 February 2000), the Bank was in disarray. In spite of some attempts to move it towards "openness" and "inclusiveness," its staff remained "far more in tune with the cold calculus of structural adjustment packages than with the complexities of sustainable development, human capital, and 'cultural economics.'" "(A)n especially useful instrument for projecting American influence in developing countries, and one over which the US maintains discreet but firm institutional control" (Wade, 2001, 127). The World Bank employs 10,000 people, compared to the IMFS' 2000. See Bretton Woods institutions, dams, displacement, economic policy, US, export-led growth, Fifty Years is Enough, international financial institutions, International Monetary Fund, Keynes, John Maynard, Morse Commission, organizations, for the promotion of capitalism and globalism, structural adjustment, There is No Alternative, Washington Consensus, World Bank loans, World Development Report, World Social Forum and links.

**World Bank loans.** By the mid-1990s the World Bank was lending around $24 million annually. This money came mainly from two sources, repayments plus interest from debtors and bonds. "(I)n the late 1980s a number of developing countries were paying more back to the Bank in principal and interest than they were receiving, and by the early 1990s the problem in a number of key nations was acute. The Côte d'Ivoire had a net negative transfer of $618 million to the Bank for the period 1989–1993, of which $209 million was for 1989–1990... in 1993, Nigeria contributed $328 million more to Bank coffers than it received, Egypt $92 million more ($890 million more for 1989–1993), and Indonesia $428 million more. In some of the most heavily indebted Latin American countries, the net negative transfers to the Bank ballooned enormously; for Brazil, $1.313 billion in 1993 ($5.3 billion for 1989–1993); for Mexico, $714 million that same year; for the whole Latin American region, $7985 billion for the years 1989–1993." The Bank has nearly $20 billion in investments, mainly in government and corporate bonds. Since 1985, this sum has never sunk below $17 billion (Rich, 1994, 184, 310). See World Bank and links.

**World Conference Against Racism, Racial Discrimination, Xenophobia and Related Intolerance (WCAR).** Held in Durban, South Africa, in early September 2001. Several irreconcilable differences arose at the conference, particularly those concerning slavery, the slave trade and colonialism and the question of Zionism. The US and Israel withdrew from the conference. See conferences, international, organizations and links.

**World Development Forum** (www.derby.ac/seas/geog/jollyfranc). Site based on Geography Department of University of Derby, UK. Discusses development issues such as debt, arms control, war on terrorism. See organizations, development.

**World Development Movement** (www.wdm.org.uk). British-based organization, founded in 1970. Founder member of Jubilee 2000. Campaigns against debt, TNCs and WTO. Present campaign against General Agreement on Trade in Services (GATS). See General Agreement on Trade in Services, Jubilee 2000, organizations and publications, human rights, transnational corporations, World Trade Organization and links.

*World Development Report.* Produced by the World Bank since 1990, the reports frame the debate for development. As Wade (1996) has shown, the reports are dogmatic in the sense of needing to show that the doctrines of the World Bank are infallible and conspicuously subject to manipulation. Their authors, overwhelmingly North Americans and Brits, are invariably trained and socialized to see economics from an Anglo-American neoclassical point of view. See theory, neoclassical, World Bank and links.

**World Disasters Report** (www.ifrc.org/publicat/wdr 2001). Joint publication of Red Cross and Red Crescent, annual report concerns disaster relief.

**World Economic Forum.** Annual meeting held in early February since 1970 of self-appointed world corporate and political elite, usually at Davos, an expensive ski resort in Switzerland (although in 2002 in New York). Participants pay $20,000+ to attend. According to its Web page: "The Annual Meeting in Davos... sets the world agenda for the year to come." Ritually, leading CEOs, World Bank functionaries and plutocrats give earnest speeches on corporate responsibility for the world's poor, demonstrating that speech making about poverty will always be on the agenda. See conferences, international and links.

**world economy, trends, since 1945.** Led by the US, the world capitalist economy grew rapidly between the late 1940s and the early 1970s. After the US, the first national economies to expand were those of Western Europe and Japan, followed by later-developing East Asian economies (South Korea, Taiwan, Hong Kong) (These are usually known as the "Newly Industrialized Countries" (NICs)). The NICs increased their combined share of world goods exports between 1965 and the 1990s from 1.2% to 13.1% (other shares: US: 11.7%, Germany, 12.7%, Japan 8.5%). The effect of the expansion of the nics, which was based on lower wages and advanced techniques, was duplication and overproduction. From the early 1970s to the early 1990s there was stagnation in the West but not the nics (known as "the long downturn" in the US). This was characterized by a declining rate of profit, with recessions being experienced in 1979–1982 and 1989–1991). In the area of political economy, this period saw the abandonment of Keynesianism and the adoption of neoliberalism. From c.1993, the US broke with the pattern of stagnation and surged ahead, becoming internationally competitive once more, dragging with it the economies of East Asia. From mid-1999 to mid-2000, US GDP growth stood at 5.2%. This expansion witnessed the greatest financial bubble in US history. This basis for this bubble, which began to rise in 1995, was the "New Economy." Supported by the devaluation of the dollar, this was fuelled by the dis-savings of millions of households, i.e., by the "wealth effect" which led to the widespread borrowing on the basis of high share prices and inflated value of household assets, especially land. Net purchases of stocks reached an all-time high. Then from c.2000, the bubble of inflated share prices burst. Many of the stars in the technology, media and telecommunications (TMT) sector, like Nortel, simply burned out, losing as much as 90% of their share value. The US now joined East Asia and Western Europe and the entire global economy slowed down radically. "As the US economy... loses momentum, it cannot be rescued by the rest of the world economy, but can only bring it down with it, further exacerbating its own difficulties. Any recovery from the deepening international downturn will have to be initiated and driven by the US" (Brenner, 2002, 273–74). The basis for the US recovery in 2003–2004 is borrowing. The US has become a debtor nation, owing its willing creditors more than $500 billion. Its current account deficit by 2004 was nearly 5% of GDP. See bubble, dot.com firms, neoliberalism, newly industrialized countries, recession, technology, media and telecommunications (TMT) and links.

**World Health Organization (WHO)** (www.who.int/whr/2000). UN agency with headquarters in Geneva. Produces *Report on World Health* (various years). In report for 2000, average life expectancy index for Japanese is in first place at 74.5 years. France is 3rd, Italy 6th, UK 14th and the US 24th. See organizations, agriculture and links.

**World Policy Institute** (www.worldpolicy.org). US-based internationalist think-tank with journal. Current interests include arms trade, missile defence tests, Iraq and Columbia. See organizations, peace/arms control, think-tanks and links.

**World Resources Institute** (www.wri.org). A Washington-based environmental NGO with publication lists which includes materials on climate change, Indonesian forests, coastal and marine ecosystems. Publishes *World Resources,* an annual summary dealing with world resources. See organizations and publications, environmental and links.

**World Scientists' Warning to Humanity.** Issued in 1992, estimated that by 2012 unless economic policies changed humankind would face a bleak future (*CCPAM*, 7, September 4, 2000, 2). See crisis, ecological, aversion of, organizations and publications, environmental, theory, crisis and links.

**World Social Forum** (www.worldsocialforum.org). Antithesis of World Economic Forum. Inaugural meeting at Porto Alegre, Brazil, on January 25, 2001. Hosted by Workers' Party, which was in power there. Among founders was Bernard Cassen, director general of *Le Monde Diplomatique*. See World Economic Forum and links.

**World Summit on Sustainable Development.** International conference held in Johannesburg from August 26–September 4, 2002. Boycotted by the US. See conferences, international, development and links.

**world trade.** The rapid growth of world trade after WWII and especially since 1960 has only brought world trade back to the level it was before WWI. The data for six capitalist countries (France, Germany, Japan, the Netherlands, UK and US) show that while between 1950 and 1987 the ration of commodity exports and imports to GDP grew from 28.8% to 40.2%, in 1913 the ratio was 42.6% (MacEwan, 1999, 26). See world economy, trends and links.

**World Trade Organization (WTO).** American-dominated organization which ostensibly seeks to remove obstacles to global free trade. Its 143 members account for 97% of world trade. Successor from 1995 to General Agreement on Trade and Tariffs (GATT). Some of its successes include getting Third World countries to sign (a) Trade-Related Investment Measures (TRIMS), which prevents them from using trade policy as a means to industrialize, (b) Trade-Related Intellectual Property Rights (TRIPS), which gave high tech transnationals like Microsoft the right to monopolize innovation in the knowledge-intensive industries and gives bio-tech firms like Novartis and Monsanto the rights to privatize past research and development, and (c) Agreement on Agriculture (AOA), which opened the markets of developing countries to highly-subsidized agriculture transnationals and as a consequence destroyed smallholder-based agriculture. The present director-general of the WTO is Supachai Panitchpakdi, a former Thai commerce minister. For 10 benefits of the world trade system which it manages, see Peet, 2003, 159–60 and for the corruption of the WTO by multinationals, especially pharmaceutical and software firms, see Bhagwati, 2004, 82–83. Check: WTOWatch.com. See Bretton Woods institutions, international community, Meltzer Commission, subsidies, world economy, trends and links.

**World Wealth Report.** An annual look at persons, worldwide, with financial assets exceeding $1 million produced by Merrill Lynch and Gemini Consulting. The collective wealth of these 7 million grew by 18% in 1999 to $25.5 trillion. Nearly one third live in North America, fewer live in Western Europe, fewer still in Asia and Latin America, almost none in Africa. The wealth of the top 55,000, those with $30 million or more in assets, grew by 16% to $7.9 billion. See Clintonomics, Forbes 500, bubble, stockmarket, of the 1990s, in the US, wealth, distribution of, US and links.

**World Wildlife Fund** (www.worldwildlife.org). Founded in 1969 and now largest privately supported conservation fund in the world. The three main objectives of the WWF are protecting endangered species, saving endangered species, and addressing global threats. WWF produces *Living Planet Report* annually. See organizations, environmental and links.

**Worldwatch Institute** (www.worldwatch.org). Founded by MIT professor, Lester Brown, in 1984, produces annual *State of the World* reports that focus on environmental decline. See organizations and publications, environmental and links.

# BIBLIOGRAPHY

Ahiakpor, James. "Multinational Corporations in the Third World: Predators or Allies in Economic Development." www.acton.org/publicat/rand 1/92 sep_oct/ahiakpor.

Allen, Tim, and Alan Thomas. 2000. *Poverty and Development into the 21st Century.* Oxford.

Anderson, Perry. 2001. "Testing Formula Two." *New Left Review.* March–April.

Arrighi, Giovanni. 2003. "The Social and Political Economy of Global Turbulence." *New Left Review,* 20, March–April.

Bacevich, Andrew. 2002. *American Empire. The Realities and Consequences of US Diplomacy.* Cambridge, MA.

Bhagwati, Jagdish. 2004. *In Defense of Globalization.* New York.

Baker, Dean, Gerald Epstein and Robert Pollin (eds.). 1998. *Globalization and Progressive Economic Policy.* New York.

Bales, Kevin. 2000. *Disposable People: New Slavery in the Global Economy.* New York.

Barlow, Maude, and Tony Clarke. 2002. "Who Owns Water?" *The Nation,* September 2/9.

Barrett Brown, Michael. 1993. *Fair Trade.* London, UK.

Beck, Ulrich. 1999. *What is Globalization?* Cambridge, MA.

Berlan, Jean-Pierre, and Richard Lewontin. 1986. "The Political Economy of Hybrid Corn." *Monthly Review,* 38, 3, July–August.

Blum, William. 1995. *Killing Hope: US Military and cia Interventions Since World War II.* New York.

_____. 2004. *Rogue State: A Guide to the World's Only Superpower.* New York.

Brenner, Robert. 2004. "New Boom or New Bubble." *NLR,* 25, January–February.

_____. 2003. "Towards the Precipice." *LRB,* 25, 3, 6 February.

_____. 2002. *The Boom and the Bubble: The US in the World Economy.* London.

_____. 1998. "The Economics of Global Turbulence. A Special Report on the World Economy, 1950–98." *New Left Review,* 229, May/June.

Bruno, Kenny. 2001. "A Convenient Confusion." *NI,* 335, June.

Brym, Robert, and James Sacouman. 1979. *Underdevelopment and Social Movements in Atlantic Canada.* Toronto.

Burrows, Gideon. 2002. *The No-Nonsense Guide to The Arms Trade.* London.

Canada, Government of. Parliamentary Research Branch. 1997. "Aid to Developing Countries." Revised 17 September (79–16E).

Cassen, Bernard. 2000. "Dans l'ombre de Washington." *LMD,* September.

_____. 2003. "On the Attack." *New Left Review,* 19, January–February.

Centre for Economic and Policy Research. August 2002. "Growth may be good for the poor... But are IMF and World Bank policies good for growth?" Washington, DC.

Chomsky, Noam. 2003. *Hegemony or Survival: America's Quest for Global Dominance.* New York.

_____. 1999. *Profit over People: Neoliberalism and Global Order.* New York.

_____. 1999. *The Umbrella of US Power: The Universal Declaration of Human Rights and the Contradictions of US Policy.* New York.

Chomsky, Noam, Ramsey Clark and Edward W Said. 1999. *Acts of Aggression. Policing "Rogue" States."* New York.

Chossudovsky, Michel. 1997. *The Globalization of Poverty: Impacts of imf and World*

*Bank Reforms*. London.

Clairmont, Frédéric F. 2000. "Menaces sur l'économie mondiale." *LMD*, 566, Mai 3.

Cockburn, Alexander, and Jeffrey St.Clair. 2000. *Five Days That Shook the World: The Battle for Seattle and Beyond*. London.

Cohen, Stephen. 2000. *Failed Crusade: America and the Tragedy of Post-Communist Russia*. New York.

Cumings, Bruce. 1998. "The Korean Crisis and the End of 'Late' Development." *NLR*, 231, September/October.

Daly, Herman E., and John Cobb. 1989. *For the Common Good: Redirecting the Economy Toward Community, the Environment, and a Sustainable Future*. Boston.

Dawkins, Kristin. 1997. *Gene Wars: The Politics of Biotechnology*. New York.

Dobbin, Murray. 1998. *The Myth of the Good Corporate Citizen: Democracy Under the Rule of Big Business*. Toronto.

Ellwood, Wayne. 2001. "Mired in Crude." *NI*, 335, June.

_____. 2001. *The No-Nonsense Guide to Globalization*. Toronto.

Epstein, Barbara. 2001. "Anarchism and the Anti-Globalization Movement." *Monthly Review*, 53, 4, September.

Featherstone, Liza. 2000. "The Student Movement Comes of Age." *Nat*, 271, 11, October 16.

Featherstone, Liza, and Henwood, Doug. 2001. "Clothes Encounters: Activists and Economists Clash over Sweatshops." *Longuafranca*, 11, 2, March.

Ferguson, Niall. 2004. *Colossus. The Price of America's Empire*. New York.

Finnegan, William. 2003. "The Economics of Empire: Notes on the Washington Consensus." *Harper's Magazine*, May.

Frank, Thomas. 2000. *One Market under God: Extreme Capitalism, Market Populism, and the End of Economic Democracy*. New York.

Garrett, Laurie. 2000. *Betrayal of Trust: The Collapse of Global Public Health*. New York.

George, Susan. 2001. "A Short History of Neo-Liberalism: Twenty Years of Elite Economics and Emerging Opportunities for Structural Change." In F. Houlart and F. Poulet (eds.), *The Other Davos*. London. See also Public Citizen Global Trade Watch.

Gill, S., and Mittleman (eds.). 1997. *Innovation and Transformation in International Studies*. Cambridge.

Gilmour, Ian. 2001. "Little Mercians." *LRB*, 23, 13, 15 July.

Godrej, Dinyar. 2001. *The No-Nonsense Guide to Climate Change*. Toronto.

Goldsmith, Edward, and Gerry Mander, (eds.). 2001. *The Case Against the Global Economy*. London

Gorce, Paul-Marie de la. 2001. "La Russie en quíte d'un nouveau rôle." *LMD*, 566, Mai.

Gray, John. 1998. *False Dawn: The Delusions of Global Capitalism*. London.

Greer, Jed and Kenny Bruno. 1996. *Greenwash*. London.

Greider, William. 1997. *One World, Ready or Not: The Manic Logic of Global Capitalism*. New York.

Gresser, Edward. 2002. "Toughest on the Poor: America's Flawed Tariff System." *Foreign Affairs*, 81,6, November–December.

Grunberg, Isabelle. 2000. "Que faire du Fonds monétaire international?" *LMD*, Septembre.

Guérin, Daniel. 1970. *Anarchism: From Theory to Practice*. New York.

Guilhot, Nicolas. 2000. "D'une vérité à l'autre, les politiques de la Banque mondiale," *LMD*, Septembre.

Harmes, Adam. 2001. "Mass Investment Culture." *NLR*, 9, May June.

Haslam, Jonathan. 1999. *The Vices of Integrity: E.H. Carr, 1892–1982*. London.

Healey, David. 2003. *Let Them Eat Prozak*. Toronto.

Hecht, Susanna. 1989. *The Fate of the Forests*. New York.

Held, David. 2004. *Global Covenant: The Social Democratic Alternative to the Washington Consensus*. Cambridge.

Held, David, and Anthony McGrew (eds.). 2000. *The Global Transformation Reader: An Introduction to the Globalization Debate*. Cambridge.

Held, David, Anthony McGrew, David Goldblatt, and Jonathan Perraton (eds.). 1999. *Global Transformations. Politics, Economics and Culture*. Stanford.

Henwood, Doug. 2000. *A New Economy?* New York.

_____. 1998. *Wall Street*. London.

Herman, Edward S., and Robert W. McChesney. 1997. *The Global Media: The New Missionaries of Corporate Capitalism*. London.

Hirst, Paul, and Graham Thompson. 1999. *Globalization in Question*. Cambridge.

Hobsbawm, Eric. 1994. *Age of Extremes: The Short Twentieth Century, 1914–1991*. New York.

Homer-Dixon, Thomas. 1999. *Environment, Security and Violence*. Princeton.

Hoogvelt, Ankie. 1997. *Globalization and the Postcolonial World: The New Political Economy of Development*. London.

Huntington, Samuel. 1999. "The Lonely Superpower." *Foreign Affairs*, 78, 2.

Hutton, Will, and Anthony Giddens (eds.). 2000. *On the Edge: Living with Global Capitalism*. London.

International Institute for Sustainable Development and World Wildlife Fund. 2001. *Private rights, Public Problems: A Guide to nafta's Controversial Chapter on Investor Rights*. Winnipeg.

International Labour Organization. 1996. *Child Labour: Targeting the Intolerable*. Geneva.

Jamieson, Fredric. 2000. "Globalization and Political Strategy." *NLR*, 4, Jul/Aug.

Jeffrey, Brooke. 1999. *Hard Right Turn: The New Face of Neo-Conservatism in Canada*. Toronto.

Johnson, Chalmers. 2000. *Blowback: The Costs and Consequences of American Empire*. New York.

_____. 2004. *The Sorrows of Empire: Militarism, Secrecy, and the End of the Republic*. New York.

Johnson, Jo. 2001. "Le Monde joins the new world." *FT*, July 21/22.

Kaplan, Robert. 2000. *The Coming Anarchy: Shattering the Dreams of the Post Cold War*. New York: Random House.

Kerstetter, Steve. 2003. "Rags and Riches. Wealth Inequality in Canada." CCPA, January.

Kinsman, Gary, Dieter K. Buse, and Mercedes Steedman (eds.). 2000. *Whose National Security? Canadian State Surveillance and the Creation of Enemies*. Toronto.

Klare, Michael T. 2001. *Resource Wars: The New Landscape of Global Conflict*. New York.

Klein, Lawrence R., and Marshall Power. 2001. *The New Russia: Transition Gone Awry*. Stanford.

Klein, Naomi. 2000. "Crackdown: When police wage war against activists." *G&M*,

November 15: A15.

_____. 2000. *No Logo.* Toronto.

Kiely, Ray, and Phil Marfleet (eds.). 1998. *Globalisation and the Third World.* London.

Korten, D. 1990. *When Corporations Rule the World.* West Hartford.

Latouche, Serge. 2001. "En finir, une fois pour toutes, avec le développement." *LMD,* 566, Mai.

Levitt, Kari. 2003. *Silent Surrender.* Montreal.

Lewontin, Richard. 2001. "Genes in the Food!" *NYRB,* XLVII, 10, June 21.

Leyro, Jeffrey, and Andrew Moravcsik. 2001. "Faux Realism. Spin versus Substance in the Bush Foreign Policy Doctrine." *FP,* July/August.

Leys, Colin. 2001. *Market-Driven Politics. Neoliberal Democracy and the Public Interest.* London.

_____. 1996. *The Rise and Fall of Development Theory.* Bloomington.

Lieven, Anatol. 2003. "The Empire Strikes Back." *Nat,* July 7.

Lieven, Dominic. 2000. *Empire: The Russian Empire and Its Rivals.* New Haven.

MacEwan, Arthur. 1999. *Neo-liberalism or Democracy? Economic Strategy, Markets, and Alternatives for the 21st Century.* London.

McFarlane, Bruce. 2001. "Politics of the World Bank-IMF Nexus in Asia." *JCAS,* 31, 2.

McHughen, Alan. 2000. *Pandora's Picnic Basket: The Potential and Hazards of Genetically Modified Foods.* New York.

McKibben, Bill. 2001. "Some Like It Hot." *NYRB,* XLVIII, 11, July 5.

McNeill, J.R. 2001. *Something New Under the Sun: An Environmental History of the Twentieth Century World.* New York.

McQuaig, Linda. 2001. *All You Can Eat: Greed, Lust and the New Capitalism.* Toronto.

_____. 1998. *The Cult of Impotence: Selling the Myth of Powerlessness in the Global Economy.* Toronto.

Malarek, Victor. 2003. *The Natashas: The New Global Sex Trade.* Toronto.

Mason, Mike. 1997. *Development and Disorder: A History of the Third World Since 1945.* Toronto.

Middledorf, G. 1998. "New Agricultural Biotechnologies: the Struggle for Democratic Choice." *MR,* July–August.

Monbiot, George. 2001. "How Europe Was Subverted." *GW,* June 28–July 4.

Morris-Suzuki, Tessa. 2000. "For and Against NGOs." *NLR,* 2, March–April.

Murphy, R.T. 2000. "Japan's Economic Crisis." *NLR,* 1, Jan/Feb.

Naylor, R.T. 2002. *Wages of Crime: Black Markets, Illegal Finance, and the Underworld Economy.* Montreal.

Ohmae, K. 1995. *The End of the Nation State.* New York.

Panitch, Leo. 2000. "The New Imperial State." *NLR,* 1, Jan/Feb.

Pallast, Gregory. 2002. *The Best Democracy Money Can Buy: An Investigative Reporter Exposes the Truth about Globalization, Corporate Cons, and High Finance Fraudsters.* New York.

_____. 2000. "IMF's shock cures are killing off the patient." *GW,* October 12–18.

Paringaux, Roland-Pierre. 2001. "Femmes D'Asie en butte la violence." *LMD,* 566, Mai.

Parpart, Jane, and Henry Veltmeyer. 2004. "The Dynamics of Development, Theory and Practice. A Review of Its Shifting Dynamics." *Canadian Journal of Development Studies,* XXV (1), Special Issue.

Peel, Quentin, and Alan Beattie. 2001. "An end to fireside chats." *FT,* July 21–22.

Peet, Richard. 2003. *Unholy Trinity: The IMF, World Bank and WTO.* London.

Petras, James. 1997. "Imperialism in Latin America." *MR*, 7, 49, December.
Petras, James, and Henry Veltmeyer. 2001. *Globalization Unmasked: Imperialism in the 21st Century*. Halifax.
_____. 2003. *System in Crisis. The Dynamics of Free Market Capitalism*. Halifax.
Pollen, Robert. 2000. "Anatomy of Clintonomics." *NLR*, 3, May–June.
Polanyi, Karl. 1944. *The Great Transformation*. London.
Prestowitz, Clyde. 2003. *Rogue Nation: American Unilateralism and the Faiure of Good Intentions*. New York.
Prowse, Michael. 2001. "Tawdry side to the global pursuit of personal gain." *FT*, July 21–22.
Ransom, David. 2001. *The No-Nonsense Guide to Fair Trade*. Toronto.
Rich, Bruce. 1994. *Mortgaging the Earth: The World Bank, Environmental Impoverishment, and the Crisis of Development*. Boston.
Rist, Gilbert. 1997. *The History of Development from Western Origins to Global Faith*. London.
Roberts, Paul. *2004. The End of Oil*. Boston.
Rosenau, James. 1997. *Along the Domestic-Foreign Frontier*. Cambridge.
_____. 1998. "Government and Democracy in a Globalizing World." In D. Archibugi, D. Held, and M. Kohler (eds.), *Re-Imagining Political Community*. Cambridge.
Ross, Andrew (ed.). 1997. *No Sweat: Fashion, Gree Trade and the Rights of Garment Workers*. London.
Sayle, Murray. 2001. "After George W. Bush, the Deluge." *LRB*, 12, 23, 21 June.
Schlosser, Eric. 2001. *Fast Food Nation: The Dark Side of the All-American Meal*. Boston.
Schwenninger, Sherle R. 2000. "America and the World: The End of Easy Dominance." *The Nation*, 271,16, November 20.
Sellers, John. 2001. "Raising a Ruckus." *NLR*, 10, July–August.
Sen, Amartya. 1999. *Development as Freedom*. Oxford.
Sharratt, Lucy. 2002. *Regulating Genetic Engineering for Profit: A Guide to Corporate Power and Canada's Regulation of Genetically Engineered Foods*. Ottawa.
Sinai, Agnès. 2001. "Comment Monsanto vend les OGM." *LMD*, 48, 568, Jillet.
Smil, Vaclav. 2003. *The Earth's Biosphere: Evolution, Dynamics, and Change*. Cambridge, MA.
Spiro, Peter J. 2000. "The New Sovereigntists: American Exceptionalism and Its False Prophets." *Foreign Affairs*, 79, 6, November/December.
Stalker, Peter. 2001. *The No-Nonsense Guide to International Migration*. Toronto.
Strange, Susan. 1996. *The Retreat of the State: The Diffusion of Power in the World Economy*. Cambridge.
Stiglitz, Joseph. 2002. *Globalization and Its Discontents*. New York.
_____. 2000. "The Insider: What I Learnt at the World Economic Crisis." *The New Republic*, April 17.
Tabb, William. 2000. *The Amoral Elephant: Capitalist Development in the Early 20th Century*. New York.
_____. 2000. "Globalization, Economic Restructuring and Democratic Implications." Paper given at Conference on Democracy and Civil Society in Asia: The Emerging Opportunities and Challenges, August 19–20, Queens' University, Kingston, Canada.
Townsend, Monica. 1998. *Health and Wealth*. Ottawa.
Tracy, Spencer. 2001. *A Review and Critique of NGOs in Jamaica*. MA thesis, Queen's University.

Tranh-Dam Troung. 1990. *Sex, Morality and Money: Prostitution and Tourism in Southeast Asia.* London.

UNDP. *Human Development Report.* (various years).

UNCTAD. *Trade and Development Report.* (various years).

_____. *World Investment Report.* (various years).

UN. *World Development Report.* New York (various years).

US Department of Interior. *Country Studies.* Washington (various years).

Veltmeyer, Henry. 2004. *Globalization and Antiglobalization: Dynamics of Social Change in the New World Order.* London.

_____. 2001. *Transcending Neoliberalism: Community-Based Development.* West Hartford, CT.

_____. 1998. *Canadian Corporate Power.* Toronto.

_____. 1997. *Economic Liberalism and Class Conflict in Latin America.* London.

Wade, Robert. 2001. "Showdown at the World Bank." *NLR*, 7, January–February.

_____. 1998. "The Asian Debt-and-Development Crisis of 1997–9: Causes and Consequences." *World Development*, 26, 8, August.

_____. 1996. "Japan, the World Bank, and the Art of Paradigm Maintenance: *The East Asian Miracle* in Political Perspective." *NLR*, 217, May/June.

Wade, Robert, and Frank Veneroso. 1998. "The Asian Crisis: The High Debt Model Versus the Wall Street-Treasury-IMF Complex." *NLR*, 228, March/April.

_____. 1998. "The Gathering World Slump and the Battle over Capital Controls." *NLR*, 231, September/October.

Watts, Mike. 2001. "Black Acts." *NLR*, 9, May/June.

Wilkinson, Richard. 1996. *Unhealthy Societies.* London.

Williamson, John (ed.). 1994. *The Political Economy of Reform.* Washington: Institute for International Economics.

Wolf, Martin. 2004. *Why Globalization Works.* London and New Haven.

World Bank. *World Development Report. 2000–2001.*

## Note from the author

This glossary was prepared for the students in History 231, "The Making of the Third World," at Queen's University, Kingston. It is meant to supplement the main text for that course: Mike Mason, *Development and Disorder: The Third World Since 1945* (Toronto, 1997). Any suggestions regarding additions or deletions are welcomed and if included in future versions will be acknowledged.

Entries are included to that the extent that they are relevant to the development of global capitalism, i.e., globalism, its effects, elements, beneficiaries, victims, personnel, proponents, hirelings, wellsprings, theories, interpreters, models, measures, organizations, misspeakings, scams, critics and downright enemies. I would like especially to thank Mary Hallard and Henry Veltmeyer as well as my colleagues in Development Studies at Queen's. Paritosh Kumar, Steve Mason, Jeff Moon, Julian Berry, Bob Shenton, Linda Freeman, Tim Smith and Dan O'Meara have all made valuable suggestions. Brenda Conroy of Fernwood Publishing, especially, has contributed to the cogency and brevity of this guide. The selection and interpretation of material here is my responsibility.

I would like to dedicate this glossary to my past students in History 231. And to Lucia and Amina bint Lucia, in celebration.